INTERNATIONAL LEGAL REGULATION OF SPACE DEBRIS

Proposal for establishment of an International Space Agency

by
Aleksandar Milanov

NEW AGE CITIZENS
FOUNDATION

SOFIA
2023

International Legal Regime of Space Debris: Proposal for establishment of an International Space Agency

Publisher: Copyright 2023 by Foundation New Age citizens, Sofia, Bulgaria.
www.newagecitizens.org

Revision of the author's doctoral thesis, 2023

Design and preparation of the book Svetozar Voynov

ISBN 978-619-90834-9-9

# *Acknowledgements*

This book is a slightly revised and enhanced version of my doctoral thesis, which I defended in 2023 in Jindal Global University. I would like to express my sincere gratitude to all my tutors, reviewers, colleagues, and editor who contributed to this version of the book.

I am sincerely grateful to my amazing mother Mariana and my beloved wife Katina for their love and constant support. I would like to dedicate this book to my son Kristo, who at the age of five already understands the importance of protecting the outer space environment.

There are different futures and we will choose which one to experience.

Aleksandar Milanov
Sonipat, September 2023

Executive Summary

This research explores the international legal regulation on protecting outer space environment from different types of space debris. The monograph focuses on the international legal gaps to regulate all major aspects of space debris and the challenges in front of comprehensive international cooperation and legal regulation. It illustrates the levels of cooperation, achievements and omissions in different international forums that address the issue of space debris. The research concludes that unless comprehensive cooperation is achieved on a global level and new international legal treaties are not established, potential military conflicts could emerge amongst space-faring nations over the right to exploit outer space resources. The book also illustrates different challenges of different space debris and proposes ways to address them. This research also examines the roles of international governmental organizations as well as international scientific organizations to address the issues of space debris production, management, and removal from outer space. Therefore, the monograph provides the steps to improve traffic management in space to provide safety to all space activities while achieving better protection of the outer space environment.

The first chapter explores into the definitions of the main legal terms such as space object, space debris, aerospace object and others. It analyses the legal norms, relevant to the space debris issue and explores the need to adopt new international legal norms. This chapter also investigates the most important legal terms, related to the space debris issue, such as ownership, jurisdiction and control over space debris. This chapter also includes the classification of different types of space debris and the different types of threats that they represent to space activities and to people on Earth. International space debris regulation has different aspects, which have to be explored in order to draw a complete picture and analyse the problem from different perspectives. These perspectives include the legality of the creation of space debris, and the different dangers from it, based on the chemical structure, size, location, traceability and the risk of loss of life and property in space and on Earth. Analysing the legal definition of "harmful contamination" and its scope in the creation of space debris is an important part of this chapter. Environmental protection of outer space and of Earth from space debris is also significant in this chapter. The legal issue of international liability is reviewed and analysed. The latest examples of good national practices to reduce the risk from space debris are also identified and analysed in the present research. Special focus is placed on the public-private partnership in space activities.

The second chapter focuses on analysing the achievements and failures in international efforts of states to improve the safety of the outer space environment. This chapter is devoted to analysing the positive as well as the negative aspects of such international cooperation on a state level and on a non-governmental level. The main challenges of international cooperation are explored in the last subchapter of chapter II. The main purpose of the second chapter is to provide an analysis and overview of the relevant leading intergovernmental organizations and international scientific organizations in the field of international space law. These organizations are UN-COPUOS, Inter-Agency Space Debris Coordination Committee, ITU, COSPAR, International Law Association and the Conference on Disarmament. Separate subchapters in this section discuss the international cooperation on banning anti-satellite tests and taking a look at the European regional structures that are involved in the mitigation of space debris. The European projects, investments, and institutional capacities are analysed from the perspective of regional cooperation that could produce good institutional practices for global cooperation. Comparative analysis of different national space policies that discuss methods to reduce the threats from space debris is separately provided in a subchapter.

Chapter three explores the most significant proposals in international law to resolve the problems related to space debris. The proposals have been selected on two distinct criteria: 1) from authors, who have published extensively in the field of international space law and 2) the proposals that distinguish themselves with originality and logic to address the issue of space debris.

The last chapter presents comprehensive proposal with resolution of the challenges from space debris production and attempts to convince the readers of the need of global space agency. I propose the establishment of an International Space Agency. This sui generis international organization includes most nations that dedicate themselves to protecting the interests of humankind as well as those of states and private actors. The holistic vision of outer space exploration is key to solving the problems in outer space policies, including the massive creation of space debris and their poor management.

The research also suggests the adoption of a global planetary quarantine protocol for the protection of the Earth from returning space objects, infection by space organisms, nuclear explosions of nuclear-powered satellites and improvements in present international bodies, which are regulating aspects of space debris.

The research aims to provide recommendations on how to deal with space debris on a global level. Although national measures adopted by space-faring states could be very useful in achieving better protection of outer space environment, the measures would not be sufficient because other states will not have the obligations to adopt them. Comprehensive international cooperation in dealing with the negative effects of space debris is essential, particularly with respect to sharing information about activities in outer space, traffic management and adoption of common standards for shielding space objects and common mitigation guidelines.

Table of Contents

Introduction

As a final frontier, outer space became immensely significant for the development of human knowledge. The usage of satellites is already the backbone of globalization. Space objects are vital assets for national security, agriculture, telecommunication, navigation, and many other areas of economic development. In the last century, the issue of space debris has been identified as a major challenge against the preservation of space assets in Earth's orbit. Despite it, we have not seen successful political and legal efforts of leading space-faring nations to deal with the risks from space debris comprehensively.

All space activities generate space debris during the launching stages and after the completion of the mission of the space system. Therefore, detailed and comprehensive legal rules are needed to define lawful and unlawful generation of debris in outer space. These rules will also clarify the legal obligations of states to prevent collisions of space objects and mitigate the risk for space missions. The life of astronauts and the safety of the people on Earth could be better protected, if such rules are adopted.

This research project adds to scholarship of international legal researches on environmental safety in outer space and contributes to the analysis of standards for the mitigation of space debris.

The research also focusses on the legal and the scientific developments in aerospace engineering in the context of improving the international legal framework for the protection of the outer space environment.

Space debris is one of the main threats to outer space activities and a constant danger to the safety of astronauts and people on Earth. Therefore, the need to perceive and explore other space activities and scientific developments related to the space sector is crucial.

The leading space-faring nations are identifying the large challenges that the space debris issue is causing to space activities, but their international legal actions are not leading to an adequate solution or decreasing the risk of collisions in outer space and on the surface of Earth. Therefore, the main research question of this project is the following: **Is there a comprehensive international legal regulation of the space debris issue and if not, what are the reasons for its absence?** This research question is in two parts. The first part presupposes that there isn't such a comprehensive regulation, because the issue is not resolved and space debris are becoming an even greater threat with the development of space activities. The second part aims to explore the main reasons for not achieving this international regulation.

The aim of the research is to identify the gaps in international regulation, analyse the reasons for these gaps, select, analyse and evaluate significant proposals to improve international space law with respect to the issue of space debris. Lastly, the research aims to formulate and present my unique proposals to resolve the issue of space debris.

The scientific and technical aspects related to the mitigation of space debris, such as innovation of launching systems, shielding standards, and the relevance of different orbits are considered, but the focus of the research remains the international legal regulation and the steps for improving international cooperation between states to increase the safety level of outer space activities.

Chapter 1

International legal regulation of space debris

This chapter "International Law on Space Debris", focusses on clarifying terminologies—terminologies that have been contested in various international fora and scholarly writings; these terminologies discuss issues surrounding international responsibility and liability, jurisdiction, and ownership; and state practice.

In order to achieve a comprehensive understanding of the space debris issue, it is useful to analyse the different threats that various types of space debris cause to outer space activities and to the safety of people on Earth. The causes for the creation of waste in outer space are different, and they have to be analysed separately to determine the adequate measures and approaches to mitigate and prevent the production of space debris.

Modern scientific and technical innovations in space activities are instrumental to reduce the threat of space debris.

Castronuovo argues that the active removal of five to ten large objects per year from the Low Earth orbit (LEO) region is the only way to prevent debris collisions from cascading. Among the three orbital regions near the Earth where most catastrophic collisions are predicted to occur, the one corresponding to a sun-synchronous condition is considered the most relevant.[1] In addition to the esti-

---

1 Marco M. Castronuovo, *Active space debris removal—A preliminary mission analysis and design* 69(9-10) Acta Astronautica, 848, 848 (2011).

mation of the approximate number of active removal of large space objects, academic scholars have argued that the location of these objects should also be considered. In the last four decades, the man-made objects' mass in Earth's orbit increased at an annual rate of about one hundred and forty-five metric tons.[2] This led to a total of more than seven thousand metric tons. The most concentrated area is LEO and the majority of the space objects—rocket bodies and functional spacecraft- are intact. There are also operational spacecraft, but they are a much smaller number. The analysis of DeLuca and other scholars predates the launches of thousands of small satellites by SPACE-X in LEO. The scholars concluded that simulations and corresponding parametric analyses illustrate that the most efficient way to prevent the emergence of long-term growth is by freeing the used and densely populated orbits from enough cross-sectional mass.[3]

A stable environment for man-made space objects could be achieved only by adopting drastic measures of active removal of space objects, as suggested by Klinkrad and Johnson.[4] Their conclusions are based on long-term projections of the orbital space debris in outer space. Even if the measures are immediate and include the complete ceasing of launches of space objects, it will not be possible to achieve a safe outer space environment with the present man-made space objects. Their projection shows that collisions of existing space objects in the next decades are likely and will lead to the generation of more orbital debris at such sizes that would lead to more collisions. The authors conclude that the active removal of large space objects, such as non-functional spacecraft, orbital stages, and mission-related objects, is the optimal solution.[5] This conclusion shows that there is an im-

2 L.T. DeLuca, et al., *Active space debris removal by a hybrid propulsion module*, 91 Acta Astronautica, 20, 22 (2013).

3 *Id.* at 22

4 Heiner Klinkrad & Nicholas Johnson, *Space Debris Environment Remediation Concepts*, Fifth European Conference on Space Debris, 8, 8 (2009).

5 *Id.* at 8

mediate danger of orbital debris to space activities. There is also a need for states and private companies to invest in active debris removal projects.

The present ban on harmful contamination (Article IX of the Outer Space Treaty) does not include the production of all space debris. Since the emergence of international space law, the performance of space activities was always related to the inevitable generation of space debris. States silently agreed that leaving non-functional satellites in orbit would not be considered a legal violation of article IX of the Outer Space Treaty.

The interpretation of article IX of the Outer Space Treaty with respect to the potential of space debris to cause "potentially harmful interference" does not include consultation for every planned space mission with all space-faring nations.[6] It is evident that space debris creation per se is not legally banned. The absence in the Outer Space Treaty of the legal obligation of states to return non-functional space objects over which they have jurisdiction is a major weakness of international space law.

Wassenbergh makes a distinction between "harmful contamination" and interference.[7] He defines harmful contamination as biological, chemical or nuclear contamination and gives an example that carbon dioxide and nitrogen oxides represent a great danger to the ozone layer of the Earth. An example of extremely dangerous harmful contamination in outer space is the distribution of chemical bromine in the stratosphere, specifically the ozone layer, which would result in the spreading of large amounts of cosmic radiation to Earth, which could destroy life on it.[8]

Interference exists if there is a collision of radio spectrums and accumulation of debris. This classification makes a clear distinction between the physical and chemical characteristics of the objects in

6 Christopher D Williams, *Space: The Cluttered Frontier,* 60 J. Air L. & Com. 1157 (1994).

7 Henri A. Wassenbergh, *Principles of Outer Space Law in Hindsight*, 71 (1991).

8 Колосов Ю., Сташевский, С. *Борьба за мирний космос*, 41, 42 Статут, Москва (2014).

outer space, which could lead to damaging consequences for the outer space environment and safety in outer space.

Despite the fact that an attempt was made in article IX to regulate the preservation of the outer space environment, it is justly defined as an unsuccessful and ineffective one. Many scholars of the space law doctrine reached this conclusion because of the perception of the governments that outer space is a "laboratory for research". Space law doctrine makes an argument for the ineffectiveness of article IX stating that if there is space mining of a celestial body that leads to its "disfiguration", it will not be a violation of Article IX.

The lack of a clear definition of the term "harmful contamination" focusses on the question whether all space debris can be included in the scope of the term. The group of authors, who have developed the European space debris mitigation guidelines, adopt the position that the spreading of space debris could be interpreted as identical to the term harmful contamination, mentioned in the Outer Space Treaty. This approach is practical, and in my research the term "spreading of space debris" will be considered as an example of "harmful contamination" of outer space.

Jasentuliana acknowledges that the Outer Space Treaty is fundamental to international space law and it is fair that the treaty is known as Magna Carta of the space law. At the same time he also rightly points out that the general character of the norm in article IX sentence two, and precisely the lack of concrete measures that the states should be obliged to take in order to prevent harmful contamination, is a major weakness of the treaty.

1.1. Legal definition of space debris

In order to explore the international legal regime of space debris, it is necessary first to clarify the terms "space object" and "space debris" and to establish the relationship between them. It is essential because the consideration of space debris as a type of space object would mean that the general international legal regime for space objects, including rules of ownership, jurisdiction and liability, are applicable to space debris as well.

The term "space waste" has been used by legal scholars to distinguish from "space debris". A group of authors asserts that "space waste" indicates that there is an intention of the owner of the space object to abandon it.[9] According to a scientific report presented to the Scientific and Technical Subcommittee of COPUOS, space debris does not always qualify as "space waste". I don't see the merit of such a distinction between the terms. There are not any legal grounds to include this criterion to distinguish both terms. Therefore, in this research, the terms will be used interchangeably as synonyms, as there is no officially accepted terminology that distinguishes both.

At the end of the 50s and 60s of the twentieth century, began the discussion of the status of objects, which have been launched into outer space.

The norm in article VIII of the Outer Space Treaty illuminates this issue and regulates ownership of space objects.[10] The article contains the first international legal norm that regulates the status of the objects launched into outer space and it is a cornerstone of international space law.

Article VIII of the Outer Space Treaty regulates significant aspects of jurisdiction, control, and ownership of the objects launched into outer space, and explicitly points that celestial bodies are included in the scope of outer space. Consequently, the objects launched from Earth and situated on celestial bodies should also be considered

---

9 Academic Study *Active Debris Removal - An Essential Mechanism for Ensuring the Safety and Sustainability of Outer Space: A Report of the International Interdisciplinary Congress on Space Debris Remediation and On-Orbit Satellite Servicing*, A/AC.105/C.1/2012/CRP.16, 31 (2012).

10 Treaty on Principles Governing the Activities of States in the Exploration and Use of Outer Space, including the Moon and Other Celestial Bodies, 18 U.S.T. 2410 610 U.N.T.S. 205, 61 I.L.M. 386 (1967) [hereinafter Outer Space Treaty] Art. VIII, sentence 2 stipulates that *"Ownership of objects launched into outer space, and of their component parts, is not affected by their passage through outer space or by their return to the earth.*

space objects. From the norm in article VIII is visible that the right of ownership of all space objects, including their component parts, stays intact, without regard to their position in space: in outer space, in the air space of Earth, or on the surface of the Earth. Since the component parts of space objects are the main type of space debris, it can be concluded that article VIII of the Outer Space Treaty directly regulates the legal status of waste in outer space. At the same time, article VIII does not provide any obligations or recommendations to states about any regulatory aspects of ownership that should be included in the legal scope of space objects.[11] The purpose of the article is to regulate that the right of ownership is not affected by the presence of object in outer |space but not to provide norms that should be included in the scope of the right to ownership. The last is left for the states to regulate it in their national legislation.

The phrase "space object or its component parts" is used in another international space law treaty – Agreement on the Rescue of Astronauts, the Return of Astronauts (from now on referred to as Rescue Agreement).[12] Legal definitions of the terms "space object" and "space debris" are not provided in this treaty as well.

Albeit not a legal definition, the article 1d of the Liability Convention provided the first legal description of the term "space object".[13] The description of the term "space object" includes component parts of a space object as well as its launch vehicle and parts thereof. In the negotiations for adopting the convention, there is an absence of mentioning of space debris and whether all space debris should be considered space objects.[14] During these negotia-

11 Рубанов Август, *Взаимосвязь гражданского права России и международного космического права: вопросы теории*, 4 Государство и право, 64 (2006).

12 Agreement on the Rescue of Astronauts, the Return of Astronauts and the Return of Objects Launched into Outer Space, Art. 5.1, 19 U.S.T. 7570, 672 U.N.T.S. 119, 7 I.L.M. 149 (1968) [hereinafter Rescue Agreement]

13 Convention on International Liability for Damage Caused by Space Objects,24 U.S.T. 2389, 861 U.N.T.S. 187, 10 i.L.M. 965 (1972) [hereinafter Liability Convention]

14 U.N. COPUOS, Legal Subcommittee, 7th Sess., A/AC.105/C.2/SR

tions, which are known as "the space object debate",[15] the Italian delegation proposed a definition of "space object", which included launching vehicles, capsule, and all their component parts, which have been detached or broken during the transit.[16] This proposed definition had been supported by Argentine, Belgium, France and Mexico, but there was no unanimous support for it in the COPUOS. Instead of a definition, the above-mentioned description was adopted which was not comprehensive and did not bring any substantial legally scientific value. Every object contains its component parts in itself. Space objects are objects; ergo, they include into themselves their component parts.

As Gorove points out, there is no indication that the drafters of the Liability Convention ever intended to make a distinction (*between component parts and other parts of a spacecraft*) when they formulated the partial definition of a space object.[17] All parts of the space system are space objects.

In the Convention on Registration of Objects Launched into Outer Space (from now on referred to as the Registration Convention), it is also not given a definition of the term space object. The term is used to describe a payload launched into outer space with its component parts.[18]

The Registration Convention addresses many questions regarding space objects, but it does not mention any of the eligible methods of localization and identification of the space objects (including space debris). These important monitoring activities have been put into practice by a small number of leading space-faring states, and

---

(August 1968).

15 Howard Baker, Space Debris: Legal and Policy Implications 124 (1989).

16 U.N. COPUOS, Legal subcommittee, 9th Sess., A/AC.105/85 (3th July 1970).

17 Stephen Gorove, *Toward a Clarification of the Term Space Object-An International Legal and Policy Imperative* 21 J. Space L. 14 (1993).

18 The Convention on Registration of Objects Launched into Outer Space, article 1b, includes the phrase "as well as its launch vehicle and parts thereof". 28 U.S.T. 695, 1023 U.N.T.S. 15, 14 I.L.M. 43 (1975) [hereinafter Registration Convention]

this situation creates many advantages for technologically more developed countries over nations that do not possess comprehensive equipment for space situational awareness.

Presently, there is no universally accepted legal definition for the terms "space object" and "space debris".

An academic study[19] was presented in the 49th session of the Scientific and Technical Subcommittee of the UN Committee of Peaceful Use of Outer Space (from now on referred to as COPUOS). It provides a conclusion that space debris is included in the term "space objects". There is a pressing need to establish a common standard and a definition that is legally accepted by space-faring nations about the characteristics of space debris.[20] The conclusions and recommendations of the authors of the report are logical and well-grounded and need to be considered by the leading space-faring states. Vaskov and Malkov concluded that after an incident in outer space in which a space system is destroyed and ends its existence, the created space debris are also considered space objects and this is a common flaw of international space law.[21]

If there is not a significant change in the political will of the leading space-faring states to cooperate to achieve common legally binding definitions, it is unlikely that COPUOS will ever produce such definitions. This is evident from the lack of progress of COPUOS members to formulate a common definition of the term "aerospace object". For the purpose to produce a common legally binding definition of the last, a questionnaire was prepared to ad-

---

19 Academic Study *Active Debris Removal - An Essential Mechanism for Ensuring the Safety and Sustainability of Outer Space A Report of the International Interdisciplinary Congress on Space Debris Remediation and On-Orbit Satellite Servicing*, A/AC.105/C.1/2012/CRP.16, (2012).

20 Academic Study *Active Debris Removal - An Essential Mechanism for Ensuring the Safety and Sustainability of Outer Space A Report of the International Interdisciplinary Congress on Space Debris Remediation and On-Orbit Satellite Servicing* STSC, report A/AC.105/C.1/2012/CRP.16, 30, (2012).

21 Васьков, Сергей Арсеньевич, and Сергей Петрович Малков, *Нормативно-правовое обеспечение космической деятельности*, 87-89 (2003).

dress all member states of the Committee.[22] The initial version of the questionnaire was completed in the 34th session of the Committee in 1995. The total number of questions was reduced to ten. The title of the questionnaire and the questions have clearly guided the addressees about the key moments which are related to the so-called "aerospace objects", and the only aim of the questionnaire is that the cCommittee can be acquainted with the positions of the member states. Presently, there have been a total of 32 states (that is less than half of all member states) that have provided their official answers. For example, there has been an official answer from the delegation of Iraq: "This question is not clear enough and should be clarified".[23] Thirty-one states have been able to understand the question but not the representatives of Iraq. Moreover, there are still no official answers from the USA, China, France, the UK, Japan, among other leading states. The lack of an attempt even to present a national position and to defend it is a clear political sign that the term "aerospace object" will not be officially defined as well.

If the major UN committee, that was established to develop international space law, is not capable of producing basic legal definitions, it will be impossible to continue the legal regulation of all major issues related to outer space exploration and exploitation. This is a significant hindrance to the development of international space law and the future of safe outer space activities. The challenges of developing international space law and improving international co-operation between states in the framework of UN COPUOS are analysed separately in subchapter 2.1.1. of the present research.

On a regional level in Europe, we can find a definition adopted by the European Space Agency in the document "Space debris mitigation, for Agency projects, Terms and definitions". It stipulates that space object includes *all man-made space systems, its components,*

22 U.N. COPUOS report *Questionnaire on Possible Legal Issues with Regard to Aerospace Objects*, A/AC.105/635/add.1 (1996)

23 U.N. COPUOS report, *Compilation of replies received from member states to the questionnaire on possible legal issues with regard to aerospace objects*, A/AC.105/635 (15.01.1996).

parts or fragments. The term space system includes *"space ships, rocket launchers and object-related with the mission"*.[24] Presently, this policy is superseded by an updated ESA document "Space Debris Mitigation Policy for Agency Project".[25] The same definition of space debris applies in both documents.

The term "space object" was also defined in the document adopted by leading European states and ESA's "European code of conduct for space debris mitigation", Annex 2. The document states that space debris is *"any man-made space system and any of its components or fragments"*.[26] Presently, this definition is still valid for ESA member states.

The predominant understanding of the term "space object" is in its narrow meaning as a synonym of space system with its components, fragments, and parts thereof and not, for example, as every object in outer space.[27] Besides man-made objects, for safety in outer space, it is vital to keep an international public register of the asteroids, which could bring harm and damage to space systems and on Earth. Presently, The International Asteroid Warning Network is focused on obtaining information on the location and sizes of asteroids and on informing the UN and the general public on their movement and trajectory.[28]

For the purpose of the present research, we will consider the term "space object" as the most commonly referred man-made object, launched or sent in a different way into outer space, including on celestial bodies.

Baslar attempts to substantiate that the legal status of the celestial bodies is that they are a common heritage of mankind,[29] but

---

24 E.S.A. Space Debris Mitigation for Agency projects, Terms and definitions; ESA/ADMIN/IPOL(2008)2 ANNEX 2 (2008).

25 E.S.A. Space Debris Mitigation for Agency projects, ESA/ADMIN/IPOL(2014)2 ANNEX 2 (2014).

26 European code of conduct for space debris mitigation, Annex 2 (2004). https://www.unoosa.org/documents/pdf/spacelaw/sd/2004-B5-10.pdf

27 Registration Convention, Article 1(b)

28 http://iawn.net/about.shtml last visit 05.12.2022

29 Kemal Baslar, The concept of the common heritage of mankind in

such a conclusion is not accepted by most of the leading space-faring nations. The Agreement Governing the Activities of States on the Moon and Other Celestial Bodies(from now on referred to as the Moon Agreement)[30] indeed stipulates in article 11 par.1 that the Moon and its natural resources are common heritage of mankind, but the leading space-faring states refused to sign and ratify the agreement and abide by such a regime.[31] From the official position of the US President, expressed in an executive order from April 6th 2020, it is evident that *"the United States does not view outer space as global commons"*.[32]

Access to the Moon, Mars and other planets in the near future will require additional legal regulation of the usage of celestial bodies from states, intergovernmental organizations, private legal entities, and natural persons. The celestial bodies are an inseparable part of outer space[33], and when we are analysing the pollution of outer space and the creation of space debris, we should also include the man-made waste generated on celestial bodies. The technological capabilities of nations and private corporations to reach the Moon, planets in our solar system, and asteroids are increasing every year. The result of human activities on celestial bodies is the production of an enormous amount of waste, some of which could be preserved as artefacts for historical purposes and the heritage of mankind, but other pieces of waste could be detrimental to future explorations.

Even small objects located in outer space are travelling with very high velocity and an eventual impact with space systems al-

international law 166-198 (1998).

30 The Agreement Governing the Activities of States on the Moon and Other Celestial Bodies, 1363 U.N.T.S. 22, 18 I.L.M. 1434 (1979) [hereinafter Moon Agreement]

31 By February 10th 2023 only 18 states have ratified the treaty.

32 Exec. Order No. 13914 (Apr. 6, 2020), 85 Fed. Reg. 20,381 (Apr. 10, 2020) ("Encouraging International Support for the Recovery and Use of Space Resources"), https://www.federalregister.gov/documents/2020/04/10/2020-07800/encouraging-international-support-for-the-recovery-and-use-of-space-resources

33 Article 1 of the Outer Space Treaty: "The exploration and use of outer space, including the Moon and other celestial bodies…"

ways possesses an enormous amount of kinetic energy. For example, the astronauts John Young and Michael Collins from US Gemini-10 threw a bag with garbage on board. The Soviet cosmonauts from Salute-7 also have thrown bags with garbage that contains "dirty clothes, packages from food and other garbage".[34] This variety of objects would not have been of scientific interest if they were not placed in the Earth's orbit and do not have the potential to destroy satellites, space stations, and other useful space systems because of the velocity with which they are orbiting. These objects are also legally considered space objects and they are space debris. They are a part of the waste of the inventory of the space system, which is non-functional and man-made.

The Treaty Banning Nuclear Weapon Tests in the Atmosphere, in Outer Space and Under Water (from now on referred to as the Partial Nuclear Test Ban Treaty) is the only international agreement, which mentions the term debris, but only in the context of radioactive space debris.[35]

The International Academy of Astronautics (IAA) adopted the definition of orbital debris.[36]

One of the most significant distinctions between the definitions of IAA and COPUOS is that IAA refers to orbital debris, taking into consideration that environmental protection of celestial bodies is also of key importance.[37] It is evident that a broad definition of

---

34 James Oberg, Eyes on the Sky, Air and Space, 42-43 (1987).

35 The Treaty Banning Nuclear Weapon Tests in the Atmosphere, in Outer Space and Under Water Article I b), 14 U.S.T. 1313, 480 U.N.T.S. 43, 2 I.L.M. 889 (1963). https://treaties.un.org/doc/Publication/UNTS/Volume%20480/volume-480-I-6964-English.pdf

36 It states that "any man-made Earth-orbiting object which is non-functional with no reasonable expectation of assuming or resuming its intended function or any other function for which it is or can be expected to be authorized, including fragments and parts thereof. Orbital debris includes nonoperational spacecraft, spent rocket bodies, material released during planned space operations, and fragments generated by satellite and upper stage breakup due to explosions and collisions", Pos. paper on Orbital Debris SG 5.01, 2001, https://iaaspace.org/publications/iaa-cosmic-studies/#Pub-Stud-C5

37 IAA Study on Protecting the Environment of Celestial Bodies (PECB) SG

space debris should include orbital debris around Earth and other celestial bodies and man-made waste on celestial bodies.

1.2. Types of space debris

Different space debris causes different types of threats to outer space activities and to people and property on Earth and should be addressed separately. For example, radioactive space debris could be dangerous for human beings, the environment of Earth and of outer space, if these remnants are released in a usable orbit or if they are deorbiting back to Earth. The non-functional elements of space objects, which are made of easily destructible material could create space debris clouds of smaller pieces. Space objects, which are made with chemical components that could be poisonous to biological species upon contact with it, are causing a different type of threat than a space object, which doesn't have such chemical molecules.

Classification of space debris in this research is designed to include different aspects of space objects and to identify the different types of threats that potentially could emerge from them. This is required in order to evaluate the international regulation of space debris and the protection of the outer space environment from different significant aspects.

1.2.1. Classification of space debris according to their orbital location

In order to develop the most reliable measures of mitigation of space debris, it is important that outer space planning should include precise models for the determination of the location and trajectory of space objects in different areas of outer space. Consequently, the legal instruments should be consistent with the specifics of these areas.

The technical possibility for localization of space debris depends, on one hand, on the size of the debris, and on the other on the distance from Earth. The closer the space debris is to the Earth, the

5.6, https://iaaspace.org/publications/iaa-cosmic-studies/#Pub-Stud-C5

bigger the possibility to locate smaller objects. The technological progress in the last decades makes it possible to be located smaller and smaller particles as well to better estimate their trajectory and damaging effect on other space objects.

Space debris is predominantly in the orbits, which are used for space activities. An exception is "graveyard" orbits that are used for transferring non-functional satellites.

The most densely populated orbits with space functional space objects are Low Earth Orbit (LEO) and Geostationary Orbit (GEO).

These orbits have their specific features, which are taken into consideration in the ITU constitution and radio regulations. These orbits are also prioritized by the Inter-Agency Space Debris Committee as very important, and the regions in closest proximity around them are referred to as protected regions.[38]

There are different theoretical models of the borders of LEO. For the purpose of this research, I choose to adopt the most common delimitation of the boundaries of the LEO, particularly the view of the leading European "space states", that objects in LEO are those that are orbiting at an altitude between 110km and 2000 km above the Earth sea level.[39] The GEO is a circular geosynchronous orbit 35786 km in altitude above the Earth's equator.

The most populated area of outer space is at an altitude between 300 km and 1000 km above sea level. There is also a massive concentration of objects in the altitudes of 1450 km as well as in GEO.

A significant component of evaluating the probability of collisions of space objects is the orbital inclination. This is the angle between the orbital field and the equator of the Earth. For example, in GEO, between 30 and 35 degrees north and south latitude is a more densely populated inclination than others.

Another component, which influences the trajectories of space objects, is the orbital perturbations. This physical phenomenon of motion of a massive body subject to forces other than the gravi-

38 IADC Space Debris Mitigation Guidelines, 8, (2002).

39 The European Space Debris Safety and Mitigation Standard annex 2, 13 (June 2004).

tational attraction of a single other massive body should also be acknowledged in space debris orbits in order to have adequate international regulation.

These scientific and technical parameters are of great importance in order to understanding the factors leading to clusters of space objects in certain orbits. The more desired and accessible an orbit is, the higher will be the risk of collisions with many space objects, which are orbiting in it. The international forum, which is the most suitable for scientific debates and recommendations is the Scientific and Technical Subcommittee of COPUOS.

In the last two decades, the technological development allowed more states to gain access to outer space and more investments in satellites to be done by leading private space companies. These factors are causing additional difficulty in managing space objects and they require serious improvement of the principles and rules of access to the limited outer space resources and management of space traffic. Jakhu and Singh are correct in pointing out that equal rights to access and sustainability are at the heart of a discussion of space security.[40]

Space debris in Low Earth Orbit

The advantages of the Low Earth Orbit (LEO) are its affordable access and useful utilization, which is due to its relative proximity to the Earth. For example LEO is valuable for satellite images, telecommunication, remote sensing activities and other activities. Most of the present functional and non-functional objects are located in the LEO. The space debris in this orbit is increasing rapidly threatening useful space payloads to be destroyed. There is a real danger in the near future about the risk of collisions between payloads and space debris to be so high that huge areas of this orbit could become unusable.

An important characteristic of LEO is that the Earth's gravitation interacts with the objects stronger than in the other orbits.

40 Ram S. Jakhu & Karan Singh, *Space Security and Competition for Radio Frequencies and Geostationary Slots* ZLW 58. Jg. 1, 76, (2009).

Therefore the orbital life of the space objects there is the shortest. In a matter of years, the orbital life of objects in LEO is from several weeks to twenty years, and after that, the objects fall on the Earth's surface. If they are small in size and weak with chemical composition, they will burn into the thermosphere without any threat to outer space or to population on Earth. However, when space debris survives the entering of the lower levels of the atmosphere, they descend to Earth at enormous speed and could cause severe damage, including the loss of life. For example, in July 2009, space debris the size of a football ball[41] fell on the house of Mr Peter Welton in Hull city, UK. The debris went through the entire roof and landed in the living room. Luckily, there were no human casualties, but the consequences would be different if the debris had crashed in a nuclear station or another high-risk facility.

In 1984, International Astronautical Federation (IAF), in its own research, made the conclusion that space debris is "particularly dangerous and are a real problem" in LEO, and it is imperative to undertake international actions to solve the problem.[42] The conclusion of this research also focusses on the immediate need for international research and the development of policies for the prevention of dangers of space debris. Almost four decades later, the space debris problem is growing at a rapid speed and still needs comprehensive legal regulation.

Space debris in Geostationary Orbit (GEO)

The geostationary orbit is one of the geosynchronous orbits where the object is making its complete revolution for a time, which corresponds to that on the Earth – for about 23h56min. Its location of 35786 km above sea level of Earth's equator makes it more difficult and more expensive for a satellite to be sent but cost-effective to be used. Jakhu and Tronchetti are absolutely correct in

41 https://www.dailymail.co.uk/sciencetech/article-1220621/Red-hot-piece-space-junk-crashes-pensioners-roof.html , last visited Nov 30th (2022)

42 UNISPACE I, The world in space: a survey of space activities and issues, (1982).

their conclusion that GEO is a strategic resource, particularly for telecommunication and broadcasting purposes.[43] Precisely for this reason, the Inter-Agency Space Debris Committee IADC has made a proposal to include an adjacent area approximately 200 km below and above GEO in order to improve the safety of satellites moving in orbit.[44] States and private actors comply so far with this recommendation of IADC.

Figure 1

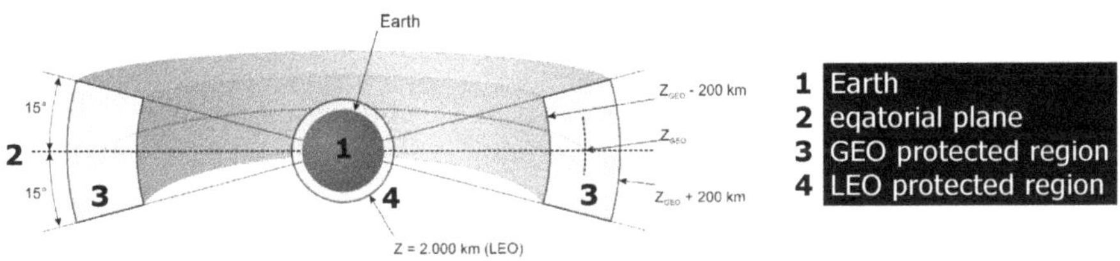

GEO is the only orbit in which a satellite has constant surveillance over a vast area of Earth, and it is seen from our planet as stationary. This simplifies its localization and sending and receiving signals through antennas from Earth. This orbit is actively used in the spheres of civil communication, meteorology, remote sensing, radio and television broadcasting and others. It is a desired orbit because GEO can provide uninterrupted contact with local Earth stations with only one satellite. It is necessary for the satellites to be placed in certain orbital slots.

These slots are of a certain number, which makes the GEO limited for use.[45] These natural restrictions are the reason for satellites to be of relatively large quantity and the risk of a collision is much higher than in Medium Earth Orbit for example. A collision between satellites or space debris and a satellite in this orbit would create a

43 Ram S. Jakhu, *The legal status of the geostationary orbit*, 7 Annals of Air and Space Law, 333, 333 (1982).

44 IADC Space Debris Mitigation Guidelines, 8, (2002).

45 Article 44(2) of the ITU Costitution declares that GEO is limited natural international resource.

devastating "tsunami" of floating space debris, which could destroy all useful payloads and turn this very important orbit uninhabitable. Because Earth's gravitational pull is not as strong as it is for objects in LEO, the space objects in GEO, including space debris, have an outage of millions of years. The International Telecommunication Union (ITU) further adopted a specific recommendation (ITU-R S.1003-2) for the environmental protection of the geostationary orbit. In this recommendation is also included an "encouragement" for the spacecraft operators "*to monitor the use of on-board propellant to ensure adequate fuel is available to achieve the required manoeuvre at the end of life.*" This guideline is important for the promotion of change in the practice of operators abandoning non-functional satellites in orbit.

In relation to the space debris, the velocity of the objects in GEO is between 0.1-0.8 km/sec, which is significantly slower than the velocity in LEO – an average of 10 km/sec. With respect to the velocity, the shock of collision is lower, which would lead to less detrimental damages and destruction. On the other hand, because of its big remoteness from Earth, the possibilities of tracking debris are more difficult. The announced technological capacity currently permits from the Earth's surface to be localized space debris in GEO, which is bigger than several decimetres.

The International Standardisation Organization (ISO) also adopted precise and concrete standards to guide private companies and states involved in space activities to re-orbit a satellite.[46]

There is no clear, legally binding requirement for the minimum distance between the satellites in GEO. In some cases, several satellites share the same slot. This logically increases the probability of collisions. In 1981, more than four decades ago, during a discussion about the effective use of GEO in COPUOS, the question

46 ISO, Disposal of Satellites Operating at Geosynchronous Altitude, ISO Standard, ISO 26872:2010, TC20/SC14, ISO/DIS 26872; Estimating the Mass of Remaining Usable Propellant, ISO Standard, ISO 23339:2010; Space Debris Mitigation Requirements, ISO Standard, ISO 24113:2019, https://www.iso.org/standard

of space debris damaging the outer space environment became a concern. During these debates, a proposal was made about the satellites launched in GEO. The proposal stated that satellites which are going to be launched in GEO have to be supplied with the necessary equipment for their removal after they become non-functional.[47] A year later in 1982, in the report of the second conference of the UN for exploration and peaceful use of outer space, a recommendation was made that the owners of satellites should have an obligation to return them safely to Earth. Such an obligation today is not mandatory and there are no legal sanctions for states and private companies to abandon non-functional space objects in any orbit, including GEO.

1.2.2. Classification of space debris according to their chemical structure

In the Chinese legal doctrine in the field of international space law, it was substantiated a classification of space debris, which is according to their chemical structure.[48]

This classification includes two major groups of space debris. The first group is called natural micrometeoroids, and the second group is known as artificial space debris. With this division, Chinese scholars include in the scope of space debris the natural micrometeoroids. It should be noted that micrometeoroids have different legal regimes from space debris. The first is natural particles for which existence the states are not legally liable, and they are not man-made objects. Space debris, on the contrary, is man-made space objects and legal ownership and jurisdiction remain the same as before they have become non-functional.

The positive element of the inclusion of micrometeoroids is that data collection for their location, size, structure and velocity

47 Report *Efficient use of the geostationary orbit*, UNISPACE I, A/CONF.101/BP/7 (1981).

48 C Li, Z Ouyang, Y Zou, J Liu, L Xu, *A proposal for chemical classification of space debris*, Third European Conference on Space Debris ESOC, Darmstadt, Germany, (19 - 21 March 2001).

should be gathered because they carry significant danger for collision with space payloads. It is methodologically incorrect to classify them as space debris.

These scholars further divided natural micrometeoroids according to their chemical structure of the following types: metals and phyllosilicates. Artificial space debris is classified into seven groups: polymers, non-metal space debris, metals and their alloys, oxides, sulfites and their analogues, halides and carbides.

The classification on the basis of chemical structure is very useful also to calculate the destructive capacity of space debris and other space objects in incidents in outer space or during re-entry on Earth. For this reason, gathering information on the chemical structure of space objects and analysing it well is a very important aspect of reducing pollution of outer space and increasing the safety of space traffic.

1.2.3. Observable and non-observable space debris

Malkov classifies space debris as observable and non-observable.[49] The observable objects could be located through different types of technological equipment. Malkov divides the space debris further in two subgroups, depending on the method of measurement. The first subgroup is space debris detected by radiolocation and the second subgroup is space debris detected by optical devices.

Both methods are important for gathering information about space debris, and they are mutually inclusive because they are used in different areas of outer space. Radiolocation is used predominantly in Low Earth Orbit, and optical devices are preferred for higher orbits, including the Geostationary orbit. The issues of space debris observation and space debris environmental modelling were extensively addressed at the COPUOS 54th session in 2011.[50]

The significance of this division of space debris is enormous because non-observable space debris carries an unforeseen threat.

---

49 Сергей Малков, Международное космическое право-учебное пособие, 218-220, 2002.

50 Report of COPUOS 54th session, A/66/20, 2011, point 102, p.16

In order to minimize the threat, it is needed localization devices of space objects to be improved. The level of detection of small-sized objects should be for particles, which are not likely to destroy a well-protected useful payload. The significant merit in Malkov's classification is that it uses functional criteria and not stationary criteria to classify space debris.

After the destruction of a satellite, most of its fragments are **untraceable** and have the potential to cause severe damage that includes destruction of payloads. In 2010, the officially declared technical capabilities of the US surveillance network for tracing objects into Low Earth Orbit were if the objects are the size of 4 cm. However, objects, which are of size 1 cm, can lead to the destruction of a payload or the piercing of a spacesuit of an astronaut who is in outer space. Taking into consideration the speed with which objects are moving in outer space, even micro-particle can produce serious damage to payloads. Therefore after the destruction of a satellite or another payload, there comes foreword the element of the **unforeseen threat**, which will increase the risk of subsequent destructions in outer space. Secondly, fragments are **scattered** in different orbits and disseminate the threat out of the orbit of the destructed satellite. Some of the produced fragments are **unstable** and will be subjected to further disintegration without crashing with other elements.

Thirdly, it is important to note that after the destruction of a satellite or other space object, dispensing the debris become **irreversible.** This is because a satellite could be removed from outer space, but it is technologically impossible to remove thousands of fragments and millions of particles.[51]

If a state or a private actor is planning the intentional destruction of a space object, they would have to calculate the size of the debris that would be deemed dangerous and the ways to avoid its creation. If the debris are small, the number of the fragments shall be large because the area-mass ratio of the fragment becomes large. The atmospheric drag becomes large too.[52]

---

51 SWF report *Advanced Debris Removal Vehicle (ADRV),* (2019)

52 Yu Jiang, *Debris cloud of India anti-satellite test to Microsat-R satellite,*

Due to an improvement in technology, smaller particles can be tracked, and shield technology of space objects is improving as well. For example, the Chinese Academy of Sciences has begun the construction of a new survey telescope to detect space debris in medium and high orbits.[53] The survey telescope should be able to detect small space debris and determine its orbit and operation law. The goal of the project is to gather early warnings of possible debris collisions and to avoid creation of space debris that is dangerous for functional space objects.

Only when scientific and technical aspects of space debris are thoroughly understood, legislative efforts could be improved. The first goal to achieve minimum "shield standards" is to provide protection for space objects and prevent their destruction from untraceable space debris and other particles. Therefore, the first goal is to achieve the protection of particles with a diameter of 4 cm in Low Earth orbit.

1.2.4. Radioactive space debris

Radioactive space debris can be generated mainly from two types of space activities. The first one is the testing of nuclear weapons in the lower layers of the atmosphere and the second type is a result of the destruction of a nuclear reactor in space.[54] Radioactive contamination, which is caused by the testing of nuclear weapons in outer space, is already prohibited by the Partial Nuclear Test Ban Treaty since 1963.[55] This treaty partially bans nuclear testing because its scope doesn't include nuclear tests on the ground and underground in the territory of the state conducting the test. Accidental nuclear explosions, such as nuclear-powered space object

---

6.8. Heliyon, (2020).

53 Xinhua *China begins construction of new survey telescope to detect space debris* Shine News Agency, (June 30th 2021) https://www.shine.cn/news/nation/2106301362/ last access 09.02.2023

54 UN Principles Relevant to the Use of Nuclear Power Sources in Outer Space, Principle 3 par.2 res.47/68, (1992).

55 Treaty banning Nuclear Weapon Tests in the Atmosphere, in Outer Space and Under Water, 14 U.S.T. 1313, 480 U.N.T.S. 43, 2 I.L.M. 889 (1963)

collisions with space debris, are not going to be considered a violation of the treaty.[56]

In this treaty as well as in other official documents and academic publications often is used the term "atmosphere" to designate several lower layers of the atmosphere, particularly the troposphere, the stratosphere, and the mesosphere. The other two upper layers of the atmosphere are the thermosphere (from 85km up to 600km) and the exosphere (from 600 km up to 10,000km).[57] They are situated, almost exclusively in what is considered to be legally outer space. This legal inconsistency with terms from physics can be interpreted as a narrow definition of the atmosphere that includes only its lower three layers.

It would be much more precise if international legal regime in the future uses the term atmosphere that encompasses five layers. The terms "airspace" and "outer space" should be used as areas with different legal regime and jurisdiction. For the outer space there is no clear, generally accepted legal boundary and the problem of delimitation between air space and outer space remains unresolved until the present day.[58]

The Partial Nuclear Test Ban Treaty is the only international agreement, which mentions the term "debris", but only in the context of radioactive space debris.[59] The total number of known conducted nuclear tests for the period 1946-1996 is above 2000, from which 500 tests have been conducted in air space, and others have been performed in low Earth orbit.

As a result of these tests, radioactive materials are produced, which have no useful purpose. If these radioactive materials are produced in outer space, they are dangerous space debris.

---

56 Kenneth F. Schwetje, *Space Law: Considerations for Space Planners*, LJ 12 Rutgers Computer & Tech, 245, 252 (1986).

57 US National weather service http://www.srh.noaa.gov/jetstream/atmos/layers.htm

58 Bin Cheng, *The legal status of outer space and relevant issues: Delimitation of outer space and definition of peaceful use*. 11 J. Space L., 94-98 (1983).

59 Treaty banning Nuclear Weapon Tests in the Atmosphere, In Outer Space and Under Water, art. I b), 14 U.S.T. 1313, 480 U.N.T.S. 43, 2 I.L.M. 889 (1963)

In 1954 the USA started Operation Castle and made the first test of a hydrogen bomb, which became the biggest radiological catastrophe in the United States of America, known as the Castle Bravo accident.[60] After this operation, the leading space-faring nations stood together united in their position that nuclear tests should be legally banned in the atmosphere, outer space, and underwater. After witnessing the risks and damages from such tests, the leading space-faring nations were persuaded to adopt the Partial Nuclear Test Ban Treaty.

The treaty was signed by the USSR, the USA, and Great Britain. The three countries already made dozens of tests. France continued its own testing program until 1974 and China until 1980. The last two nations have not signed the treaty but have made a declaration that they will follow it. Such absence of official legally binding commitments presents a risk for the future if their national policies change.

In the process of the adoption of the treaty, the USA and the USSR discussed mechanisms of control and methods for monitoring nuclear testing and a comprehensive test ban treaty in the future, which should also prohibit ground and underground tests.

Initially, the position of the USSR from October 17th 1956, is that it is not necessary to create an international legal mechanism for surveillance and control, arguing that it is technically impossible to conduct a nuclear test without this being registered by other states and that nuclear testing cannot be secret.[61] In a public statement, President Eisenhower rejected this argument stating that only the biggest nuclear tests can be registered and considering the vast area of the USSR, a smaller test might not be registered by other states. Consequently, on June 14th 1957 the USSR proposed the creation of a system for international control, that includes international commission and control posts

60 The United States Department of Defense; Defense Nuclear Agency (1982). Castle Series. Washington DC: United States Government Printing Office.

61 Partial Nuclear Test Ban Treaty, Narative Partial Nuclear Test Ban Treaty, Narative, 1963,

in the territories of the USSR, the USA, Great Britain, and the Pacific Ocean area.[62] The proposal was rejected by the United States. Despite the appeal to stop nuclear testing from Khrushchev in 1958, the US continued with the tests during the negotiations for the treaty. It needs to be stressed that during this period of negotiations, the first satellites in outer space were successfully launched and the beginning of the space age had started. For the two superpowers became a real possibility to send nuclear weapons in outer space and to militarize it with weapons of mass destruction.

In July 1958, an expert conference was held on the prohibition of nuclear weapons testing in Geneva. At the conference USA, USSR, Great Britain, France, Canada, Poland, Czechoslovakia and Romania participated. On August 21st, after the agreement on the technical parameters for control and monitoring of nuclear tests underwater in the atmosphere and in outer space, the conference concluded a report that offers the establishing of 160 earth posts, 10 posts on a ship, and regular specialized flights for control.[63] After the failure to negotiate a comprehensive test ban treaty and after the declaration of a temporary moratorium of nuclear tests USA and USSR, in July 1963 negotiations were held in Moscow to adopt a legally binding treaty to ban nuclear testing. They concluded with the adoption of the Partial Nuclear Test Ban treaty, which is still in force today. The weakness of the treaty is that it did not create an international system of control, but only a verification system to monitor the nuclear tests.

Outer space is explicitly stated as an area where nuclear testing is forbidden, and considering the fact that after 1980 there are no shreds of evidence that such tests have been conducted, it can be concluded that the treaty regulates the issue adequately and prevents the creation of radioactive space debris as a result of nuclear weap-

62 Ibid.

63 Thomas Schmalberger, In pursuit of a nuclear test ban treaty, (1991).

ons testing.[64] One of the main goals of the treaty is to prevent the global distribution of radioactive waste.[65]

The treaty differs from the following adopted five space treaties with the absence of the expression "including the moon and other celestial bodies" after outer space. Therefore, arises the question, are the states allowed to test nuclear weapons on the Moon and on other celestial bodies? The answer is: definitely no. It is not allowed because all celestial bodies are part of outer space, and secondly, even if there is a state that has a different interpretation of what includes in the scope of outer space, article I 1b) stipulates that nuclear testing is forbidden in any other environment if the explosion causes radioactive debris.[66] Article II of the Outer Space Treaty regulates that outer space must not be nationally appropriated.[67] The celestial bodies are not part of the territory of any state and are not under state jurisdiction and control. Therefore, the legal ban includes them too.

In article I p.2 is envisioned the obligation of the parties to refrain from causing, encouraging, or participating in, the conducting of any nuclear weapon test explosion in outer space. This commitment of the state parties to the treaty is an important addition to the ban, and it shows a declaration of will to prevent sharing of knowledge and technology for the development of the nuclear potential of other states, which might conduct a test in outer space. Despite this commitment, other states have already developed and are develop-

---

64 Article I p.1. states that "*Each of the Parties to this Treaty undertakes to prohibit, to prevent, and not to carry out any nuclear weapon test explosion, or any other nuclear explosion, at any place under its jurisdiction or control... including outer space.*"

65 Irene Atney-Yurdin, *Space Debris Legal Research Guide*, 3 Pace YB Int'l L., 167, 184 (1991).

66 Partial Nuclear Test Ban Treaty, Article I 1b) foresees the following: "*in any other environment if such explosion causes radioactive debris to be present outside the territorial limits of the State under whose jurisdiction or control such explosion is conducted.*"

67 Article II of the Outer Space Treaty foresees that *"outer space, including the Moon and other celestial bodies, is not subject to national appropriation by claim of sovereignty, by means of use or occupation, or by any other means."*

ing their own nuclear potential, and the risks of nuclear weapons being tested in outer space are rising every year.

In 1978, the international community was put on high alert when an incident took place with a Soviet satellite "Cosmos 954" with a nuclear reactor, which crashed in the territory of Canada. This accident clearly showed that space objects with nuclear power sources is not only dangerous for the safety of outer space operations but also for the life and safety of people on Earth's surface. The Canadian government's Whiteshell Nuclear Research Establishment looked into the debris, produced from the crash and concluded that "highly radioactive and dangerous debris from the satellite had been deposited on Canadian territory."[68]

It was evident that this incident was not a unique event, and a similar or more dangerous impact could occur in the future.[69] After the crash, Canada introduced a proposal to the legal subcommittee of COPUOS, which contained seven principles related to the safety of nuclear power sources in outer space.[70] The fourth principle of the proposal stipulates that each space object with a nuclear power source on-board shall be assessed thoroughly and comprehensively prior to each launch.[71]

Despite this proposal for a requirement for safety assessment, the problem remains that such an evaluation would be conducted by the launching state. This lack of objective international independent monitoring leads to uncertainty and a lack of guarantee for the effective protection of the outer space environment or safety on Earth. Every state has its own policy on what is an acceptable risk. In addition, states could choose to become a "flag of convenience"

---

68 Protocol of Settlement of Claim between Canada and the Union of Soviet Socialist Republics for Damage Caused by "Cosmos 954", point 27 (Released on April 2, 1981).

69 Andrew Brearley, *Reflections upon the notion of liability: The instances of Kosmos 954 and space debris*. 34 J. Space L., 300 (2008).

70 UN, GAOR, COPUOS, *The elaboration of draft principles relevant to the use of nuclear power source in outer space*, A/AC.105/C.2/L.154/Rev.2, (1987).

71 Report LS, COPUOS, AC.105.484E, 14 (1991). http://www.oosa.unvienna.org/pdf/reports/ac105/AC105_484E.pdf

for private actors and require less contingent safety rules and review of the launch.[72]

The third proposed principle envisions concrete steps and criteria for the safety assessment, which should be used when the object is reviewed. This principle points out that the risk of radiological contamination should be minimized according to the requirements in the recommendations of the International Commission on Radiological Protection. The same principle proposes that in order to prevent radiological contamination of Earth from space objects with nuclear power sources, the states should try to place the objects in the so-called nuclear-safe orbits. The space object in these orbits would last for a minimum of three hundred years. The responsibilities of considering which orbits are sufficiently high and whether nuclear reactors are those that use exclusively highly enriched uranium 235[73] remain only to the launching states.

The principles are not adapted to accommodate future technological developments in nuclear propulsion systems. It would have been preferable for the principles to include a statement that particular requirements applied to nuclear propulsion cannot yet be formulated at the present state of technological development.[74]

The issue of using nuclear sources of energy in outer space is raised for discussion in the GA of the UN, and in 1980 on the 35th session, the dangers of using these power sources are acknowledged.[75] During the session, attention was given to safety of using

72 Kai-Uwe Schrogl & Charles Davies, *New Look at the Concept of the Launching State-The Results of the UNCOPUOS Legal Subcommittee Working Group 2000-2002, A/Der Begriff des Startstaats-Ergebnisse der UNCOPUOS Arbeitsgruppe zum Launching State/Le Terme Etat de Lancement: Resultats du Groupe de Travail de l'UNCOPUOS*, 51 ZLW, 366 (2002).

73 Resolution of G.A. U.N., Principle 3, par.2 c), 47/68 (December 1992).

74 Marietta Benko, Gerhard Gruber & Kai-Uwe Schrogl, *UN Committee on the Peaceful Uses of Outer Space: Adoption of Principles Relevant to the Use of Nuclear Power Sources in Outer Space and Other Recent Developments*, 42 ZLW, 40 (1993).

75 Report of COPUOS, 45, A/35/20, (1980) http://www.oosa.unvienna.org/pdf/gadocs/A_35_20E.pdf

nuclear power sources and reaffirmation that nuclear power sources in outer space exploration are needed to be used.[76]

The focus was also drawn to international law on the subject, but it was only stated that only the legal regime should be reviewed.[77] In 1992 the GA of the UN adopted a resolution of the "Principles relevant to the use of nuclear power sources in outer space unanimously".[78]

Considering the fact that the principles were adopted through the instrument of resolution of GA of the UN, they are not legally binding principles. This is due to the fact that GA resolutions are not legally binding. Since it is not a declaration of a pattern of behaviour of the state, due to international legal obligation, this particular resolution does not reflect customary international law.

These principles are not recognized by states as general principles of international law, and they are not norms *jus cogens*. Their characters are merely legally non-binding declaration for partial mitigation of the risks of using nuclear power sources in outer space. The scope of the principles includes only nuclear sources for electricity but not for using nuclear energy in the propulsion system or nuclear substances, which are in outer space.[79]

There are eleven adopted principles. The third principle foresees the restriction of usage of nuclear power sources to only those missions in space, which cannot operate optimally with non-nuclear energy sources. The aim is to minimize the generation of radioactive materials in outer space.[80] What constitutes a reasonable way for the operation of a space mission is going to be decided by the operator of the mission. This signifies that states are not willing to allow common international safety standards monitored by an independent international body.

76 Report of COPUOS, A/35/20;p. 46 and 47

77 Ibid. p. 48 http://www.oosa.unvienna.org/pdf/gadocs/A_35_20E.pdf

78 UNGA Res.47/68 (Dec.12, 1992). http://www.oosa.unvienna.org/oosa/en/SpaceLaw/gares/html/gares_47_0068.html

79 UNGA Res.47/68 (Dec.12, 1992); See more Lotta Viikari *The environmental element in space law*, 83, (2008).

80 *Id.* at Principle 3

It became obvious that these principles were carefully negotiated in order to not obligate the states legally. The aim was to provide a formal response to the growing concern of states, private organizations, and individuals after the incident with the Soviet satellite "Cosmos 954".

The massive usage of nuclear power sources for spacecraft was on hold for a period of almost three decades after 1988. The usage of NPS was not performed after 1988.[81] However, the new impetus for missions to Moon and Mars has given new life to NPS innovation for propulsion systems of different countries. For example, NASA initiated Project Prometheus, whose main aim is to develop nuclear systems.[82] In September 2020, NASA and the Department of Energy (DOE) issued a formal request for proposals for a lunar nuclear power system.[83]

Roscosmos is also planning to launch a spacecraft utilizing nuclear-powered propulsion systems for missions to the Moon, Venus and Jupiter.[84]

Future deep space missions would require the usage of nuclear power sources until safe technological alternatives are not introduced to the general public and academia. This means that the risk of nuclear space debris due to collisions will increase.

The international legal framework has to be further developed by the leading space-faring states to adopt international legally binding norms, guidelines, and standards in order to avoid a disastrous nuclear incident.

1.2.5. Debris on celestial bodies

Space debris should not be equated terminologically to orbital debris. Space debris is also produced on celestial bodies. The legal issues with respect to space waste creation activities are analysed

81 N. Johnson, *A new look at nuclear power sources and space debris*, Fourth European Conference on space debris, 4,(2005).

82 Report *Prometheus Project*, NASA/JPL.,191 (October 1st, 2005).

83 https://www.nasa.gov/press-release/nasa-announces-nuclear-thermal-propulsion-reactor-concept-awards, last accessed on 05.12.2022

84 https://tass.com/science/1113827, accessed on 05.12.2022

separately as the produced waste is causing threats of different nature compared to debris in orbit.

Exploration and exploitation of celestial bodies result in the generation of a large number of debris. Although these non-functional objects are not in orbit and cannot pose a threat to functioning space systems and human life on Earth, it should be included in the scope of space debris. The three elements that define space debris exist cumulatively. These are 1) man-made objects; 2) that are non-functional; 3) that are located in outer space. Celestial bodies are considered part of outer space.[85] The risk of polluting the Moon, Mars and other celestial bodies in the near future is increasing with the advancement of space technology and with the rapid increase of investments from the private sector.

Viikari correctly summarized that the dominating attitude of treating outer space, including celestial bodies, is to be a mere resource reserve and a dump for the refuse produced by space activities.[86] This attitude is the main risk of polluting celestial bodies.

Private companies, which are planning to use celestial bodies for the purpose of tourism, are interested in a safe ecosystem and aim for lack of pollution. Other companies, on the other side, have plans to exploit asteroids or the Moon through the mining of valuable resources. These activities would cause pollution and production of space debris that could jeopardize touristic activities or important scientific projects.

There are private companies that encourage space travel for tourism purposes, such as Virgin Galactic L.L.C., offering suborbital flights in outer space.[87] Leading private companies like Space X and Blue Origin are also engaged in space touristic activities and plan to continue in the future on celestial bodies.[88]

---

85 Stephen Gorove, *Interpreting article II of the outer space treaty*, 37 Fordham L. Rev.37, 349, (1968).

86 Lotta Viikari, *The environmental element in space law*, 14, (2008).

87 http://www.virgingalactic.com/ last access 10.02.2023

88 Private passenger program is functioning https://www.spacex.com/human-spaceflight/, last accessed on 10.02.2023

Sreejith is correct in his observation that space science is split into fragments and further divided into scientific projects for bids.[89] It is true that space activities include much more private actors presently than in the past and that space law development is dependent on the interests of private actors in outer space.[90] The biggest problem that privatization of outer space activities presents to the development of international space law and to achieving safety in the outer space environment is the lack of a common philosophy to utilize outer space in the interest of humankind and its many scientific areas. The rapid increase of privately owned satellites in outer space, especially after the launching of thousands of Starlink satellites in the last three years, requires the adoption of adequate and comprehensive liability rules, covering damages caused by space debris to the outer space environment.[91]

Chimni is absolutely correct in his overall conclusion that the ongoing "privatization of the UN system" reduces the possibility of UN forums to serve as the centre for collective action of states from the so-called "third world".[92] The internal structure and decision-making process of international organizations such as ITU and COPUOS show that the interests of third-world countries are not well-protected in the most significant international space law forums. The private space sector is influencing global international space policy development to prioritize its aims of profit-making from space activities instead of global sustainable investments in the service of all humankind.

The lack of motivation to invest in space projects which are not generating economic profit, the competition for the usage of orbital

---

89 S.G. Sreejith, *Unmaking a National Space Legislation for India: Indigenizing Space Law through the Organic Science of the Indian Space Program.* 83 J. Air L. & Com.,118, (2018)

90 Marietta Benkö, Kai-Uwe Schrogl, Denise Digrell, and Esther Jolley, eds. 2*Space law: current problems and perspectives for future regulation*, 2 (2005).

91 Isabella Henrietta Philepina Diederiks-Verschoor & Vladimir Kopal, *An introduction to space law*, 121, (2008).

92 Bhupinder S. Chimni, *International institutions today: an imperial global state in the making*, 15/1 European Journal of International Law, 15 (2004).

slots, and territory on celestial bodies, and the mentality of cost-savings instead of the application of higher standards are additional mental obstructions from the private sector. This lack of vision is causing the unsustainable and inequitable usage of outer space that we are presently witnessing.

This status quo could be overcome by introducing comprehensive legal regulation from states on a national and international level and by considering the interests of humankind in all space activities.

In order to avoid the emergence of military conflict between competing space-faring nations, it would be very practical to adopt governing mechanisms and long-term plans for the utilization of celestial bodies that is acceptable by all space-faring nations, in the interest of developing nations and in the interest of humankind.

Such a higher perspective of governance that is inclusive of different national, commercial, and scientific interests is also needed because particular locations on celestial bodies carry different significance today in scientific fields. For example, in the field of radio astronomy, specific craters on the far side of the Moon have been identified to become "lunar quiet zones", as defined by ITU.[93] Other locations, one of them being the Daedalus crater, have been identified as suitable to become a new radio-quiet zone, and a proposal was made in 2010 for receiving official status as such.[94] Maccone also substantiated that on the far side of the Moon needed to be chartered a special zone with a diameter of 1820 km only for scientific studies. This zone is referred to as Protected Antipode Circle.[95] Mining activities and tourism on celestial bodies should not be allowed to occur without regard to the interests of other scientific fields, such as radio astronomy. The production of waste on the Moon should also be extremely careful not to affect radio frequencies significantly. Tourism in outer space should be per-

93 Presently the crater Saha is designated such status after the adoption of ITU recommendation 479-4

94 Claudio Maccone, Proposing a New Radio-Quiet Zone on the Farside of the Moon, COPUOS 53 Tech.S. (June 11th 2010).

95 Ibid.

ceived as an increased risk for the generation of space debris but also as a source of financial resources necessary to fund orbital space cleanup.[96] Controversial scientific experiments have been already conducted on the Moon, which is causing unpredicted effects for future scientific studies or commercial initiatives. An example of such an experiment is the NASA Lunar Crater Observation and Sensing Satellite impactor LCROSS mission, which became known as the "NASA Moon bombing".[97] The purpose of the mission was to determine whether there is water on the Moon crater Cabeus. The project was conducted by crashing the satellite in the crater and performing a spectral analysis of the debris after that. The danger of such questionable experiments lies in two aspects. The first one is that they are conducted without prior consultations with other states, such as China, India, Japan and Russia that were conducting or planning to conduct scientific experiments in the area during this intentional collision. The actions of NASA could be interpreted as aggressive by other nations and a violation of Article IV of the Outer Space Treaty. The second aspect of conducting scientific experiments without prior consultations with states, COPUOS, ITU and other international organizations, which are responsible for scientific studies in outer space, is that activities such as intentional collisions of satellites and explosions could jeopardize the further study and use of this particular area for the future generations. The knowledge of the importance of a specific location, crater, or underground resources may be discovered in the future and activities in the present should be planned not to harm the optimal utilization of the celestial body in the interest of humankind. If we accept the purpose of this mission and the methods of this scientific experiment as stipulated, it is illogical and unjustifiable for a scientific project to aim to discover water in a Moon crater by polluting the location with space debris and

96 Agatha Akers, *To infinity and beyond: Orbital space debris and how to clean it up*, 33 U. La Verne L. Rev., 285, 295-296 (2011).
97 News of Huffington post https://www.huffpost.com/entry/nasa-lcross-mission-to-bo_n_311038 accessed last on 10.02.2023

by destroying the frozen reservoirs for future missions. There is no legitimate scientific purpose in applying aggressive scientific methods to discover a vital resource, such as water in outer space if the scientific team is polluting it in the process.

Conducting scientific missions, that are destroying resources and creating a huge amount of debris, illustrates the need for a holistic approach and clear international legally binding mechanisms, which have to be adopted by leading states and by private actors. It is essential that states and private organizations engage in an open debate about plans for utilizing celestial bodies. Elon Musk has publicly announced ideas for bombing Mars and using nuclear weapons to terraform the planet.[98] Such plans have to consider all aspects of environmental protection of outer space.

1.2.6. Debris from anti-satellite tests (ASAT)

The usage of anti-satellite weapons and testing of such weapons is not an explicit violation of international law, even if their own targets are destroyed. The USSR and the USA conducted dozens of tests during the cold war. The Russian Federation conducted the last deliberate satellite destruction with an ASAT weapon on 15th November 2021[99] and previously on December 16th 2020.[100] India conducted a test in March 2019, China in January 2007 and, the USA in February 2008. The Chinese government acknowledged that they were testing their anti-satellite weapon, while the actions of the USA were presented as a rescue operation in which a dangerous satellite was destroyed. Russia had conducted a series of non-destructive ASAT tests - the last two were on 16th December 2020, according to the US Space Command[101] and on 15th Novem-

---

98 News reported by the website Popular Mechanics https://www.popularmechanics.com/science/a32588385/elon-musk-terraform-mars-nuclear-missiles/ last access on 10.02.2023

99 https://www.nasa.gov/press-release/nasa-administrator-statement-on-russian-asat-test, last access on 10.02.2023

100 Pavel Podvig Pavel, *Nudol ASAT system tested from Plesetsk*, Russian Strategic Nuclear Forces. (December 17th 2020).

101 U.S. Space Command Public Affairs Office, News Nov. 15th 2021, https://

ber 2021.[102] The United States Vice President Harris announced on April 18th 2022 that the U.S. will place a ban on the "destructive direct-ascent anti-satellite missile testing." This is a positive step, but it indicates also that kinetic anti-satellite tests would continue to be a possibility in the future.

Presently, there is no international legal treaty banning or severely restricting the conduct of destructive anti-satellite tests. This lack of legal regulation means that states have not prohibited the deliberate production of space debris from this activity.

In order to understand whether there is a norm from international legal custom, which prohibits the anti-satellite tests, we should review whether there is a relevant practice of the states and if the representatives of the states consider such practice as an international legal obligation.

To fulfil abstention from testing the anti-satellite weapon, it is necessary for the states to be in possession of such a weapon or at least have the technological capacity to develop it. Only if the state has the option to test the weapon and it chooses not to do so, then the prerequisite for state practice exists.

In its detailed research for international custom and anti-satellite tests, Koplow points out that the majority of testing was conducted by the USA and USSR until 1985, and after that, only the USA, China and recently India have conducted a total of dozen of tests.[103] The fact that EU states, Japan, Canada, and Brazil have the potential to test, but they have not performed anti-satellite tests, could shows abstinence. What needs to be analysed is the subjective element-- (opinio juris) -- whether the states consider their behaviour of abstinence from testing as an international legal obligation.

---

www.spacecom.mil/Newsroom/News/Article-Display/Article/2842957/russian-direct-ascent-anti-satellite-missile-test-creates-significant-long-last/ last access on 10.02.2023

102 https://www.nasa.gov/press-release/nasa-administrator-statement-on-russian-asat-test, last access on 10.02.2023

103 David Koplow, *ASAT-isfaction: Customary International Law and the Regulation of Anti-satellite weapons*; 30 Michigan Journal of International Law, 1187, 1239 (2008).

Most states are unwilling to declare explicitly that their behaviour is due to an international legal obligation because it would be a restriction for them in the international arena.

On the contrary, all major space-faring nations consider the conduction of ASAT tests as legally allowed. For example, in the adopted national space policy of the United States from August 31 2006, by the Bush administration, it was mentioned that conducting anti-satellite and other tests in outer space are activities part of the American national interests and that the US "will oppose the development of new legal regimes or other restrictions."[104]

The US space policy, from June 2010, adopted by the Obama administration, focussed on reducing space debris, but in no way it was referred that abstinence in anti-satellite testing is due to international legal obligation.

Another possibility for understanding the attitude of a state towards these tests is to study the situations when a state is expressing its position and attitude towards a test made by another country. For example, after the Chinese test in 2007, the US had expressed that the actions were "regrettable"[105] and had characterised the test as "very worrisome", "destabilising", and "quite unpleasant",[106]

104 National Space Policy of the United Space of America, point 2 „The United States will oppose the development of new legal regimes or other restrictions that seek to prohibit or limit U.S. access to or use of space. Proposed arms control agreements or restrictions must not impair the rights of the United States to conduct research, development, testing, and operations or other activities in space for U.S. national interests." (August 31st 2006).

105 Christina Rocca, Ambassador, U.S. Permanent Representative to the United Nations, Prevention of an Arms Race in Outer Space, Statement to the Conference on Disarmament (Feb.13th, 2007), http://www.usmission.ch/Press2007/0213PAROS.html (last accessed on 10.02.2023) (expressing the U.S. government's view that China's 2007 ASAT test was "regrettable").

106 Theresa Hitchens, *U.S.-Sino Relations in Space: From "War of Words" to Cold War in*
Space? 5 China Security 12 (Winter 2007); (quoting U.S. Department of State Deputy Spokesperson Tom Casey, who, referring to debris-creating ASAT tests, stated, "[w]e don't believe anyone should be doing these kinds of activities"); Wade Boese, Chinese Satellite Destruction Stirs Debate, Arms Control Today, Mar. 2007, at 27, 28 (quoting U.S. government officials labeling the Chinese test

but not once it was mentioned that this test is a violation of international law.

The assessment of Russia, EU member states, India, Brazil, Australia, Taiwan, and South Korea towards the Indian, Chinese and US anti-satellite tests are also negative, but they do not point out that this is a violation of international law.[107]

Only the reaction of the Japanese prime minister at that time, Shinzo Abe, in relation to the Chinese test, can be interpreted as that anti-satellite tests are a violation of international law.[108] However, Japanese government's position is not sufficient to determine if there is evidence of international legal custom because the international community and particularly the other space-faring nations consider ASAT tests legally allowed.

Therefore, it can be concluded that there is not any norm from international legal custom or international treaty, which prohibits the anti-satellite testing and generating of space debris from it.

The danger that outer space is used as a polygon where a state can demonstrate their military power is the most dangerous aspect of space debris creation. Destruction of satellites via ASAT weapons could lead to extremely difficult usage of Earth's orbits and challenging outer space traffic management.

Hobe rightly points out that damage to international objects, which are "common" or common heritage of mankind (Antarctica, High Sea, seabed, and Outer Space), cannot be compensated *per se,* and the calculation of such harm is nearly impossible.[109] At the same time, states should be liable for damages to the high seas, for example, as they have failed to comply with their legal obligation to

---

as "very troubling," "very worrisome," "destabilizing" and "quite unpleasant").

107 Theresa Hitchens, *U.S.-Sino Relations in Space: From "War of Words" to Cold War in Space? 5 China Security*, 14, (2007)

108 Space Daily, Japan's Abe Charges China Satellite Test Illegal, Space Daily, Jan. 31, 2007,available at http://www.spacedaily.com/reports/Japan_Abe_Charges_China_Satellite_Test_Illegal_999.html (last accessed on 10.02.2023).

109 Stephan Hobe*, Space Debris: A proposal for its international legal regulation, Proc. 34th Colloquium L. Outer Space,* 195-199 (1992)

protect the marine environment,[110] which is reflected in international legal custom and in the UN Convention on the Law of the Sea.[111]

Anti-satellite weapons are a much-desired military system by many states because they could severely destroy the outer space assets of leading space-faring nations.

Firstly, the destruction of military space assets of the US or other space-faring nations results in severe limitation of the military operational capacity of the damaged state. The US Strategic Command, US Army and other US agencies have concluded that the land, sea, air and outer space arena for military operations have become "very dependent on outer space resources".[112]

Secondly, the conclusion of US military agencies in the war games scenario is that if nuclear detonations are conducted by the "neighbouring country of Ukraine" in outer space to destroy US military assets, the result will be the almost complete annihilation of the US space-based capabilities. The US military leadership since the 1990s concluded that in case of war, the "Space Pearl Harbour" would be "virtually certain" and a very effective way for a US adversary to reduce the US military superiority.[113]

India's anti-satellite test called "Mission Shakti" was conducted in Low-Earth Orbit and was planned in a way not to create long-term orbital debris.[114] From a national military perspective, the ASAT test was a huge success for India. Analysing the military test

---

110 Pierandrea Leucci, *Outer space and the marine environment: responsibility of states for damages caused by man-made space debris to the marine environment of areas beyond national jurisdiction*, 19 (2017).

111 United Nations Convention on the Law of the Sea, art.212-222, Dec. 10, 1982, 1833 U.N.T.S 1833 U.N.T.S. 397, 21 ILM 1261. [hereinafter Law of the Sea Convention]

112 Benjamin S. Lambeth, *Mastering the ultimate high ground*, 100, (2003); William B. Scott, *Wargames Underscore Value of Space Assets for Military Ops*, 146(18)Aviation Week and Space Technology, 60, (April 28, 1997).

113 Report of the Commission to Assess United States National Security Space Management and Organization, 100,(January 11, 2001), [hereinafter Space Commission Report]

114 Vladimir Akhmetov, Vadym Savanevych, and Evgen Dikov, *Analysis of the Indian ASAT test on 27 March 2019*, (2019) arXiv preprint arXiv:1905.09659

from the perspective of environmental protection and the amount of space debris that was created, it can be concluded that the mission was very successful, and the parameters of the test were chosen to minimise the risk for space objects from the created debris, and the orbital life of the non-functional parts was planned to be less than 45 days.[115] At the same time, immediately after the mission, NASA reported that the risk of collision of the debris with the ISS had increased by 44% after the test and that the agency tracked about 60 debris objects larger than 10 cm.[116]

Taking into consideration that the destruction of the space assets of space-faring nations is very effective, prompt for execution and very feasible to achieve, the outer space environment and the whole space sector are extremely vulnerable to a military conflict between space-faring nations, which possess anti-satellite weapons and nuclear weapons.

In order to preserve its military superiority, or at least advantage, the US has adopted a strategic policy goal to deny other states access to outer space, if it becomes necessary.[117] The international response to this national policy is that states that are striving to maintain their national security and independence from the USA, such as China, Russia and India, are investing in anti-satellite weapons and are aiming to test them. The result is a much less safe outer space environment, increased difficulties for space traffic management and tension in international relations. The adoption of an international legal ban on ASATs is analysed in subchapter 3.5., which is explored the international cooperation at the Conference of Disarmament.

---

115 Vladimir Akhmetov, Vadym Savanevych, and Evgen Dikov, *Analysis of the Indian ASAT test on 27 March 2019*, (2019) arXiv preprint arXiv:1905.09659

116 Yu Jiang, *Debris cloud of India anti-satellite test to Microsat-R satellite*, 6.8. Heliyon, (2020).

117 William B. Scott, *Commission Lays Foundation for Future Military Space Corps*, 154(3) Aviation Week and Space Technology, 433, 2001

1.3. Ownership, jurisdiction and control over space debris

In order to begin the steady minimisation of the risks from space debris and gradual solving of this problem, it is necessary to clarify the issues of ownership, jurisdiction, and control over functional space objects and space debris.

The increased activities of private space actors in conducting outer space activities led to the legal condition that many of the satellites in outer space are owned by private organisations: corporations and other non-governmental organisations. Despite the fact that private organisations have enormous influence in space law both in its development and its decline, according to the norm in Article VI of the Outer Space Treaty,[118] the states are the legal subjects that have to exercise control over their non-governmental organisations.

Many of the corporations are multinational, and they conduct their activities in many states, and it is possible that difficulties may arise in determining which is the "appropriate" state that should maintain supervision. The legal status of a space object of a private organisation is that the private organisation has ownership, and the state where the object is registered has jurisdiction and control over it. Consequently, if a private company acts in breach of the Outer Space Treaty, the state of registry can be held responsible for that breach.[119]

The definition of the launching state in the Registration Convention and in the Liability Convention affirms the possibility for several states of being launching states, and therefore they will be jointly and severally liable.[120]

The norm in article VIII paragraph 1 of the Registration Convention stipulates that the object over which the state retains ju-

118 Article VI of the Outer Space Treaty, 1967 stipulates "*The activities of non-governmental entities in outer space, including the Moon and other celestial bodies, shall require authorization and continuing supervision by the appropriate State Party to the Treaty.*"

119 Ram S. Jakhu & Paul Stephen Dempsey, eds. *Routledge Handbook of Space Law*, 7, (2016).

120 Article IV par.2 of Liability Convention, 1972

risdiction should be registered in the national register of a state party of the treaty. The question arises whether the state retains jurisdiction over an object that has been launched in outer space and is property of the state or owned by its private organisation, but the object has not yet been registered. This hypothesis is very real because, in practice, states are delaying their registration, and states could have secret space objects, which are either non-registered, or information about their registration may not be provided to UN Secretary-General.[121] The last is an obligation under the Registration Convention.[122] Evidence for these practices can be seen in a list that contains more than 1374 space objects, for which detailed information has not been provided to UNOOSA.[123] Jakhu, Jasani and McDowell are absolutely correct in their observation that one of the most important purposes of sharing information about the registration of space objects is to achieve full international transparency.[124] At the same time, there is no legal obligation for a state to register unsuccessful attempts to launch a space object. Precisely in this kind of unsuccessful launch, an accident may occur and an object that has not entered outer space can destroy itself on the territory of another state. Despite the fact that for such an object, there is no obligation to be registered, for the state in which territory the object has landed, there is an obligation to inform the launching state[125] and return the object upon request.[126] The state, which makes the request, should prove that it is a launching state.

---

121 During the writing of the research 1374 space objects have not been registered, according to the UNOOSA online index: https://www.unoosa.org/oosa/osoindex/search-ng.jspx?lf_id, last accessed on 10.02.2023

122 Article II of The Registration Convention, 1974

123 UNOOSA online index: https://www.unoosa.org/oosa/osoindex/search-ng.jspx?lf_id=, last accessed on 10.02.2023

124 Ram S. Jakhu, Bhupendra Jasani, & Jonathan C. McDowell, *Critical issues related to registration of space objects and transparency of space activities*, 143 Acta Astronautica, 406, 413, (2018).

125 Article V par.1 of The Rescue Agreement, 1968

126 *Id.* Article V par.3

Pusey argues that the registration of space objects should be automated, and the information should be provided continuously and not only at the time of launch.[127] She is correct in her assessment that this would increase the utility of the UN registry, and it would be beneficial for those space actors who are trying to evaluate the risks associated with space debris.

Hobe analysed the definition of the term "jurisdiction". According to him, it stands for the meaning that it is the authority to make practical binding pronouncements on legal matters and to administer justice within a defined area of responsibility.[128] States have the general jurisdiction to prescribe applicable national laws and enforce them, and usually require private organisations to apply for authorisation and licenses to conduct space activities.[129]

Malkov gives a similar definition of the term "jurisdiction" that focusses on the aspects to carry out legislative, executive and judicial authority over persons, and objects, which are in outer space, including on the celestial bodies.[130] In my opinion, this definition is an accurate one and it can be broadened to include objects that were launched but have not reached outer space and also for objects that are returning to Earth from outer space and are in air space or have landed.

The meaning of the word "control" in article VIII of the Outer Space Treaty is ambiguous. There are several hypotheses on the meaning of control, and they are the following: 1) part of jurisdiction; 2) actual control of the object, or 3) authority (the right and duty) to control the object.[131]

---

127 Natalie Pusey, *The case for preserving nothing: The need for a global response to the space debris problem*, 21 Colo. J. Int'l Envtl. L. & Pol'y, 425, 438, (2010).

128 Stephan Hobe, Geradine Meishan Goh & Julia Neumann, *Space Tourism Activities-Emerging Challenges to Air and Space law*, 33 J. Space L. 33, 359, 365, (2007).

129 *Id.* at p.365

130 Сергей П. Малков, Международное космическое право-учебное пособие, 49, (2002).

131 George T. Hacket, *Space debris and the corpus iuris spatialis*. 2. Atlantica

The norm of article VIII stipulates that the state "retains control" over the space object in space; therefore, it should not be interpreted as actual control over the object because the law cannot guarantee that this will always be a fact. It is logical to assume that the term "control" was used to signify the authority of control, which is part of the jurisdiction over an object or a person. This authority includes the rights and duties of the state.

Diederiks-Verschoor argued that jurisdiction and control over space objects and crew should be permanent and should be retained without regard to their position.[132] This view, which represents the logical extension and continuation of jurisdiction over space objects is shared by Hall as well.[133]

This view of permanent jurisdiction is not shared by Cheng, whose interpretation of Article VIII of the Outer Space Treaty is that legal control and jurisdiction over registered space objects ceases to exist when there is an expressed or implied act of abandonment due to a loss of *animus dominandi (the intention to control)*.[134] Baker also expressed the view that permanent jurisdiction and control over space debris should not be applied because this will hinder the possibility of non-functional space objects being removed from outer space.[135]

In my opinion, it is methodologically incorrect to change the legal regime of a space object because there might be a danger that the state, which has jurisdiction over it, might not be interested in retaining control of that object.

What would happen if we consider that the jurisdiction of functional objects is changing and the state has no jurisdiction over these objects at the moment when they are becoming useless? A certain change of jurisdiction would discharge the state from the responsi-

Séguier Frontières, 192, (1994).

132 Isabella Henrietta Philepina Diederiks-Verschoor, *Environmental protection in outer space*, 30 German YB Int'l L.,146, (1987).

133 Cargill R. Hall, *Comments on salvage and removal of man-made objects from outer space*, 33.2 Journal of Air Law and Commerce, 288, 291 (1967).

134 Bin Cheng, *Studies in international space law*, 416, (1997).

135 Howard Baker, Space Debris: Legal and Policy Implications 69 (1989).

bility to remove the objects or make them safe for the environment. States and international organisations are allowed to remove space debris, which is in their own jurisdiction, or they have permission from the state or international organisation, which has jurisdiction over the non-functional space object. States are reluctant to remove even the objects under their jurisdiction to save costs.

It should be noted that the legal regime of jurisdiction over space debris is not different from the legal regime over any other space object, as space debris is a type of space object. Subsequently, retaining jurisdiction over objects, which are not functional and have become space debris, is not excluding the possibility of another state removing a foreign space object under certain conditions.

The statement of White, who argues that jurisdiction ceases to exist from the moment the object is abandoned or returned to Earth, contradicts the legal norm in art. VIII of the Outer Space Treaty and it has to be disputed.[136] According to him, the jurisdiction and control are limited in time and are valid as long as it is necessary for the exploration and exploitation of outer space. He argued that jurisdiction ceases to exist from the moment when the activity is halted. White provides an example that abandoned space objects or even space systems that are returned to Earth don't have jurisdiction.

There is no international norm, which regulates that the jurisdiction of a space object ceases to exist, and such a legal vacuum is illogical to be accepted. I disagree with the statement and arguments of White.

Article VIII of the Outer Space treaty envisions that jurisdiction and control are retained over space objects and crew when they are in outer space.[137] It is logical to raise the question of what is the legal regime of jurisdiction and control over objects and crew, which are in foreign air space or have landed on the territory of another country. Many representatives of the legal doctrine have the opinion that juris-

---

136 Wayne N. White, *Real Property Rights in Outer Space*: Proceedings, 40th Colloquium on the Law of Outer Space, 370 American Institute of Aeronautics and Astronautics 373 (1998).

137 Francis Lyall & Paul B. Larsen, *Space Law. A Treatise* 469 (2009).

diction and control over space objects and crew should be permanent and should be retained without regard to their location.[138]

Sentence two of article VIII of the Outer space treaty states that the ownership of objects launched in outer space, including their component parts, is not affected by their presence in outer space or by their return to Earth. From this norm, we can conclude that the ownership of all space debris is also not affected by their location because they are a type of space object and are with the same legal status. We should explore whether there is a change in the legal regime of space debris depending on its location.

As was already stated above, if jurisdiction ceases to exist, then no state will have the obligation to remove a space object, render it safely or give back the space object to the launching state when the space object has landed on its territory. Jurisdiction is a legal term that provides rights and obligations. There is no solid legal argument that liberates the states from their legal bond with space objects when they become non-functional. Despite the fact that the leading space-faring nations and private organisations do not have the willingness to invest significant financial resources for grounding their space waste, it does not mean that damages from their space debris would not lead to liability for the state, which has jurisdiction over it. In the last decade, we have witnessed scientific projects and investments in space systems that are aiming to reduce the amount of space debris in specific orbits. An example of such a project is ELSA-d, which has been developed by a Japanese satellite service company called Astroscale. The main objective of this mission is to locate and retrieve space debris. This project is the first of its kind by a commercial satellite operator. The demonstration of this mission was launched in 2021. This project involves the use of two satellites, the service and the client satellites. In the demonstrations, the service satellite attempts to catch the client satellite by using cutting-edge GPS and navigation technology. The service satellite

138 Cargill R. Hall, Comments on salvage and removal of man-made objects from outer space, 33.2 Journal of Air Law and Commerce, 288, 291 (1967).

catches the client using magnetic technology and then lowers it into the Earth's atmosphere so that both the objects can burn up on re-entry.[139]

The increased involvement of private space companies in space activities has led to the situation that private corporations are sending thousands of satellites into outer space[140] without having the explicit duty to return them back to Earth or at least to remove the non-functional space systems in a "graveyard" orbit. According to article VI of the Outer space treaty, the international responsibility is for the states. The lack of a comprehensive legal framework for the protection outer space environment and the present disinterest in space traffic management safety has led to the present ecological outer space crisis and higher risk of conducting space activities. I cannot agree with the postulate of Lewis that outer space exploration needs a minimally invasive domestic and transnational legal and administrative regime in order to reach its full potential.[141] If such a policy is pursued, the private sector will saturate the outer space environment with tens of thousands of satellites for similar purposes, which are going to become space debris in a matter of a few years. If those space objects are not removed from orbit, they would hinder significantly space traffic and the capacity of space actors to safely launch space objects.

The third sentence of Article VIII of the Outer Space Treaty and the Rescue Agreement stipulated the obligation of a state on which territory has landed a space object to return it to the state where the object is registered. The state where the object is registered should provide identification data prior to the return upon request on behalf of the state on which territory has landed the space object, which will probably be space debris.

---

139 David Leonard, *Space Junk Removal Is Not Going Smoothly,* 14 Scientific American (2021).

140 Business Insider, SPACE-X plans to send 42000 satellites in less than 10 years. https://www.businessinsider.com/how-elon-musk-42000-starlink-satellites-earth-effects-stars-2020-10#

141 Lewis D. Solomon, *The privatization of space exploration: Business, technology, law and policy*, 94 (2017).

What would happen in a situation when the state of registry refuses to acknowledge that the object is under its jurisdiction? For example, the crash of a satellite of one state on the territory of another is leading to absolute international liability and is related to serious compensation depending on the size of the damages, and expenses for recovering and returning the object.

In such a crash, it is very likely to become difficult to identify the owner of the space debris and the state to which it should be returned upon request.

It would be fair to presume that the state, which has jurisdiction over the object, is going to refuse to admit ownership and jurisdiction, and the government will try to avoid international liability.

In a similar situation, when space debris cannot be identified, the state which receives the debris will prove its contention that a particular state has jurisdiction over the space debris. The weakness of the norm in article VIII sentence three regulates only an obligation to return a space object, which in many cases will be useless for the state that has jurisdiction over it. The practical difficulties of identifying the state that has jurisdiction over smaller space debris particles are leading to the impossibility of the damaged state to address its claim for compensation.

Lyall and Larsen correctly conclude that the legal regime of ownership remains consistent and permanent in national legislation as well. The ownership rights established under appropriate national laws, therefore, continue to exist even when a space object is outside the territory of the launching state.[142] For example, the Russian national space legislation foresees that "*the rights of ownership over space objects shall remain unaffected, during the ground time of such objects, at any stage of a space flight or stay in outer space, on celestial bodies and also on return to the Earth, unless otherwise specified in international treaties of Russian Federation*".[143]

142 Francis Lyall & Paul B. Larsen, *Space Law. A Treatise* 274 (2009).
143 Art. 17 of the Law of the Russian Federation "About Space Activity, Decree No. 5663-1 of the Russian House of Soviets, translated by UNOOSA https://www.unoosa.org/oosa/en/ourwork/spacelaw/nationalspacelaw/russian_

The legal obligation to return the object to the launching state which has registered the object also exists for states non-parties of the Outer Space Treaty because according to the norm of customary international law, the states are guided by the principle of cooperation and mutual assistance and have to conduct all their activities in outer space for the corresponding interests of the other states.[144] International legal custom has existed in international space law from the beginning,[145] and the above norm is an example of that.

There is no legal barrier to the space debris not being returned if the two states agree on that.

The states have different levels of technological development, and this also affects their technological capacity to detect space debris on Earth and also identify them when these objects are returning to Earth.

The norm article 5 par.1 of the Rescue Agreement stipulates that the state which has information about space debris, which has landed on any territory on Earth without regard to the jurisdiction, should inform simultaneously the authorities which have conducted the launch and the Secretary-General of the UN.

When a space system has made an emergency landing on foreign territory, the object may be functional or non-functional—it may or may not have significant economic value; a circumstance dependent upon the evaluation of the launching state. If the launching state decides that it is in its interest that the space system or the produced space debris has to be recovered, the state can make a request to the state on which territory the space object has landed.[146] To acknowledge the expenses for recovering the landed space object or its component parts, it is necessary for the operation to start after a request from the launching state. Otherwise, in the absence of a request, the launching state can substantiate

federation/decree_5663-1_E.html

144 Nandasiri Jasentuliyana, International space law and the United Nations, 190, (1999).

145 Bin Cheng, *The commercial development of space: the need for new treaties*. 19 J. Space L. 17, 19 (1991).

146 Rescue Agreement, Article 5 par.2, 1968

not paying the expenses for recovery because it does not want its object to be recovered.

The prerequisite for addressing a request to the state on which territory has landed the space object signifies that the jurisdiction over the object when it is located on foreign territory is not exclusive to the state, which has jurisdiction over it in outer space. This is evident also by the right of the state, on which territory the object has landed, to conduct an operation for recovering, investigating the substances of the object and placing it under quarantine in order to avoid contamination.

The norm in article 5 par. 3 from the Rescue Agreement elaborates further on the norm in article VIII sentence 3 from Outer Space Treaty, which envisions an obligation to return the space object. Space objects, including space debris, should be returned to the authorities conducting the launch, if they make a request. The identification of space debris often is very difficult, and in the list of UN for discovered space objects on territories of states, a significant number of the objects have been put in the category "believe to be ...."[147]

If the launching state is not interested in recovering the space object, it is highly likely that such a request is not made on its behalf due to the fact that the crash will lead to international liability. If there is no economic or political advantage for the state to accept the crashed space object, and the last cannot be identified, it is highly likely that the launching state will not be identified too, unless a modern Space Situational Awareness system is used. This problem is not solved by the current international legal regime. The space situational awareness system can be useful for the prevention of collisions and assessment of a potential collision of space objects to have physical and mathematical models for hypervelocity impact on pressurised structures.[148]

---

147 Section for unidentified space debris –"Believe to be" http://www.oosa.unvienna.org/oosa/natact/sdnps/unlfd.html

148 N.N. Smirnov, V. F. Nikitin, and A. B. Kiselev, *Peculiarities of space debris production in different types of orbital breakups,* 393 In Second European

On the other hand, the obligation of the launching state to furnish identifying data prior to the return of the space object is important to guarantee that the space object will be placed in possession of the launching state. It is a possible hypothesis that the space object is given to another state which did not present identifying data, or from the presented data, it is evident that the state did not have jurisdiction over the space object in outer space. Then the state which gives the space object will bear international responsibility for violation of article VIII, sentence 3 from the Outer Space Treaty and Article 5 of the Rescue Agreement. If from this act of wrong return of the object has occurred damages, the state that delivered the object will be liable and will have to compensate the launching state. Such damages could announce the secret technology of the launching state or its private organisation.

The Rescue Agreement regulates in article 5 par. 4 the hypothesis when dangerous space debris had landed on the territory under the jurisdiction of a state.[149]

Such dangerous space debris could be a radioactive satellite or space debris that had brought extra-terrestrial organisms, which are capable of causing biological contamination or other threats. The measures for rendering the safety of the crashed space object should be performed by both states; one on which territory is the object and the other that is the launching state. These obligations for cooperation between the states could be interpreted as shared jurisdiction over the space object until it is returned to the launching state.

If such a crash takes place, it is most probable that the state in which territory the space object has landed will perform all actions

---

Conference on Space Debris, 465, 469, (1997).

149 Rescue Agreement, Art.5 par.4, 1968. The article foresees: "*Notwithstanding paragraphs 2 and 3 of this article, a Contracting Party which has reason to believe that a space object or its component parts discovered in territory under its jurisdiction, or recovered by it elsewhere, is of a hazardous or deleterious nature may so notify the launching authority, which shall immediately take effective steps, under the direction and control of the said Contracting Party, to eliminate possible danger of harm.*"

for preventing and containing the dangers from the space object. The measures should be efficient, and this will be decided by all states concerned, particularly the state on which territory the dangerous space object has landed.

Article 5 par. 4 does not stipulate explicitly that the launching state should provide all available relevant information about the space object and its potential dangers, but this obligation is part of the principle for cooperation and mutual assistance between the states.

A serious weakness of this norm is that the problem of back contamination is left to be resolved only by the launching state and the state on which territory the space object has landed. This is the location from which the contamination will start to spread. This means that two developing nations with humble economic and technological capabilities for protecting their environment from space contamination will have to be responsible for taking all actions on this matter.

Article 5 par.5 of the Rescue Agreement regulates the expenses for recovery and returning of the space object. It states that the expenses for recovering and returning the space object, without regard to whether it is space debris or not, is the responsibility of the launching state. The article does not regulate which state has to pay the expenses for discovering the space object. In my opinion, these expenses should be levied on the launching state too, because its space object creates a danger for the state on which territory the space object has landed.

If the states have negotiated that the space debris should be destroyed or preserved, then these expenses should be a financial burden for the launching state unless the states have negotiated something different.

Different states have different standards of living, and the costs of the mission could vary significantly. From the salaries of the experts to the type of used equipment, the expenses for rendering safety should be borne by the launching state. In my opinion, the question of paying all of the expenses should be perceived from the point, of what expenditures would have been made by the state the space object has crashed — depending if the object was its own property or property of its private organisation.

In the case of the incident in 1978 when the Soviet satellite with nuclear reactor "Cosmos 954", which crashed on the territory of Canada, a dispute arose between Canada and the USSR in regards to the compensation for the expenses that the Canadian government has made to discover, render safety and return the space debris from this satellite.

The USSR made a request to be included in the operation for search and rescue, but the Canadian government did not allow their participation. USSR made an argument, referring to article 2 par. 3 from the Rescue Agreement,[150] for paying a smaller sum for compensation than the one that Canada claimed. The dispute between the two states did not go to court or ad hoc commission, and it was solved by bilateral diplomatic negotiations. As a result of these negotiations, it is not acknowledged that USSR bears international liability for the crash of the satellite.

The question of jurisdiction over the space object cannot be fully explained without analysing whether states have legal rights to deorbit or change the orbit of foreign space objects.

Bordunov substantiates that encroachment on foreign space objects without permission of the state of the registry is forbidden.[151] If it is recognised that exists unilateral right of a state to move foreign space objects without the consent of the state, which has jurisdiction over it, this will create tension and uncertainty in international relations. At the same time arises the question whether exceptions exist from the absolute character of the jurisdiction over space objects in outer space, including space debris.

---

150 Rescue Agreement, Art.2 par.3 foresees that "*if assistance by the launching authority would help to effect a prompt rescue or would contribute substantially to the effectiveness of search and rescue operations, the launching authority shall cooperate with the Contracting Party with a view to the effective conduct of search and rescue operations.*"

151 Vitaliy D. Bordunov, *Rights of States as Regards Outer Space Objects*, 24 Colloquium L Outer Space, 91 (1981).

As substantiated above, the jurisdiction over space debris is the same as the one over every other space object. The obligation which states have to cooperate and to take due regard to the corresponding interests of the other states is the legal norm of article IX Outer Space Treaty. The obligation should be interpreted to include moving or deorbiting of space objects that constitute a danger to space traffic, collision in outer space, destruction on Earth or other threats. Lach rightly summarised that the purpose of the "due regard" principle is to set the limitation of the activities of states in outer space.[152] However, such a general rule could be perceived as vague and unclear about the precise obligations of the states[153] and where those legal boundaries are. An example of a concrete legal measure that could be implemented to decrease the risk of space debris is the introduction of a rule for deorbiting the non-functional space objects in Low Earth Orbit in a period of fewer than 25 years[154] before they have disintegrated into many smaller fragments.

Therefore, the refusal to change the orbit of a space object from outer space or to provide permission for another state to do so when the space object constitutes a significant danger is a violation of the principle of cooperation. It could be argued that the refusal of the state, which has jurisdiction over the space object, to act accordingly gives the concerned states the right to take all appropriate measures to prevent the danger.

The freedom of every state to interpret, according to their national standards and at their discretion, what activities are causing danger and what measures are appropriate, signifies that serious disputes could arise in the future. If foreign space objects are destroyed or removed from space without permission, there is a high risk of

152 Manfred Lachs, *The Law of Outer Space: An Experience in Contemporary Law-Making, by Manfred Lachs, Reissued on the Occasion of the 50th Anniversary of the International Institute of Space Law*, 42-45, (2010).

153 John S. Goehring, *Can We Address Orbital Debris with the International Law We Already Have? An Examination of Treaty Interpretation and the Due Regard Principle*, 85 J. Air L. & Com., 318, (2020).

154 Paul B. Larsen, *Solving the space debris crisis*, 83 J. Air L. & Com., 496, (2018).

confrontation and acts of aggression, which could decimate space assets, create clouds of space debris, and hinder space activities in a severe way.

If space debris or a useful payload enters in foreign airspace of a state, then this state is legally allowed to destroy the space object in order to avoid the danger of a crash on its territory. This legal possibility exists because the airspace of a state is under its national jurisdiction. Since international law does not regulate precisely where the boundary between outer space and airspace is set, this creates a gap and uncertainty for the safety of space objects. Every state without a clear position about the delimitation of outer space and air space could claim that the space object is passing through its airspace and could cause harm. These significant lapses in international law could justify the initiation of a military conflict that could paralyse the whole space sector.

Carns advocates for the legality of the active removal of space debris, which is smaller than 10 cm.[155] He argued that this specific size of the space object was derived from the technological capabilities of ground-based sensors and the conclusions of NASA.[156] He stated that the legal regime of ownership and perpetuity of a large non-functional object (for example, an 8-ton satellite) and 1 cm particle should not be the same, and the particle could be removed without the consent of the original owner. Although such a conclusion was drawn from the practical need of improving the safety of space activities and decreasing the risks from space debris collisions in orbit, such an approach, in my view, is counterproductive. The reason is that the legal regime cannot be changed without clear criteria that are specified in a legal norm. The size of the space object and its functionality are not changing the legal jurisdiction over it.

155 Marc G. Carns, *Consent Not Required: Making the Case that Consent is Not Required under Customary International Law for Removal of Outer Space Debris Smaller than 10cm*. 77 AFL Rev., 173 (2017).

156 *NASA handbook for limiting space debris*, STD-8719.14 "*Because of the inherent limits of ground-based sensors, debris events can only be known and discussed if there are pieces larger than approximately 10 cm.*", 33, (2008).

Ownership on Earth and in outer space never has an absolute character. It always consists of certain legal obligations towards others. The right to remove a foreign-owned space object, irrelative of its size, could arise if the state, which has jurisdiction over it, is legally obligated to deorbit the space object or place it in a specific zone, such as a graveyard orbit.

There is no need to use the danger of space debris as a pretext to create a new legal regime of space objects. The analysis of the present international legal regime and particularly of Article III of the Liability Convention shows that the active removal of foreign-owned non-functional space objects will not immediately result in international liability. It is because the state that has jurisdiction over the removed space object has to provide explanation of the damages that have occurred from the removal. Considering the tension that the unsanctioned removal of foreign non-functional space object could lead to between the involved states, it is logical for them to seek cooperation for all activities. After seeking and obtaining consent from the state of registry,[157] the active debris removal would not lead to additional space security concerns.

Are there legal obstacles for a state to remove or even destroy outer space objects, which are unidentified, and which are not registered in the national register of any state? As mentioned above, there are at least 1374 unregistered space objects orbiting Earth and the answer to this question is important to avoid serious tension between states.

The ownership of the space object is not dependent upon its registration or lack of such. This conclusion is logical upon analysing the norms of the Registration Convention and particularly the absence of such a condition that registration of space objects will determine their ownership.

157 Academic Study *Active Debris Removal - An Essential Mechanism for Ensuring the Safety and Sustainability of Outer Space A Report of the International Interdisciplinary Congress on Space Debris Remediation and On-Orbit Satellite Servicing*, A/AC.105/C.1/2012/CRP.16, 33 (2012).

The legal difficulty of a state to prove its jurisdiction over a satellite or other unregistered space object that is destroyed by another state creates uncertainty in international relations, because such acts could be interpreted as acts of war.

The importance all space objects in outer space to be identified was recognised in the early years of the development of international space law.[158] It is necessary that a modern international system exists for the registration of space objects. Such monitoring system should be capable to identify all space objects and associating them to the relevant states.[159]

One of the most important benefits of the identification of space objects is the evaluation of the risk from eventual crashes in outer space and on Earth. When the object is properly identified, it can be understood what materials it is made of, whether it has a nuclear reactor, and what types of shielding it possess. In order to maintain this information, it is important for the launching state to provide full and timely data. Presently, there is no precise legal obligation for any state to provide comprehensive data on the object, the materials it is made of and the types of space systems that are used.

The Registration Convention regulates the predominant part of the issues with the registration of space objects, but there are no legal norms that regulate the rules for tracking and identifying space objects, including space debris. In practice, the functions of technological tracking and identifying space objects are carried out separately by the leading space-faring states. The information that they gather could be released at their sovereign discretion. These conditions create possibilities for states that are technologically more advanced to conceal information from other states and the public. The Registration Convention has serious lapses in regulating the legal regime of space debris.

---

158 Myres S. McDougal, Harold D. Lasswell, and Ivan A. Vlasic, *Law and public order in outer space*, 569, (1963).

159 Paul G. Dembling & Swadesh S. Kalsi, Pollution of Man's Last Frontier: Adequacy of Present Space Environmental Law in Preserving the Resource of Outer Space, 20.2 International Law Review, 125, 142, (1973).

A major problem in the convention is that the language is not clear and precise about the obligations of the states to register space objects. What is included in the term "space object", and which objects should be registered are aspects that are not precisely defined. The lack of explicit obligation to register non-functional satellites leads to a situation where every state will decide for itself which objects to register.

Secondly, article II par.1 of the Registration Convention stipulates that after the launch of the space object, the launching state has the obligation to register the space object in an appropriate national register that it has to maintain. This norm is interpreted by most states that there is no legal obligation for them to register unsuccessful launches.

Article IV par.3 of the same convention envisions that the information will be provided "*to the greatest extent feasible and as soon as practicable*". Such formulation creates uncertainty not only about whether the information will be delivered on time to the Secretary-General of the UN but also if it will be delivered at all.

Article V of the convention foresees a voluntary regime for marking with a designator the space objects, and this non-compulsory regime is one more prerequisite for difficulties in the identification of space objects. On the matters of identification and registration of space objects, the technical and scientific subcommittee of COPUOS, during its seventh session, proposed four different possibilities for signifying space objects.[160]

The four proposals include the following:

1) Special marking with placing of metal numbers;

2) Detailed description of the structure of the space object, including the materials and components that are used;

3) Registration of frequencies of the radio transmitter;

4) Information for the sojourning trajectory of the space object.

The issue is still discussed in the committee for the last four decades, without reasonable expectation of reaching a successful con-

160 UN GAOR, COPUOS, Report of the Scientific and Technical Subcommittee on the work of its 7th session, par.39-43, (1970).

clusion. This prolonged debate illustrates that a major change of the international mechanisms is required in order to develop international legal space regulation to respond to the old and new challenges.

Article VI of the Registration Convention explicitly states that if it is impossible to identify the object, which has caused the damage or is dangerous for a state and its private persons, the other states have the obligation to respond to the greatest extent feasible to a request for assistance in the identification of the object.

Such technological dependence of most of the states, which cannot afford space monitoring and tracking facilities creates tension in international relations and uncertainty about international space law being obeyed.

Presently, there are no international legal norms that regulate procedures for the prevention of collision between space objects in outer space. These procedures are crucial for avoiding space debris creation from crashes. For example, if there is a danger of a crash between two satellites and the states, which have jurisdiction over them, are aware of the situation, there is a need for international compliance with a legal procedure which includes urgent actions to be taken in order to prevent the crash and to inform the Secretary-General of the UN and the Office of the Outer Space Affairs about the situation.

If one state changes the trajectory of a functional satellite or space debris that is under the jurisdiction of another state and there is no permission from this state, these actions shall be considered a violation of the norm in article VIII par.1 of the Outer Space Treaty. If these actions lead to damages, the state will be internationally liable, according to the Liability Convention.

The International Court of Justice has the following position concerning the threat from nuclear weapons: *"The existence of the general obligation of States to ensure that activities within their jurisdiction and control respect the environment of other States or of areas beyond national control is now a part of the corpus of international law relating to the environment."*[161]

161 Legality of the Threat or Use of Nuclear Weapons, Advisory Opinion,

This advisory opinion is very significant for understanding the legal obligations of states to protect the outer space environment. The last is an example of an area "*beyond national control*". This advisory opinion of the International Court of Justice includes all activities in outer space.

The obligation for cooperation and mutual assistance of states is hindered by the mindset of constant competition and even rivalry that exists between leading space-faring nations. The freedom of states to use outer space is still understood as the right for competitive action of the states to explore and exploit outer space exclusively for their own national interest, including for military purposes. In this stream of thought, it is not necessary to be in the national interest of one state to deorbit its non-functional satellites because it will be an economic disadvantage. If space-faring states continue to pursue such irresponsible policies of leaving space debris in outer space, it will significantly increase the risk for space navigation.

1.4. International liability for damages from space debris

The creation of space debris threatens the life of astronauts, as well as the life of people on Earth when the space waste is landing. Space junk can cause significant property damage to useful payloads in outer space and on Earth. Therefore, it is important to review the legal regime of international liability from space debris and to make conclusions about its efficiency.

Firstly, it should be mentioned that international space law, as a branch of international law, is developing in correspondence with the general principles of international law.[162] Among these principles is the international liability.

1996 LC.J. 15, at 29 (Jul. 8 1996).

162 Outer Space Treaty, Article III "*States Parties to the Treaty shall carry on activities in the exploration and use of outer space, including the Moon and other celestial bodies, in accordance with international law, including the Charter of the United Nations, in the interest of maintaining international peace and security and promoting international cooperation and understanding.*"

There are several academic views about the difference between the terms "responsibility" and "liability".[163]

In my opinion, the proposed definition by Cheng provides a comprehensive understanding of the different aspects of the terms, and it states the following:

"Responsibility means essentially answerability, answerability for one's acts and omissions, for their being in conformity with whichever system of norms, whether moral, legal, religious, political or any other which may be applicable, as well as answerability for their consequences, whether beneficial or injurious...The term liability is often used specifically to denote the obligation to bear the consequences of a breach of a legal duty, in particular the obligation to make reparation for any damage caused...."[164]

Under the current technological development of space activities, every launch of a space object is always concomitant with a generation of space debris. Therefore, not every generation of space debris can be considered a violation of space law that will lead to international consequences. At the same time, this should not be an excuse for creating space debris and polluting the outer space environment when these actions could be avoided. The criteria for legally permissible generation of space debris should be clarified.

For example, today, we are witnessing technological innovations, which allow the states and private actors to apply reusable launch systems, which would decrease the creation of space debris in the launching phase significantly.[165] Achieving safe space traffic management is possible only after the adoption of higher technological standards for all state and private space actors. In the near future, one such standard could be that the launching of space objects in outer space must be conducted by reusable launch systems.

---

163 George T. Hacket, *Space debris and the corpus iuris spatialis*, 2 Atlantica Séguier Frontières, 153-160, (1994).

164 Bin Cheng, *Article VI of the 1967 Space Treaty Revisited: 'International Responsibility', 'National Activities', and 'The Appropriate State'*, 26.1. J Space L,7, 9-16, (1998).

165 Falcon-9 is an example of reusable rocket, that was built by SPACE-X

1.4.1. Subjects of international liability for damages from space debris

The question of international liability for outer space activities was considered at the earliest stage of the development of international space law. Article VI of the Outer Space Treaty provides that the subjects, which can bear international responsibility are states and international governmental organisations.

Sentence one of this article stipulate that the state parties to the treaty bear international responsibility, but at the same time, less than half of the countries in the world have ratified this international treaty. Therefore, arises the question: What is the legal status of space-faring nations, which are not parties to the Outer Space Treaty or the Liability Convention? In settlement of the claim between Canada and the USSR for damages, caused by "Cosmos 954", Canada concluded that the standard of absolute liability for outer space activities, in particular activities involving the use of nuclear energy, has become a general principle of international law.[166] The Canadian government also elaborated that the principle of absolute liability has been accepted as a general principle of international law. Canada argued that the principle of absolute liability applies to fields of activities with a high degree of risk. They also acknowledged that it is repeated in numerous international agreements and as stipulated in Art. 38 of the Statute of the International Court of Justice, it is one of the general principles of law recognised by civilised nations.[167]

Jasentuliana elaborates on the issue of the obligations of the states to comply with the norms of the Outer Space Treaty, as the last is widely regarded as customary international law.[168]

It should be pointed out that the conclusion of the UN International Law Commission in relation to the responsibility of states for internationally wrongful acts is that "*Every internationally wrongful*

166 Protocol of Settlement of Claim between Canada and the Union of Soviet Socialist Republics for Damage Caused by "Cosmos 954", point 22 (Released on April 2, 1981).

167 Ibid.

168 Nandasiri Jasentuliyana, International space law and the United Nations, 190, (1999).

act of a State entails the international responsibility of that State."[169] The work of the UN International Law Commission is instrumental in understanding the allocation of loss in the case of transboundary harm arising out of hazardous activities.[170]

Morin and Richard correctly observe that the International Court of Justice cannot apply the general principles of international law to impose legal obligations of state to treat all space debris as a form of environmental pollution beyond national borders.[171] Such an approach is contrary to the principle of state sovereignty.

The Liability Convention provides different possibilities for claiming compensation to the launching state for damages that occur.

Hermida substantiates that in relation to the legal bond between states and the actions of private actors in space, the Outer Space Treaty adopts a revolutionary approach towards the development of the institute of international liability in article VI because the states are internationally liable for the damages from their natural and juridical private organisations.[172] He also argues that absolute liability in international space law is unique to international law. It should be clarified that absolute liability is not unique to international space law as it was introduced before the adoption of the Outer Space Treaty in relation to damages from aircraft[173] and for damages in the event of nuclear incidents.[174]

---

169 UN International Law Commission: Responsibility of States for Internationally Wrongful Acts, 2001 General Assembly resolution 56/83 (December 12, 2001), and corrected by document A/56/49(Vol. I)/Corr.4

170 GA Resolution 61/36, (December 4, 2006) and Resolution 74/189, GA (December 18, 2019).

171 Jean Frédéric Morin & Benjamin Richard. "*Astro environmentalism: Towards a polycentric governance of space debris.*" 12.4 Global Policy 568, 570, (2021).

172 Julian Hermida, Legal Basis for a National Space Legislation, 6-25, (2004).

173 Convention on Damage Caused by Foreign Aircraft to Third Parties on the Surface, October 07, 1952, 310 U.N.T.S. 181 [hereinafter Rome Convention]

174 Convention on Third Party Liability in the Field of Nuclear Energy of 29 July 1960, as amended by the Additional Protocol, January 28, 1964, 956

Article 8, par.1 of the Liability Convention foresees that if damages occur to natural or juridical persons of a state, this state may claim a compensation. This norm places the private persons, who endure losses, in the position of being dependent on their state to protect their legitimate interests. In order to avoid this dependence on one's own state in article 8 par. 2 is envisioned an alternative. If the State of nationality has not presented a claim in respect of damages in its territory by natural persons or legal entities, another State is given the opportunity to make a claim to a launching state. If there is a damage from space debris on a territory of a state, it is much more probable that this state will present a claim for compensation.

Article 8 par.3 of the Liability Convention regulates the legal possibility of a state to present a claim to a launching state if its permanent residents suffer damages from the space object.[175]

These norms provide additional opportunities for private persons to defend their interests.

A large part of contemporary outer space activities is accomplished in cooperation between several states, which have different forms of participation in every particular space project. This cooperation provides political guarantees that benefits and burdens will be shared, and duplication of activities could be avoided. This form of cooperation results also in major cost savings. According to article 5 par.1 of the Liability Convention, the states will be jointly and severally liable for any caused damage.

The internal relations between states, which conduct joint launches, are regulated in the next two paragraphs of article 5. In article 5, par. 2 is envisioned the possibility of a preliminary agreement for apportioning among themselves the financial obligation in respect of which they are jointly and severally liable. This norm regulates only the internal character of the relations between states

UNTS 264

175 Liability Convention, Art.8 par. 3 stipulates that "*If neither the State of nationality nor the State in whose territory the damage was sustained has presented a claim or notified its intention of presenting a claim, another State may, in respect of damage sustained by its permanent residents, present a claim to a launching State.*"

and does not forbid the possibility of the damaged state to seek full compensation from any of the jointly liable states.[176] This norm provides the possibility for the damaged state to choose from which state to seek compensation among the states that are conducting jointly the launch.

The second type of international subject, which is legally capable of bearing international responsibility, is an international governmental organisation. The legal norm from Article VI of the Outer Space Treaty stipulates that international responsibility also bear international governmental organisations. The international governmental organisation and its member states are also jointly responsible and liable for any damages from their space objects.

The development of international space law has led to an unprecedented international legal experiment, which is the privatisation of international governmental organisations. For example, INTELSAT was created in 1964 as a classical international governmental organisation, which had the aim to make accessible to all nations the benefits of radio and telecommunication broadcasting from a satellite. The activity of the organisation is recognised internationally as very successful, and it includes political achievements such as establishing a hotline between the White House and the Kremlin during the cold war, broadcasting of Olympic Games to a large number of states, and broadcasting the Moon landing of astronauts. After a process of long-term lobbying on behalf of the US corporation PanAmSat, INTELSAT was privatised, and every member state was "compensated according to its participation" in the organisation. The privatisation of international governmental organisations is a *de facto* refusal of developing international relations. Poor management of the private organisation Intelsat led to the filing for bankruptcy in US courts on May 13th 2020, with over

176 Liability Convention, Art.5 par.2 sentence 3 stipulates: "*Such agreements shall be without prejudice to the right of a State sustaining damage to seek the entire compensation due under this Convention from any or all of the launching States which are jointly and severally liable*".

US$15 billion in total debt.[177] Before its bankruptcy, the corporation Intelsat acknowledged publicly that it provided its satellites for the US army and NATO for conducting military activities as an intergovernmental organisation[178] and later as a private company. The organisation had its private interest and did not have the aim of developing international relations and implementing the principles of international law as the international governmental organisation had in the past. Before the privatisation, the international responsibility and liability were borne jointly by all member states, and after the privatisation, the state, which would be internationally liable, is the USA, according to the rules of Article VI of the Outer Space Treaty, because Intelsat had become a private US corporation.

1.4.2. Types of international liability

In the Liability Convention are envisioned two types of international liability for damages from space objects. In article 2 of the convention is stipulated that "*a launching State shall be absolutely liable to pay compensation for damage caused by its space object on the surface of the Earth or to aircraft in flight.*"

In this norm is regulated a type of liability, which is absolute. This means a strict liability that emerges without fault on behalf of the launching state or any other subject of international law.[179] Another characteristic of absolute liability is that there is no limit on the amount of compensation,[180] and the liable state owes to pay all damages that have occurred from the crash of a space object. In the

---

177 Intelsat S.A., et al, S.A., 20-32299, U.S. Bankruptcy Court, Eastern District of Virginia, Richmond, USA

178 Richard A. Morgan, *Military use of commercial communication satellites: a new look at the Outer Space Treaty and peaceful purposes*, 60 J. air L. & com., 237, (1994).

179 Volker Roeben, *Responsibility in international Law*. 16.1 Max Planck Yearbook of United Nations Law Online, 99, 107, (2012).

180 Marietta Benkö & Kai-Uwe Schrogl, *Space Debris in the United Nations: Aspects of Law and Policy*, 393 In Second European Conference on Space Debris, 749, 752-753, (1997).

settlement of the claim between Canada and the USSR for damages, caused by the satellite "Cosmos 954", Canada argued the application of the relevant criteria, established by the general principles of international law. According to these criteria fair compensation is to be paid, by including in its claim only those costs that are *reasonable, proximately caused by the intrusion of the satellite* and deposit of debris and *capable of being calculated with a reasonable degree of certainty.*[181] In my opinion, such an approach is logical and balanced.

Diedriks substantiates that the most probable reason for the adoption of absolute liability in the convention is the initial high risk of space activities in the early years of the development of international space law.[182]

Another strong incentive for negotiating absolute liability is the fact that states, in particular, developing states, might become innocent victims of the activities of space-faring nations, if space objects are crashing on their territory. If such accidents occur, there is also the risk for space-faring nations that they might not receive their space object, or even the crashed space system could be sold to other states if there is no legal obligation to return the space object. For this reason, the Liability Convention should be analysed systematically with the Rescue Agreement as an agreement between space-faring nations and developing states, which provided for both sides legal guarantees that all damages on the Earth and in airspace will be compensated without the need to prove fault. At the same time, crashed space objects have to be returned to the launching state, which has jurisdiction over it.

The second type of international liability is fault liability, which is regulated in article 3 of the Liability Convention.[183]

---

181 Protocol of Settlement of Claim between Canada and the Union of Soviet Socialist Republics for Damage Caused by "Cosmos 954", point 23 (Released on April 2, 1981).

182 Isabella Henrietta Philepina Diederiks, An Introduction to Space Law, 33-34, (1993)

183 Liability Convention, Art.3 stipulates that "*in the event of damage being caused elsewhere than on the surface of the Earth to a space object of one*

The distinctive criterion of the two types of liabilities is whether it is necessary for the damaged state to prove the fault of the launching states. In order to understand which liability is applicable, it is needed to establish the location of the damage.[184] If the damage had occurred to a foreign state on the surface of Earth or to aircraft in flight, the liability should be absolute.[185] If the damage is caused "*elsewhere than on the surface of Earth*"[186], the liability shall be fault. Outer space is the main area, which is not on the surface of Earth and damages that occur in outer space should be compensated, if they are due to fault of the state or private organizations, for which it is responsible.

The absence of a standard of care, or at least a precise common understanding of such a standard among space-faring nations, is problematic for the implementation of fault liability.[187]

The imperfections of this legal regime of international liability can be illustrated with an example, which is a probable hypothesis and is a rule and not an exception when we refer to damages from space debris: Unidentified space debris which is sojourning in space is destroying a functional satellite (or any other useful space payload) of a state. As a result of this collision, after a period of time, part of the destroyed space object is falling to the surface, survives its entrance into the lower levels of the atmosphere and is crashing on the surface of another state. The crash results in damages for the last state. The damaged state has managed to identify the object and relate it to the state, which has jurisdiction over the crashed satellite. According to Liability Convention, there will be an absolute liability for the state, which has jurisdiction over the satellite, and it

---

launching State or to persons or property on board such a space object by a space object of another launching State, the latter shall be liable only if the damage is due to its fault or the fault of persons for whom it is responsible".

184 Liability Convention, Article 4

185 Liability Convention, Article 4 par. 1 a)

186 Liability Convention, Article 3

187 James P. Lampertius, *The Need for an Effective Liability Regime for Damage Caused by Debris in Outer Space.* 13 Mich. J. Int'l L., 447, 456-457, (1991).

should compensate fully for all damages that occurred, even though this state is not faulty for the accident in outer space or on the surface of Earth.

The liable state will not be able to lay a regressive claim against another state because the original cause of the crash is space debris, which could not be identified. Even if the state is capable of identifying that initial space debris (which is highly unlikely), it should prove the fault of another state which has jurisdiction over the space junk because the destruction had happened in outer space and the liability is fault.

This example of the application of international liability shows how ineffective this legal term can be when space debris is causing damages.

Young has made well-grounded proposals, with which I agree, that if there is a technology for removing dangerous non-functional space objects and the state of the registry does not remove the space object then this behaviour of the state should be considered as negligent.[188] It is important to stress that such technologies already do exist.

The criticism of international liability in Article III of the Liability Convention is well-substantiated. Christol rightly criticized this article for the lack of definition of the fault of the state, the absence of common standards for care and also the inability to determine negligence.[189]

The lack of a common definition of "fault" provides the opportunity for mutable interpretations on behalf of the states in order to avoid liability. The absence of common standards for "maintaining good care" has led to the present situation of satellites, which are not useful to be abandoned in orbit, and this is increasing the risk of collisions in outer space.

Several representatives of the international legal doctrine have made proposals for the adoption of standards, which are supposed

188 Andrew J. Young, Space Transportation Systems, 299 (1984).

189 Carl Q. Christol, *International liability for damage caused by space objects,* 74.2 American Journal of International Law, 346, 368, (1980).

to be a landmark for the "fault" of a state.[190]

For example, the launching state would be negligent if it:

1) abandons on purpose functional satellite, if exists a technology to return it to the Earth;

2) does not fulfil the requirement for safety distance of satellites in geostationary orbit;

3) does not remove a non-functional satellite in a safer orbit, which is available;

4) does not attempt to mitigate the generation of new space debris;

5) refuses to relocate its space debris which has been generated from its activities.

These interpretations are good steps on behalf of academia to propose solutions for the contemporary issues with space debris. Presently, these standards are not legally binding for any state.

The absence of a legal requirement for states to use modern technologies and standards in relation to the safety of space objects is a major gap in international space law.

1.4.3. Damages caused by space debris

For a state to be internationally liable, it is necessary to exist a violation of an international legal obligation and damages of another state have to occur. The Liability Convention provides the meaning of the term "damage" in article 1a.[191]

The legal scope of the term "damage" includes damage to property or physical injury of people. The legal doctrine accepts that environmental damages of outer space are not included in this particular norm.[192]

---

190 Nandasiri Jasentuliyana, *Space debris and international law* 26 J. Space L., 139, 153 (1998).

191 Liability Convention, Art.1a) stipulates that "*the term "damage" means loss of life, personal injury or other impairment of health; or loss of or damage to property of States or of persons, natural or juridical, or property of international intergovernmental organisations".*

192 Isabella Henrietta Philepina Diederiks-Verschoor, *The legal aspects of space activities with potentially harmful effects on the earth and space*

Consequently arises the question of whether abandoning non-functional satellites in outer space constitutes damage to the environment and is a violation of the Liability Convention. Abandoning non-useful space objects, predominantly satellites is *de facto* pollution of outer space, but under the present international legal regime, it is not considered harmful contamination and it is not illegal. Despite the fact that geostationary orbit is defined as a limited natural resource, abandoning satellites in it is recommended not to be performed but is also not an international legal violation.[193]

The main reason for the rapid growth of the space debris problem in the last five decades is due to the practice of leaving non-functional objects in outer space instead of deorbiting them or placing them in a graveyard orbit. All space-faring nations are morally responsible for the magnitude of the space debris crisis. We cannot rely on the possibility of the emergence of international legal custom from the fact that many states follow the legally non-binding space debris mitigation guidelines of COPUOS or IADC.[194] Many states are not going to be willing to restrict space debris production without legally binding regulations.[195]

This lapse in international law is enormous, and bold new international initiatives are required to address the issue of environmental damages of outer space comprehensively and timely.

The current international legal regime does not prohibit explicitly even the deliberate creation of unnecessary space junk. The intention of creating space debris exists in performing deliberate explosions in outer space.

Deliberate explosions could be conducted for several reasons:

a) to test anti-satellite weapon (ASAT)

---

environments 15 Colloquium L Outer Space, 268-273, (1972).

193 Lotta Viikari, The Environmental Element in Space Law, 115, (2008).

194 Martha Mejía-Kaiser, *Out into the Dark: Removing Space Debris from the Geostationary Orbit*, Proceedings of the IISL Colloquium on the Law of Outer Space, 7, (2019).

195 Marietta Benkö & Kai-Uwe Schrogl, *Space Debris in the United Nations: Aspects of Law and Policy,* 393 In Second European Conference on Space Debris, 749, 750 (1997).

b) to prevent the recovery of a satellite by another state and extract information from it.

c) to create space debris intentionally in a particular orbit in order to create interference or to destroy a space object of another state.

d) to destroy a deorbiting satellite in outer space in order to avoid destruction on Earth with potential damages and loss of life.

In order, for a state or international organisation to bear international responsibility, it is necessary to establish the causal link between the damaging object and the damage itself and secondly, to identify which state or private organisation owns the damaging space object.

In February 2009, a major incident took place in outer space between the functioning US privately-owned satellite Iridium 33 and Russia's non-functional satellite Cosmos 2251.[196] Even though the two space-faring nations possess their own tracking capabilities and modern space situational awareness systems, the collision between the two large objects took place, and at least 1307 fragments have been catalogued.[197] The aftermath of this incident has shown that international legal liability is not going to be applied, and the USA and the Russian Federation reached a diplomatic understanding about the incident. The outer space environment was polluted with thousands of more dangerous debris from a collision that could have been avoided. This incident clearly illustrated the low regulatory effect of international liability in international space law.

The difficulties in establishing the owner of the space object creates uncertainty that international liability could be applied against the liable state and could result into compensation of the caused damages.

---

196 More about the incident read here: https://www.space.com/5542-satellite-destroyed-space-collision.html Last access on 10.02.2023

197 A. Tan, T.X. Zhang & M. Dokhanian, *Analysis of the Iridium 33 and Cosmos 2251 collision using velocity perturbations of the fragments*, 3.1.Advances in Aerospace Science and Applications, 13, 13 (2013).

Therefore, international liability for damages in outer space is not an effective instrument and it cannot protect the outer space environment and serve as deterrence in a possible conflict in outer space.

The state would bear international liability if its space objects, including space debris, have caused damages to another state. Therefore, it will not be internationally liable under the Liability Convention if in outer space there is a crash of two space objects owned by private organisations from the same state.

International liability cannot be invoked in the cases when space debris or a functional space object under the jurisdiction of one state crashed in its own territory and caused damages to its citizens.[198] In this scenario, the national legislation of the state would be applicable.

1.4.4. Active debris removal

Active debris removal (ADR) became an important topic for discussion among representatives of states, private companies, and academia in the last two decades.[199] ADR is an essential mechanism for ensuring the safety and sustainability of outer space.

According to the conclusion of the comprehensive COPUOS report on ADR from 2012, there will be minimal apparent benefits to operating satellites in a short period of time. However, in the long run, it will minimize the possibility of uncontrolled space debris creation and limitation on future space activities.[200]

Analysing the current legal framework, it is clear that the unauthorised removal of foreign objects from outer space will carry liability implications for the state or group of states that are making such an endeavour.[201]

Incentivising private companies to invest in active debris removal technology and projects is a crucial step in achieving the

---

198 Liability Convention, Article 7a

199 Maureen Williams, *2. Outer Space*. 26 Yearbook of International Environmental Law, 237, 238, (2015).

200 COPUOS report A/AC.105/C.1/2012/CRP.16, 28, (2012).

201 COPUOS report A/AC.105/C.1/2012/CRP.16, 30, (2012).

goal of safe outer space activities and minimisation of space debris threats.

Ansdell is correct in her conclusion that the real concern is the rapid increase of the population of space debris in the next decades.[202]

If states are willing private companies to invest in such projects, the governments should be the actors that are funding and promoting ADR businesses significantly in order to achieve sustainability and predictability of the private projects.

In 2021 several space-faring nations improved their space policies with respect to providing governmental support for ADR projects. Among the positive examples is the successful launch of the End-of-Life Services by Astroscale demonstration (ELSA-d) mission on March 22nd 2021. The company is one of the leaders in satellite servicing and long-term orbital sustainability across orbit. This became the world's first commercial mission to prove the core technologies necessary for space debris docking and removal.[203]

Ansdell focusses on four key areas with different requirements that need to exist simultaneously to establish the "ideal debris removal system".[204] These are technical, economic, political and legal. She summarised that the technical requirements include the deployment of rapid development of technologies and minimum launches of new space objects into Earth's orbits. The technological aspect of the development of the ADR systems needs to be understood well by experts in the other three areas, as it shows the limits of the system and its functionality. The economic requirement according to Ansdell should be based on a reasonable cost-to-benefit ratio. The invested efforts should produce a visible

---

202 Megan Ansdell, *Active Space Debris Removal: Needs, Implications, and Recommendations for Today's Geopolitical Environment,* 21 Journal of Public & International Affairs, 13 (2010).

203 Astroscale website, https://astroscale.com/astroscale-celebrates-successful-launch-of-elsa-d/ Last access 10.02.2023

204 Megan Ansdell, *Active Space Debris Removal: Needs, Implications, and Recommendations for Today's Geopolitical Environment,* 21 Journal of Public & International Affairs, 14 (2010).

improvement in the outer space environment. Here we could add that if the ADR system is meant to be funded and operated by a private company, the business model and return on the investment should also be taken into consideration by the governments. Among the political requirements, Ansdell also rightly noted that the transparency in development, deployment, and operations, would help space-faring states to trust each other that the system will not be used for the purpose of intentional removing of foreign functional satellites from orbit. With respect to the fourth legal aspect, she concludes that the activities should be in compliance with the five UN treaties and international standards. The Moon Agreement arguably could be left out from the legally binding commitments of the space-faring nations, as it has not been ratified by most of them.[205]

In the report from the COPUOS International Interdisciplinary Congress on Space Debris Remediation and On-Orbit Satellite Servicing, the participants have identified a serious obstacle in the initiation of projects to conduct ADR. The obstacle is related to possible liability for the state that has jurisdiction for the ADR operation against third parties that have been negatively affected by it. Due to the operation of removing a satellite, there might be the need to cross orbits, the expert team argue.[206] This could increase the risk of the organisation conducting the removal operation in terms of liability which, in turn, "*creates an incentive to leave satellites in their orbits even after they are no longer functional*".[207] The legal solution that the expert team suggested is an international agreement to exempt active debris removal from the scope of application of the Liability Convention's fault standard. The duty of cooperation between states includes not only notifications and consultations but also a genuine attempt to promptly respond to the

205 With the exception of Australia; See ratification status of all states in UNOOSA website and updated reports on treaties status - A/AC.105/C.2/2022/CRP.10

206 COPUOS report A/AC.105/C.1/2012/CRP.16, 32 (2012).

207 Ibid.

concerns of other states[208] and find implementable solutions to all emerging challenges.

Popova and Schaus argued that self-help in a state of necessity could be invoked to justify measures aiming at cleaning up the outer space environment, and they stated that specific conditions for such justification should be given in order to safeguard an essential interest from a "grave and imminent peril".[209] They also concluded that the interests of the international community as a whole, not only those of single states, have been recognised by the International Law Commission as a legitimate ground to invoke necessity. The recommendation of COPUOS that initial active debris removal missions be carried out on non-controversial debris is very important because these are high-risk operations, and accidents could lead to mistrust and tension in international relations.[210] Non-controversial debris are those that is either removed by the state that is having jurisdiction and control over it, or the state has granted permission to other entity to remove it.

In order to avoid violation of international space law and international conflict in outer space, states should follow the principle that removing foreign space debris should happen with the prior consent of the state of registry.

The chart below provided the results of a study, conducted with the participation of leading Canadian space companies on the most important issues that need to be performed presently to improve the long-term sustainability of space activities. The study is incorporated in the above-quoted report on ADR, which was provided to the COPUOS. This study clearly illustrates the actions that the states and the space private sector need to address in order to decrease the risk of space debris for space activities.

---

208 Barry Kellman, *Space: the Fouled Frontier: Adjudicating Space debris as an international environmental nuisance*. 39 J. Space L., 202, (2013).
209 Rada Popova & Volker Schaus. *The legal framework for space debris remediation as a tool for sustainability in outer space*, 2 Aerospace 5, 55, 64, (2018).
210 COPUOS report A/AC.105/C.1/2012/CRP.16, 38 (2012).

Figure 2

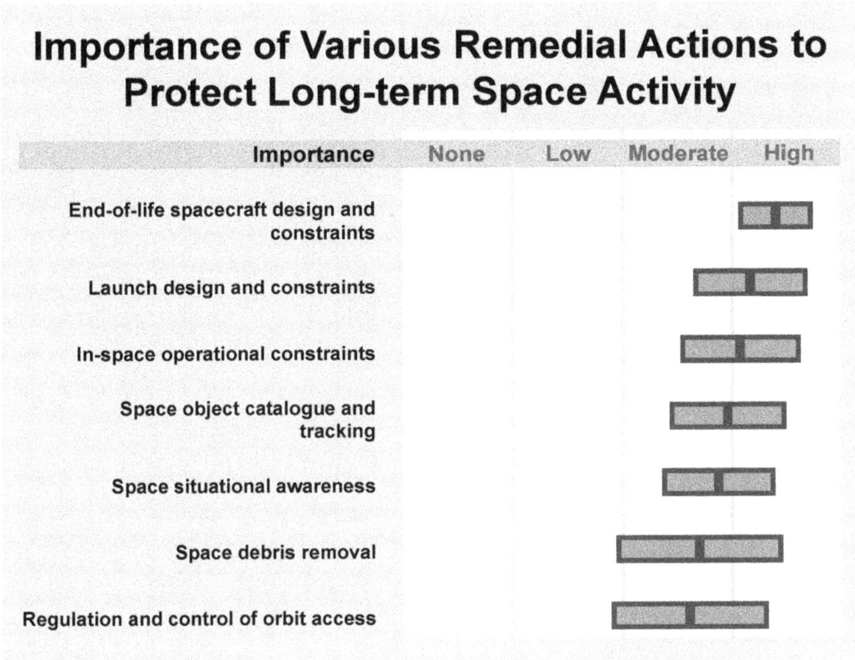

1.4.5. Compensation for damages from space debris

The compensation for damages from space debris will never substitute the necessity for the prevention of the generation of space waste. The Liability Convention envisions two ways of settling the dispute with compensation.

The first one includes the already existing diplomatic channels through which negotiations are taking place about the occurred damage. Article IX par. 1 stipulates that the damaged state should present its claim to the launching state through diplomatic channels. The next sentence foresees the hypothesis that between the damaged state and the launching state are not established diplomatic relations. In this rare scenario, the claim could be presented by another state, which will represent the interests of the damaged state. This norm illustrates that the states, which have ratified the Liability

Convention understood the pragmatic need of resolving a dispute between states that are not acknowledging their existence or have refused to have official diplomatic relationships.

The norm of the third sentence in article IX of the Liability Convention states that if the launching state and the damaged state are members of the UN, the claim can also be presented through the Secretary-General of the UN. In this hypothesis, the Secretary-General presents the claim of the damaged state, but this does not mean that he/she would represent only its interests. In this situation, the Secretary-General is supposed to mediate the process of settling the dispute without taking the side of any of the concerned states.

The Liability Convention regulates that the damaged party has a one-year period from the date that the accident occurred to present the claim to the launching state. The period starts on the same date as the occurrence of the damage or the date on which the launching state was identified as liable.[211] This period serves the needs of both damaged and damaging states, as it is not quite long and at the same time provides enough time for the damaged state to prepare its claims and legal arguments. The convention also considers the possibility that the state might not be aware of the occurrence of the damage or it might not be capable to identify the launching state. Then the state has the right to present a claim within one year following the date on which it became aware of the aforementioned facts.[212] These prerequisites are subjective to some extent because they are related to the ability of the damaged state to identify the liable state. In order to avoid delays in presenting the claim, the negotiating states agreed that the period should not be more than one year following the date on which the damaged state could reasonably be expected to have learned of these facts through the exercise of due diligence.[213]

The period of one year is applicable also in a situation when the liable launching state is identified, but it is difficult to determine the

---

211 Liability Convention, Article X par.1

212 Liability Convention, Article X par.2

213 Ibid.

full extent of the damage.[214] In this hypothesis, the claimant state is entitled to revise its claim and submit additional documentation after the expiration of the time limits until one year after the complete extent of the damage is known.

The Liability Convention explicitly regulates that presenting the claim for compensation for damages to the launching state does not require the prior exhaustion of local remedies, which may be available to a claimant state or natural persons or juridical persons it represents.[215] Such local remedies are, for example, national courts or administrative jurisdictions of the launching state.

However, if the state or natural and juridical persons that it represents are using such national juridical means for resolving the issue, it is not allowed to present the claim to the launching state for compensation for this issue.[216]

If the damages have occurred to private citizens, they should choose carefully which of the two options to apply. If they would rely on the state to make a claim, this means that they trust the effectiveness of the national authorities, and they could provide assistance in estimating the damages.

The second option of settling the dispute is active only if the diplomatic negotiations have failed. In article XIV of the Liability Convention is envisioned that if a settlement is not achieved through diplomatic negotiations, then the parties concerned could establish a Claims Commission.

This commission should be composed of three members: one should be appointed by the claimant state, one should be appointed by the launching state and the third member, which is going to be the Chairman, has to be chosen jointly by both parties.[217] If two or more states are on one of the sides, they should choose the member of the Commission from their quota together, or in another procedure, they have agreed on.

214 Liability Convention, Article X par.3
215 Liability Convention, Article XI par.1
216 Liability Convention, Article XI par.2
217 Liability Convention, Article XV par.1

In article XV par.2 is stipulated that if the state is unable to reach an agreement on the choice of the Chairman within a period of four months of the request for the establishment of the Commission, either party may request the Secretary-General of the United Nations to appoint a Chairman within two months. The dispositive character of this norm creates uncertainty that the members of the Commission will be formed, considering the fact that the launching state will most probably try to avoid liability and pay compensation.

In spite of the possibility to create an ad hoc commission, the states prefer to settle disputes through diplomatic channels when there is such an accident. In the case of the crash of the Soviet nuclear satellite "Cosmos 954" on the territory of Canada, the states agreed on a payment on behalf of the USSR without settling a commission. The settlement did not specify whether the Soviet Union bears international liability or not.[218]

The principles for determining the amount of the compensation are regulated in article XII of the Liability Convention, and it is envisioned that the compensation has to be determined in accordance with international law and the principles of equity and justice in order to restore the situation, which would have existed if the damage had not occurred.

This means that if a non-functional satellite of a state is destroyed in outer space by another state, then there should be no liability and no compensation because a non-functional satellite does not possess (or has very limited) economic value. Perek also substantiated that the important criteria for distinguishing space objects in outer space are whether they are a valuable asset for the owner/launching state or not.[219] Deorbiting the satellite if it was not destroyed would cost probably more than the materials that it is made of, he rightly argued.

---

218 Protocol of Settlement of Claim between Canada and the Union of Soviet Socialist Republics for Damage Caused by "Cosmos 954", (Released on April 2, 1981).

219 Lubos Perek, *Space debris mitigation and prevention: how to build a stronger international regime,* 2.2. *Astropolitics* 2, 215, 220, (2004).

One possible substantiation of legal interest and value of the non-functional satellite would be if the damaged state could prove that its satellite was going to be used as a target for anti-satellite weapons. Despite the fact that these tests are detrimental to the outer space environment, they are legally allowed. This means that they have a legitimate economic value for the states that have jurisdiction over them.

States might make an attempt to conclude bilateral and multilateral treaties which foresee that they will exclude international liability for damages in outer space or on the surface of Earth. The legal condition of these norms in the treaties, which are ratified by states that are parties to the Liability Convention, is that they are not in force because the norms violate the norm in article 41 par.1 b) of the Vienna Convention on the law of treaties.[220]

In the case of the Liability Convention, these norms of the bilateral or multilateral treaties would derogate the purpose of the convention as it is described in its preamble.[221]

1.5. Relevant national practices for reducing the risks of space debris

The achievement of a comprehensive international legal agreement to resolve space debris is a very difficult effort that requires competing states and private companies to agree on a common framework for space activities. For this reason, Mirmina and other representatives of the academia rightly advocate that the implemen-

---

220 Vienna Convention on the law of treaties, art.41 par.1 b*) "Two or more of the parties to a multilateral treaty may conclude an agreement to modify the treaty as between themselves alone if: (ii) does not relate to a provision, derogation from which is incompatible with the effective execution of the object and purpose of the treaty as a whole."*, 1155 U.N.T.S. 331, 8 I.L.M. 679.

221 in particular paragraph 5: *Recognising the need to elaborate effective international rules and procedures concerning liability for damage caused by space objects and to ensure, in particular, the prompt payment under the terms of this convention of a full and equitable measure of compensation to victims of such damage.*

tation of national measures to prevent and mitigate space debris is a more appropriate means of achieving the global goal to resolve the issue than aiming to adopt an international legal instrument.[222]

This approach is practical and it doesn't exclude the possibility of a future international treaty. Researching and comparing the national space policy priorities of leading space-faring nations with respect to the space debris issue is key to understanding the progress and readiness of states to protect the outer space environment and to improve the safety of space activities.

1.5.1. US national policy on space debris

The issue of space debris was acknowledged by the US government in the early stages of the development of the national space program, but it was included in the US National Space Policy for the first time relatively late in 1988.[223] The policy directive made a small effort to address the issue, which at that time was not a considerable national security threat. It is evident from the fact that the directive foresees that the reduction or minimisation of space debris should strive to be consistent with cost-effectiveness. This means that the functional space objects are going to be used as much as possible, and they are not going to be deorbited when their fuel is about to finish.

The US national space policy from 2020 declares that the US will have the goal to create a safe, stable, secure, and sustainable environment for space activities with the implementation of measures to mitigate orbital debris.[224] The policy elaborates that preserving

222 Steven Mirmina, *The regulation of orbital debris through national measures,* 29 Air & Space L, 137, 138-144, (2004).
223 Presidential Directive on National Space Policy, (February 11, 1988). "The directive further states that all space sectors will seek to minimize the creation of space debris. Design and operations of space tests, experiments and systems will strive to minimize or reduce accumulation of space debris consistent with mission requirements and cost effectiveness." https://fas.org/spp/military/docops/national/policy88.htm last access 12.02.2023
224 National Space Policy of the USA, 5 (Dec. 9, 2020). https://trumpwhitehouse.archives.gov/wp-content/uploads/2020/12/National-Space-

the outer space environment should be achieved by the adoption of international and industry standards, such as the UN Space debris mitigation guidelines.[225] On one side, this is a good sign that the US administration not only understands the magnitude of the problem, but also accepts that it cannot be resolved by one nation, and it requires mutual commitments and acceptance of common standards by most, if not all, space-faring nations. At the same time, it is worrying that the US administration considers legally non-binding standards and guidelines as sufficient to resolve the challenges from space debris. Secondly, the US administration plans to "*pursue research and development of technologies and techniques to characterise and to mitigate risks from orbital debris, reduce hazards, and increase understanding of the current and future debris environment*".[226] It is a positive step to focus on research and aims to improve technological capabilities for tracking space debris or introducing more advanced active debris removal systems and methods.

Implementing the guidelines of the US Space Policy from 2020, the Federal Communications Commission adopted a report with the title Mitigation of Orbital Debris in the New Space Age.[227] An important conclusion in this document, based on research that is not referenced, is that there are regions in the Low-Earth Orbit that have sufficient densities of orbital debris. Those regions are estimated to reach (or close to reaching) a "runaway" status, where the debris population will grow indefinitely due to collisions between debris objects.[228] This prognosis serves as a warning for all actors in space exploration and exploitation, and the conclusion is that space debris mitigation should be taken seriously by the operators. One difficulty in regulation is identified in this report, and this is the unwillingness of leading private companies[229] to accept regulation of

Policy.pdf

225 *Id.* at 14

226 *Id.* at 15

227 FR, volume 85, 52422, document number 2020-13185, (Aug.25, 2020). https://www.govinfo.gov/content/pkg/FR-2020-08-25/pdf/2020-13185.pdf

228 *Id.*

229 FR, volume 85, 52422, document number 2020-13185, (Aug.25, 2020).

spacecraft design, specifically for geostationary satellites. European leading companies like Eutelsat also refrain from accepting regulatory obligations for spacecraft design. Design flaws could lead to unpredicted flaws in satellites usage and stability, and for this reason, the Federal Communications Commission requires conducting tests of a certain number of satellites in a lower orbit for a certain number of years before deploying larger numbers of satellites, to avoid the generation of debris.

Besides changes in satellite design of the spacecraft, FCC sought comments from the private industry on the following regulatory aspects to address space debris: fewer launches; changes in operations and disposal procedures; use of economic incentives; active collision avoidance and active debris cleanup. The same leading companies from the space sector agree that changes in operations and disposal procedures are key measures to achieve the goals of mitigating orbital debris and supporting their adoption.

The role of the private sector is very important, as they would have to implement the obligations, and they have very strong lobbying power in many countries. It is important to acknowledge the efforts of dozens of private companies involved in space activities to form a Space Safety Coalition, which has published a set of best practices for the long-term sustainability of space operations. This forum and its published practices are valuable for all space-faring states to understand which measures could be accepted by private actors without any compromises and without difficult negotiations.

1.5.2. National policy on space debris of the Russian Federation

In Russia, the planned activities on space debris mitigation are included in the Russian Federal Space Program for 2016-2025. The national regulatory framework for space debris mitigation is the stan-

---

"Global NewSpace Operators states that while the government has a role to play in incentivizing industry, it does not recommend mandating specific satellite design concepts or active collision avoidance, rather preferring that these elements emerge as industry best practices."

dard of the Russian Federation GOST R 52925 «Space technology items. General requirements for mitigation of space debris population».[230] Russia is improving its methods and means of spacecraft protection of space objects and micrometeoroids.[231] An example of such a method is the restriction of the formation of space debris during regular operations by means of an exception of separating elements during the orbit-inserting of spacecraft and their operation.

An important synchronisation of methods and good practices between national space agencies is achieved in the Inter-Agency Space Debris Committee, which is researched separately in chapter 3.2.

Russia and China deepened their bilateral relations and transformed them into a strategic partnership in space activities, including adopting civil scientific and technical cooperation on space debris research.[232] This bilateral cooperation has deepened since the Russian invasion of Ukraine in February 2022 and the imposed sanctions from the USA and its allies.

1.5.3. National space policy on space debris of China

The origin of Chinese space technology is closely linked with Russian space technological development.[233] As a state that is rapidly progressing economically in the last two decades, China has made significant investments in their national space program and consequently has taken steps to address the issue of space debris in various ways. A recent example from April 2021 is the launching into the Low-Earth orbit of a Chinese robot that can "scoop up" debris left behind by other spacecraft with a big net.[234] Previously,

---

230 Yury Makarov, Anna Prokopchik, Mikhail Simonov, Alexey Gorlov, I. Usovik & M. Yakovlev, *Major trends for space debris mitigation in near-Earth space in the Russian Federation*, In Proceedings of the International Astronautical Congress, IAC, 3601, (2017).

231 *Id.* at 3606

232 Florian Vidal, *Russia's Space Policy: The Path of Decline?*, Études de l'Ifri, Ifri, January, 20, (2021).

233 Paul B. Larsen, *Outer space arms control: can the USA, Russia and China make this happen*, 23.1. Journal of Conflict and Security Law, 137, 149, (2018).

234 Reuters Agency,https://www.reuters.com/lifestyle/science/china-launches-

The Chinese government launched the AoLong-1 (ADRV) 'Roaming Dragon' satellite in 2016 in order to test target capture with a robotic arm; results are presently not publicly available.[235] China has conducted a total of five tests of co-orbital operations in the last decade, consisting of the manoeuvre of a satellite closer to another orbiting object, with the purpose of inspecting, seizing or removing it from its orbit with the help of a robotic arm. Julienne is correct to conclude that the interest of China to initiate such projects is most probably because of their dual-use – cleaning the outer space environment from space debris and using the technology to destroy, spy on or sabotage foreign satellites.[236]

The Chinese government has changed its attitude towards space activities and protecting the outer space environment after the successful Chinese anti-satellite test in 2007, which resulted in an unprecedented amount of newly created space debris in usable orbits. Presently, space debris monitoring, and early-warning systems are improved and standards and legal regulations are enhanced.[237] China innovated protection design technologies against space debris. The positive effect on the outer space environment from this technology is that the Long March carrier rockets already have upper-stage passivation, and discarded spacecraft are moved out of usable orbit.

1.5.4. Space debris policies of European countries

In 2001, the European Space Debris Centres Network developed the "European Space Debris Mitigation Guidelines". This

---

robot-prototype-capable-catching-space-debris-with-net-2021-04-27/ last access on 10.02.2023

235 Jason L. Forshaw, Guglielmo S. Aglietti, Simon Fellowes, Thierry Salmon, Ingo Retat, Alexander Hall, Thomas Chabot et al, *The active space debris removal mission RemoveDebris. Part 1: from concept to launch.* 168 Acta Astronautica, 293, 295, (2020).

236 Marc Julienne, *China's Ambitions in Space: The Sky's the Limit*, Études de l'Ifri, 24, (2021).

237 China's Council Information Office, (Dec 27, 2016). http://www.scio.gov.cn/zfbps/ndhf/34120/Document/1537022/1537022.htm

document is not legally binding, but it is of considerable political importance as it demonstrates the involvement of a large part of European countries in the problem and shows that cooperation at a regional level is achievable. ESA used the European Code of Conduct as a basis to draw up an official document for the Agency, and on June 28th 2004, it published a "European Guide to Space Debris Mitigation".[238]

The guidance explicitly states that its elements are in line with the Space Debris Mitigation Guidelines prepared by the Inter-Agency Space Debris Committee, and the European manual provides more detail and greater justification.

The introduction to the European Code of Conduct outlines the obligations that countries have under articles I and IX of the Outer Space Treaty, which require outer space to be free for exploration and use for all countries (Article I) and activities to be carried out to prevent harmful contamination (Article IX). Focus is also placed on compliance with the Liability Convention. Viikari rightly argues that the regional efforts in Europe, particularly in the format of the ESA Space Debris Working Group and the adopted European Code of Conduct for Space Debris Mitigation, are environmentally oriented. The efforts on a European level are consistent with IADC guidelines but are more detailed and provide more instructions to the ESA member states.[239]

Despite its adherence to international space law, guidance is not a legally binding document, as in point 2.2. it states that the implementation of the measures is voluntary and should be implemented by ESA, national space agencies and private companies.[240]

The legal nature and form of the harmonised documents at a regional level, with regard to all aspects of space debris mitigation, are consistent with the legal nature and form of rules at a universal

238 European Code of Conduct for Space Debris Mitigation, 2, (28.06.2004). http://www.cnsa.gov.cn/n615708/n676979/n676983/n893604/appendix/2008529151013.pdf

239 Lotta Viikari, The environmental element in space law, 95, (2008).

240 European code of conduct point 2.2. par.1

level. This is justified because legally binding regulations for European companies to invest significantly in outer space safety and minimization of space debris would increase the price of their operations, and place them in competitive disadvantage comparing to companies, which are not investing significantly in the protection of outer space environment and in safety of the space activities. If only European companies prioritize the issue of space debris and invest in its minimization, the issue will still be unresolved on a global level.

An important feature of the European Code of Conduct is the introduction of the position of Space Debris Manager and the development of a space debris reduction plan for each space project.[241]

The Space Debris Manager is also assigned to each space project. He has the authority and the responsibility for how the given plan for space mitigation is implemented during all phases of the project.[242]The space debris manager must certify that the space project adheres to the space debris mitigation specifications applicable to the project. The Code of Conduct also provides standards that are directly related to the decision-making process for a space project. The space debris manager must approve decisions relating to activities that generate space debris. The Code of Conduct also stipulates that it should coordinate the activities of space-debris generation and ensure their compliance with safety and quality activities.[243]

The creation of this position demonstrates the European institution's commitment to the problem and suggests that European space projects will be implemented to minimise the generated space debris. With regard to the Space Debris Mitigation Plan, the European Code of Conduct states the minimum requirements for the plan.[244]

In addition to management measures, the Code of Conduct also includes space systems design and operational measures. An example of such a measure involving the design of space systems is a

241 *Id.* at point 3.2
242 *Id.* at point 3.2. b)
243 *Id.* at point 3.2. e)
244 *Id.* at point 3.3. SD - 05

limitation of elements used in launching. Accordingly, the design of the elements must minimise the number of elements in orbit.[245] This will allow the tracking of the large element and its registration, as well as the fact that it will be space debris, not a multitude. Hypothetically, such an element can be moved, or even removed, if necessary, as opposed to many small elements, for which it is much more difficult or technologically impossible, at this stage of technological development. The Code of Conduct stipulates that an individual mitigation plan should include an assessment of the risk of space debris, as well as recommended measures to prevent collisions. Next, the Code of Conduct identifies LEO and GEO for protected regions and stipulates that their safety and continued use in the future must be ensured.

Annex 2 to the guidance also provides definitions that are in accordance with the European standard ECSS-P-001. The definition of the term "space debris" provides the following: "*Any man-made space object, including fragments and elements of it, which is in orbit of the Earth and which enters into the Earth's atmosphere and is non-functional.*" This is the same definition given by the IADC, which confirms that regional space mitigation measures will follow those achieved at a global level among the leading space agencies.

Good practices to address the issue of space debris are conducted by separate European countries with national funding. An example of this is Italy and the project "Debris collision alert system "DeCAS. It is an ongoing project initiated by Aviosonic Space Tech, which is an Italian start-up company.[246] This project aims to develop innovative technology, which addresses the issue of re-entry risk mitigation through onboard debris tracking management. A monitoring device that is lightweight, small and high in precision is fitted into the vehicle during the construction phase and remains in a dormant state until the spacecraft stops functioning. Once the

245 European code of conduct for space debris mitigation, point 4.1. SD – 01 (2004).

246 Aviosonic Space Tech website, https://www.aviosonic.it/themission.html last access on 10.02.2023

spacecraft stops functioning, the DeCAS system is activated and starts providing information regarding the space debris area.

The idea of tracking the debris from inside the spaceship is a unique idea. This project is completely different from all the other recent tracking projects because the DeCAS system manages to collect data "from the inside" of the spacecraft. The objective of the project is to follow the evolution of the debris cloud and provide valuable data. Since the device is small and light in weight, it can be used in most of the existing systems in the field of re-entry risk mitigation management.

The DeCAS project is a good practice from an Italian company that illustrates that space debris mitigation could be improved by private investments and research.

1.5.5. National policy on space debris of India

The rapid and unique development of the Indian space policy and program, led today by the Indian Space Research Organization (ISRO), is a result of a doctrine of self-reliance and ingenuity. It was initiated in the early age of national space exploration by one of the most prominent figures of India's Space policy development - Vikram Sarabhai.[247] This policy has continued today also in the field of addressing the space debris crisis. An example is the ISRO-initiated project "NETRA", which provides an early warning system in space to detect space debris and other dangerous hazards to the space assets of India.[248] The development of a national Space Situational Awareness Control Centre[249] is showing that the national steps of India to maintain sovereign control on tracking and monitoring of space objects is a priority for the state in order to guarantee

247 Yuichiro Nagai, Mukund Rao, Hideaki Shiroyama, K. R. Murthi, Motoko Uchitomi, and Baldev Raj, Policy Analysis: Space Programmes of Japan And India, 7, (2015).

248 Official website of ISRO: https://www.isro.gov.in/update/16-dec-2020/isro-ssacontrol-centre-inaugurated-dr-k-sivan-chairman-isro-secretary-dos#:~:text=NEtwork%20for%20space%20object%20TRacking,ISTRAC%20campus%20at%20Peenya%2C%20Bangalore. Last access 10.02.2023

249 Formally initiated on December 14th 2020

self-reliance and self-sufficiency in space policy. The SSA control center foresees the establishment of labs that are dedicated to space debris mitigation and remediation, compliance verification of UN and IADC mitigation guidelines, and research and development activities, including the fields of object fragmentation and break-up modelling and space debris modelling.[250] Those national projects of India are showing readiness to cooperate on an international level in the established forums and political will to invest in the protection of space assets by minimisation the generation of space debris.

Other countries that have adopted national legislation with explicit or implicit reference to the re-orbit guideline are Austria, Belgium, Canada, Japan, Denmark, Finland, France, Germany, Japan, New Zealand, Ukraine, and the United Kingdom.

250 Official website of ISRO: https://www.isro.gov.in/update/16-dec-2020/isro-ssacontrol-centre-inaugurated-dr-k-sivan-chairman-isro-secretary-dos#:~:text=NEtwork%20for%20space%20object%20TRacking,ISTRAC%20campus%20at%20Peenya%2C%20Bangalore. Last access 10.02.2023

Chapter 2

International cooperation to reduce the threats from space debris

Chapter II of the research explores the significant international forums of cooperation for the resolution of the space debris problem. Such forums are leading international governmental and non-governmental organizations regulating or proposing regulations to address the issue of space debris. The inclusion of the achievements of leading international non-governmental organizations is necessary to better analyse the various problems from different space debris. Comparing expert conclusions and recommendations with policy decisions and regulations on the issue will help alleviate the space debris problem.

The comprehensive review of the international cooperation of states requires research not only of international legal framework but also of national policies, official positions, and national interests of leading space-faring states. International cooperation in any branch of Public International Law illustrates the inseparable axis between international law and international politics.

The universal international principle that notes that states have the duty to cooperate in accordance with the UN Charter is one of the fundamental legal principles identified in the Declaration on Principles of International Law Friendly Relations and Co-operation among States in Accordance with the Charter of the United Nations.[251] This principle will remain a mere recommendation without any legal significance and regulatory effect if all states do not develop their national policy and foster international relations with the intention to weaken their respective rival states. In order to promote a genuine partnership between states, they should have a common goal that cannot be achieved by either of them alone.

The vast resources and future possibilities that outer space offers are a primary cause for competition among developed states and an aspiration for dominance among the leading space-faring nations. The competing interests for limited outer space resources are based on both economic and security needs. There is a serious likelihood that these vital resources could become a source of contention among many space-faring states.[252]

The legal subjects that should address the problem of space debris are states that have a leading role in space exploration and use and international organizations that have a direct or indirect connection with the issue. For this reason, it is crucial to synchronize national interests and states' policies to reduce space waste. The role of international organizations is accordingly to become helpful forums for the implementation of this synchronization.

One weak point in the Outer Space Treaty is the provision of international consultations in article IX. This is because the state, which is carrying out space activities, has sole discretion on whether its activities are threatening the interest of other states. In addition to the ineffectiveness of the procedure of international consultations is the fact that the obligation to participate in the consultations is not bound by the need for any particular results. Hobe proposes that such results could be, for example, an agreement, an obligation for exchanging data and others.[253] Malanczuk concludes that in prac-

---

251 Principles a), b) and d) of the Declaration on Principles of International Law Friendly Relations and Co-operation among States in Accordance with the Charter of the United Nations, (Oct. 24, 1970). A/RES/2625(XXV)

252 Ram S. Jakhu & Karan Singh, *Space Security and Competition for Radio Frequencies and Geostationary Slots* 58.1 ZLW, 74, 75, (2009).

253 Stephan Hobe, *Space Debris: A proposal for its international legal regulation*, 34 Proc. Colloquium L. Outer Space, 194, 196, (1992).

tice, the procedure for international consultation is exhausted with a simple notification for planned activities in outer space on behalf of the launching state. The states, which could be potentially affected, have no veto rights.[254]

The absence of significant cooperation between the states on this issue is evidenced by the conclusions set out in the previous chapter. Among these conclusions are the lack of clear international legal definitions, the absence of an independent body to monitor and control activities in outer space, and the pursuit of a policy of abandoning non-functional or uncontrolled space systems[255] aimed at short-term cost savings. The saved costs in the past and present will lead to a larger problem with space debris, which would require larger financial investments in the near future. The desire of leading space agencies and major private space actors to save costs and to refrain themselves to deorbit the majority of the non-functional space objects is one of the main reasons for not attempting and not achieving a comprehensive legal regulation of the space debris issue.

Even if one leading space-faring nation does not agree to adopt higher standards for the launching of space objects, deorbiting of space objects before they become uncontrolled, and investing in better systems and technological equipment to track and remove space objects, it would mean a lack of international progress to improve the international legal norms on the issue. The reason is that states that are willing to preserve a legal regime that does not include an obligation of the private company to deorbit their satellite will have a competitive advantage over other states that are applying higher safety standards and mandate more safety requirements to space companies.

In order to achieve long-term comprehensive minimization of the risk from space debris, it is necessary to analyse different forms

254 Peter Malanczuk, *Review of the regulatory regime governing the space environment*, 45 ZLW, 37, 52, (1996).
255 Edward G Lee & D. W. Sproule, *Liability for Damage Caused by Space Debris: The Cosmos 954 Claim*, 26 Canadian Yearbook of international Law/ Annuaire canadien de droit international, 273, 275, (1989).

of international cooperation that are resulting in better utilization of outer space and regulated space traffic management. The International Space Station is an example of a long-term project that is established through separate agreements[256] in the spirit of international cooperation in the areas of design, development, operation and utilization of the International Space Station. Sattler substantiates that NASA could continue to serve as the coordinator for future commercialization projects and settlements on celestial bodies unless an NGO is agreed upon by the participating nations.[257] She proposes cooperation that is pioneered by the USA and other countries would contribute funds and place technology on the Moon through their space agencies. These space agencies would secure the technology and funding from private businesses that enter into contracts for such services with these agencies. In accordance with the terms of the IGA and the Outer Space Treaty, each country, or space agency, would retain jurisdiction over its crew, its spacecraft, and any structures or equipment.[258]

International cooperation for addressing the issue of space debris exists at the official governmental level and also at a non-governmental level in respected forums and international non-governmental organizations. This chapter is organized to analyse both groups separately.

2.1. International cooperation at a governmental level

Governmental cooperation could be at a global level - including most states; regional - including states from a specific region; and bilateral – including two states. New mechanisms of interna-

256 Agreement among the government of Canada, governments of Member States of the European Space Agency, the government of Japan, the government of the Russian Federation, and the government of the United States of America concerning Cooperation on the Civil International Space Station, (Jan. 29, 1998). [hereinafter IGA]

257 Rosanna Sattler, *Transporting a Legal System for Property Rights: From the Earth to the Stars,* 6 Chi. J. Int'l L., 23, (2005).

258 *Id.* at 39

tional governmental cooperation emerged with the adoption of the Artemis Accords. This mechanism is not multilateral, but a set of bilateral agreements between NASA and other space agencies. It deserves to be analysed separately from the perspective of mitigation of space debris and the risks from them, because it is a new format for global governmental space cooperation.

2.1.1. International cooperation in COPUOS

COPUOS remains the most prominent international organization, which has charted international space law, particularly the five outer space treaties, guidelines and principles in relation to outer space activities. The forum has expressed its serious concerns about space debris and formulated legally non-binding guidelines, which have been accepted by the majority of space-faring states.

After the first two decades of successful legal regulation through the adoption of the five major UN space treaties, it became a common practice to adopt soft law guidelines and principles.[259] The unique decision-making process in the COPUOS, namely the requirement of consensus, predisposed the application of the "corridor negotiation".[260] The result was that less developed countries received the opportunity to participate in the decision-making process after a general understanding is struck by the leading space-faring nations.

Examples of such acts are the UN Space Debris Mitigation Guidelines and the International Code of Conduct for Outer Space Activities (ICOC). I disagree with Lim's conclusion that the ICOC represents the most promising "spiritual successor" to the OST within international soft law.[261] The reasons are that soft law documents do not possess the same regulative value as legally binding treaties. The Outer Space Treaty is still accepted by major space-faring

259 Jack M. Beard, *Soft Law's Failure on the Horizon: The International Code of Conduct for Outer Space Activities,* 38 U. Pa. J. Int'l L., 335, 345-358, (2016).

260 S.G. Sreejith, *Whither International Law, Thither Space Law: A Discipline in Transition*, 38 Cal. W. Int'l LJ, 331, 342, (2007).

261 Jonathan Lim, *The Future of the Outer Space Treaty–Peace and Security in the 21st Century*, 4.2. Global Politics Review, 72, (2018).

nations as a cornerstone for the International Space Law.[262] Jakhu rightly concludes that the international doctrine of the "persistent objector" would prevent soft law documents from becoming rules of customary international law.[263] Self-interest could not be considered a sufficient driver for states to keep outer space free from debris congestion.[264]

Ganev correctly observes that when more states are participating in an international organization where the decisions are taken with consensus, more compromises are made in the decision-making process. This results in the deterioration of the quality of the adopted acts. Consequently, the regulative function of the international organization is severely weakened.[265] Jasentuliana rightly criticizes the work of COPUOS after the adoption of the Moon Agreement. From the early 80s of the XX century, the international legal doctrine made fair criticism of the work of the UN and, in particular, the absence of legally binding agreements adopted in COPUOS.[266]

After the insistence of consultations in the Scientific and Technical Subcommittee, the member states were united around the position that in regard to space debris mitigation, it will be adopted a new document that should be approved by the Committee and by the GA of the UN.[267]

In the 41st session of the Subcommittee was established a working group that was given the task to take into consideration

---

262 Executive Order of the US President confirms the acceptance of the norms of OST –Encouraging International Support for the Recovery and Use of Space Resources, Exec. Order No. 13,914, 85 Fed. Reg. 20,381 (Apr. 6, 2020)

263 Ram S. Jakhu, *The Future of the Outer Space Treaty.* Fifty Years of the Outer Space Treaty, 185, 188, (2017).

264 Ram S. Jakhu & Joseph N. Pelton, eds. Global Space Governance: an International Study, 289, (2017).

265 Маргарит Ганев, Специализираните организации от системата на Организацията на обединените нации, Институт по международно право, 143-149, (2005).

266 Nandasiri Jasentuliyana, International space law and the United Nations, 102-119, (1999).

267 Report of the Scientific and Technical Subcommittee: A/AC.105/823, par. 97, (2004).

the comments and positions of separate states. It was decided that the new act will be in the form of guidelines, and they will be based on the report of the Inter-Agency Space Debris Committee. This Committee was specifically created as a forum for discussion of the problems of space debris, and it is different from the structure of UN organs. Its role is analysed separately in the next subchapter.

In the session of the Scientific and Technical Subcommittee was foreseen that the guidelines should consider the work of the Inter-Agency Space Debris Coordination Committee and use it as the basis for the UN Space Debris Mitigation Guidelines.[268] The second consideration is that the level of technical stringency should not exceed that level, which was set in the IADC guidelines. The third consideration stipulates the legal character of the UN Space Debris Mitigation Guidelines and it is legally non-binding under international law. The fourth consideration clarifies the intention of the guidelines to be voluntary implements and carried out through relevant national mechanisms. According to the fifth consideration exceptions from the guidelines could be justified. The next clarification is that the document is living and could be updated with the evolution of national and international practices on space debris mitigation, technological innovation, and research. The next consideration clarifies that the document is applicable for newly designed spacecraft and only if possible to existing ones. The legally binding norms in the UN treaties on outer space have to be considered in the guidelines. Lastly, the instructions on the document are to be concise, to contain high-level qualitative guidelines and to make a reference to the IADC space debris mitigation guidelines.

The acknowledgement of the work of IADC and the usage of the results of this committee as a basis signifies the good level of cooperation between the two forums and the intention to have consistency in both guidelines.

---

268 Report of the Scientific and Technical Subcommittee: A/AC.105/848, Annex II par.5, (2005).

In 2007, during the 44th session of the Subcommittee space debris mitigation guidelines were conclusively adopted.[269] Contrary to the established procedure in the past, the guidelines were not discussed in the Legal Subcommittee and were directly adopted by the Committee in its 50th session. The states expressed their great satisfaction with the adoption of the guidelines.[270]

On 22nd December 2007, the GA of the UN adopted resolution 62/217, confirmed the mitigation guidelines of the Scientific and Technical Subcommittee and renamed them UN Space Debris Mitigation Guidelines.

Guideline 1: Limit debris released during normal operations[271]

Perek emphasized the importance of designers creating the spacecraft in such a way to prevent loose parts to separate from the vehicle and covers to be attached to the vehicle even "*if they are not needed anymore*".[272] For example, the execution of Design for Demise (D4D) tests has proven to be very useful to understand the demise of concrete materials and structures used in constructing a space payload.[273] The European team of the project ReDSHIFT shared good practices in relation to research of design with all private space companies in order to reduce the risk from space debris.

---

269 Report of the Scientific and Technical Subcommittee, A/AC.105/890 par. 99, (2007). http://www.oosa.unvienna.org/pdf/reports/ac105/AC105_890E.pdf

270 Report of the COPUOS, A/62/20 par.117, (2007). http://www.oosa.unvienna.org/pdf/gadocs/A_62_20E.pdf

271 Space systems should be designed not to release debris during normal operations. If this is not feasible, the effect of any release of debris on the outer space environment should be minimized. During the early decades of the space age, launch vehicle and spacecraft designers permitted the intentional release of numerous mission-related objects into Earth orbit, including, among other things, sensor covers, separation mechanisms and deployment articles. Dedicated design efforts, prompted by the recognition of the threat posed by such objects, have proved effective in reducing this source of space debris.

272 Lubos Perek, *Space debris mitigation and prevention: how to build a stronger international regime*, 2.2. Astropolitics, 215, 218, (2004).

273 Alessandro Rossi, Camilla Colombo, Kleomenis Tsiganis, James Beck, Jonathan Becedas Rodriguez, Scott Walker, Federico Letterio, et al., *ReDSHIFT: A global approach to space debris mitigation*, 5.2 Aerospace, 64, (2018).

The team provided a publicly accessible software tool that could "*help the users to conceive a debris compliant space mission from the design to the disposal phase*".[274]

Even minimizing the usage of decaying paint on the space object is a positive example of reducing the risk of space debris release.[275]

Guideline 2: Minimize the potential for break-ups during operational phases[276]

Guideline 3: Limit the probability of accidental collision in orbit[277]

Guideline 4: Avoid intentional destruction and other harmful activities[278]

Guideline 5: Minimize potential for post-mission break-ups re-

---

274 *Id.* at 65

275 Jennifer M Seymour, *Containing the cosmic crisis: a proposal for curbing the perils of space debris*, 10 Geo. Int'l Envtl. L. Rev., 891, 913, (1997).

276 Spacecraft and launch vehicle orbital stages should be designed to avoid failure modes which may lead to accidental break-ups. In cases where a condition leading to such a failure is detected, disposal, and passivation measures should be planned and executed to avoid break-ups. Historically, some break-ups have been caused by space system malfunctions, such as catastrophic failures of propulsion and power systems. By incorporating potential break-up scenarios in failure mode analysis, the probability of these catastrophic events can be reduced.

277 In developing the design and mission profile of spacecraft and launch vehicle stages, the probability of accidental collision with known objects during the system's launch phase and orbital lifetime should be estimated and limited. If available orbital data indicate a potential collision, adjustment of the launch time or an on-orbit avoidance manoeuvre should be considered. Some accidental collisions have already been identified. Numerous studies indicate that, as the number and mass of space debris increase, the primary source of new space debris is likely to be from collisions. Collision avoidance procedures have already been adopted by some Member States and international organizations.

278 Recognizing that an increased risk of collision could pose a threat to space operations, the intentional destruction of any on-orbit spacecraft and launch vehicle orbital stages or other harmful activities that generate long-lived debris should be avoided. When intentional break-ups are necessary, they should be conducted at sufficiently low altitudes to limit the orbital lifetime of resulting fragments.

sulting from stored energy[279]

Guideline 6: Limit the long-term presence of spacecraft and launch vehicle orbital stages in the low-Earth orbit (LEO) region after the end of their mission[280]

Guideline 7: Limit the long-term interference of spacecraft and launch vehicle orbital stages with the geosynchronous Earth orbit (GEO) region after the end of their mission.[281]

A special merit of the guidelines is that they provide an internationally recognized definition of space debris, even though it is not legally binding.[282] The definition foresees that space debris is "*all*

---

279 In order to limit the risk to other spacecraft and launch vehicle orbital stages from accidental break-ups, all onboard sources of stored energy should be depleted or made safe when they are no longer required for mission operations or post-mission disposal. By far, the largest percentage of the catalogued space debris population originated from the fragmentation of spacecraft and launched vehicle orbital stages. The majority of those break-ups were unintentional, many arising from the abandonment of spacecraft and launch vehicle orbital stages with significant amounts of stored energy. The most effective mitigation measures have been the passivation of spacecraft and launch vehicle orbital stages at the end of their mission. Passivation requires the removal of all forms of stored energy, including residual propellants and compressed fluids and the discharge of electrical storage devices.

280 Spacecraft and launch vehicle orbital stages that have terminated their operational phases in orbits that pass through the LEO region should be removed from orbit in a controlled fashion. If this is not possible, they should be disposed of in orbits that avoid their long-term presence in the LEO region. When making determinations regarding potential solutions for removing objects from LEO, due consideration should be given to ensure that debris that survives to reach the surface of the Earth does not pose an undue risk to people or property, including through environmental pollution caused by hazardous substances.

281 Spacecraft and launch vehicle orbital stages that have terminated their operational phases in orbits that pass through the GEO region should be left in orbits that avoid their long-term interference with the GEO region. For space objects in or near the GEO region, the potential for future collisions can be reduced by leaving objects at the end of their mission in orbit above the GEO region such that they will not interfere with, or return to, the GEO region.

282 Stephan Hobe, *UN Space Debris Mitigation Guidelines*, 58/3 ZLW, 394, (2009).

man-made objects, including fragments and elements thereof, in Earth orbit or re-entering the atmosphere that is non-functional".[283] The definition is explicitly limited to be used for the purpose of this document. It can be used as an additional guideline in the international discussion in regard to technical and juridical complications related to space debris. Another constraint of the definition is seen in regards to the location of space debris, which is limited to Earth orbit or re-entering the atmosphere.

The importance of the guidelines was highlighted by Sachdeva, and despite their legally non-binding nature, they should be considered by states as ethically obligatory.[284]

It is evident that this understanding of the location of space debris can generate many disputes in the future when more space objects will orbit other celestial bodies or be on their surface. The present definition will not include those non-functional space objects and will not provide guidance on how they should be handled. For example, by the time of publishing of this research, the total amount of waste on the Moon is more than 181 tons.[285] As analysed in the previous chapter, this waste is also space debris, and it should be taken into consideration what should be the legal obligations of the states and international organizations that have produced them. The scope of the definition of space debris should not exclude waste on different celestial bodies.

The guidelines also mentions that space debris is only non-functional objects, and their location is provided by the state of registry. There is a serious international safety concern that the status and location of the space debris are confirmed by the registered state and not by an independent international organization.[286] This status

283 UN Space Debris Mitigation Guidelines, GA of UN Res/62/217, Background, (2007).

284 Gurbachan S. Sachdeva, *Space Doctrine of India*, 14.2-3 Astropolitics, 104-119, (2016).

285 For All Mankind website, https://www.forallmoonkind.org/about/the-declaration/ last access on 10.02.2023

286 Stephan Hobe, *UN Space Debris Mitigation Guidelines*, 58/3 ZLW, 394, (2009).

quo carries the risk that the given information will not be accurate or on time if it does not suit the national interest of the state that is providing it. In the incident with the Soviet satellite "Cosmos 954", Canada insisted that prior notification of the imminent re-entry of the nuclear-powered satellite was not provided and that USSR did not provide complete answers in a timely manner to the Canadian questions, concerning the satellite.[287] The example clearly shows that safe outer space traffic management cannot be achieved on the basis of reciprocal obligations of states to share information, and instead, there is a need for a global international space situational awareness system.

The UN space debris mitigation guidelines are applicable to mission planning and operation of newly designed spacecraft and orbital stages and, if possible, to existing ones.[288] This characteristic shows the lack of international unity to resolve the challenges that space debris is presenting today, particularly the need to remove non-functional satellites from usable orbits.

In the guidelines were not pointed out any measures or recommendations for removing space debris, nor any guidelines for solving the problems of international liability, insurance of space systems, and distribution of financial burden for compensation and for taking healthy actions for removing a dangerous space object.

Lastly, it should be noted that the guidelines do not mention any standards for the quality of space objects which are launched into outer space. The most probable reason for the lack of common quality standards is the unwillingness of some of the international space actors to be bound with economic investments for scientific exploration, which should lead to the mitigation of polluting the outer space environment.

---

287 Protocol of Settlement of Claim between Canada and the Union of Soviet Socialist Republics for Damage Caused by "Cosmos 954", (Released on April 2, 1981).

288 UN Space Debris Mitigation Guideline 2007, GA of UN Res/62/217, Rationale par. 3, (2007).

An example of such international standards is ISO 24113:2011.[289] According to ISO, this is the top-level standard of a family of standards that addresses the issue of space debris mitigation. The standard is reviewed every 5 years, which provides an opportunity for updates and improvements, which correspond with the scientific progress or an improved negotiating climate between parties.

There are not any scientific difficulties to analyse the legal status of the guidelines because paragraph 3 of the rationale explicitly foresees that they are not legally binding under international law. Even without this paragraph, the fact that the guidelines were negotiated only in the Scientific and Technical Subcommittee without being presented and considered in the Legal Subcommittee is further evidence of the legally non-binding character of the guidelines.[290]

The space debris mitigation guidelines could be adopted partially or fully in the national legal systems of all states. Their voluntary character shows that presently there are insurmountable political obstacles to adopting a comprehensive international legal framework for protecting the outer space environment.

Guideline 4 recommends the avoidance of intentional destruction of any on-orbit spacecraft or other harmful activities that generate long-lived debris.

Concerning the issue of sharing information about space debris, the guidelines do not foresee any recommendation of an international organ or even a state to conduct accurate sharing of information about space objects, including space debris. This lack of mandatory regulation preserves the high risk of collision between space objects and the creation of additional space debris.

Despite its lapses and lack of determination to resolve the issue of space debris comprehensively, the guidelines are an important in-

289 ISO standard 24113:2011. It defines the primary space debris mitigation requirements applicable to all elements of unmanned systems launched into or passing through, near-Earth space, including launch vehicle orbital stages, operating spacecraft and any objects released as part of normal operations or disposal actions. ISO website, www.iso.org/57239.html

290 Stephan Hobe, *UN Space Debris Mitigation Guidelines*, 58/3 ZLW, 396, (2009).

ternational instrument for achieving international political consensus for the mitigation of pollution in the outer space environment. The lack of legal norms which should regulate this critical issue adequately is mentioned in the 49th session of the Legal Committee.[291]

Vereshchetin provides an illustrative example of cooperation between states in relation to the use of outer space. This is the mutually reciprocal self-restraint of national sovereignty of leading space-faring states in regard to the flights of foreign space objects over their territory and the conditions under which these restrictions are implemented.[292]

Despite their legally non-binding character, the UN Space Debris Mitigation Guidelines have been referred extensively by the GA of the UN as a document that is recommended to be complied with by all nations.[293]

2.1.2. International cooperation in IADC

The Inter-Agency Space Debris Coordination Committee (IADC) is an international governmental forum, which includes leading space agencies to achieve global coordination of activities related to the issues of man-made debris and natural debris in outer space.[294] It was established in 1993, and its main purpose was to support the exchange of information on space debris research activities between leading national space agencies, to promote opportunities for cooperation in the research of space debris, to monitor

---

291 Some delegations expressed the view that there should be greater coordination and interaction between the Scientific and Technical Subcommittee and the Legal Subcommittee with a view to promoting the establishment of binding international norms addressing critical issues such as space debris and the use of nuclear power sources in outer space; A/AC.105/942; p.19; http://www.oosa.unvienna.org/pdf/reports/ac105/AC105_942E.pdf

292 Vladlen Vereshchetin, International control and the concept of "open skies", From Coexistence to Cooperation: International Law and Organization in the Post-Cold War Era, 34-43, (1991).

293 GAUN Resolution 68/74 Recommendations on National Legislation Relevant to the Peaceful Exploration and Use of Outer Space, (Dec 11th 2013).

294 Terms of Reference for the Inter-Agency Space Debris Coordination Committee, IADC-93-01, par.1, (2018).

the progress of ongoing cooperative activities, and to identify space debris mitigation options.[295] This committee is the leading specialized international forum in which states cooperate on the practical and technical issues of space debris mitigation. The IADC was also created to identify the activities of the participating space agencies, which are of common interest to the member states.

Members of the IADC are the space agencies of the United States, Russia, Great Britain, France, Germany, Japan, Italy, China, India, Ukraine and the European Space Agency. New members can be accepted with a unanimous decision.

In order to fulfil its tasks, the committee was given[296] the following competencies:

1. Review all ongoing cooperative space debris research activities between member organizations;
2. Recommend new opportunities for cooperation;
3. Serve as the primary means for exchanging information and plans concerning orbital debris research activities;
4. Identify and evaluate options for debris mitigation.

All specific actions in cooperation in the committee are conducted through agreements between participating organizations, and decisions are with consensus. These agreements could be formalized in legally binding international treaties or in the form of non-binding acts of recommendation and guidance.

The structure of IADC comprises a steering group and four specialized working groups:[297]

Working Group 1: Measurements

Working Group 2: Environment and DataBase

Working Group 3: Protection

Working Group 4: Mitigation.

There are a number of similarities and differences between the IADC and the Scientific and Technical Subcommittee of the COPUOS.

---

295 *Id.*

296 *Id.*at 7

297 *Id.* at 8

The relevant similarities between the two organizations are that they are international governmental forums with leading experts on space activities that discuss and take decisions on space debris mitigation. It is important to note that members of both forums include the major space-faring nations that are the leading actors for polluting outer space. Another important resemblance is that both are expert forums that discuss the major issues of space debris in depth. The two organisations are complementary to each other, and this is evident by the reciprocity of the space debris mitigation guidelines that have been produced in the past by them.[298] The IADC space debris mitigation guidelines are explicitly pointing out that they were based on the common principles of space debris mitigation –already adopted in other space debris mitigation standards and handbooks of national and international organizations.[299]

On the other hand, the differences between the two organisations are also significant. The IADC is a specialized body that was established specifically for discussions of the mitigation of space debris, whereas the Scientific and Technical Subcommittee of COPUOS is a specialized organisation in which all major scientific and technical issues related to space law are discussed.

Another significant distinction is the membership structure of both institutions. In IADC, all members are space agencies, and their states have made significant contributions to space research and are leading space-faring nations. In the Subcommittee, on the other hand, there are currently 102 states, a large number of which do not have significant input in space exploration and do not have ample space industries.

The work of the IADC is featured with high expertise and a systematic approach when dealing with the issue of space debris. For example, in the IADC Space Debris Mitigation Guidelines from 2002, definitions of the terms like space debris, spacecraft, launch

298 UN Space Debris Mitigation Guidelines, GA of UN Res/62/217, Introduction, (2007).
299 IADC Space Debris Mitigation Guidelines, Introduction, (2007). http://www.iadc-online.org/index.cgi?item=docs_pub

vehicle, orbital stages, orbits and protected regions were adopted.[300] Definitions on mitigation measures that include passivation, de-orbiting, re-orbiting and break-ups. The guidelines also point out the definitions of the operational phases of the missions. The members of the committee have specified that the terms and definitions are added for the convenience of the readers of this document, from which we have to conclude that the guidelines are not legally binding.

Despite the legally non-binding character of the guidelines, their significance is important to understand better various legal issues of space debris. They are a result of cooperative efforts between states, and many of the recommendations and measures are incorporated by their national legislation and in non-binding acts of COPUOS.

Viikari rightly points out that the work of IADC is anthropocentric, and the focus of the work of the committee is not the protection of the outer space environment but improving the safety of space activities.[301] The absence of obligations of states to preserve the outer space environment in the Space Debris Mitigation Guidelines of the Inter-Agency Space Debris Coordination Committee illustrates the need for a holistic approach toward policymaking, particularly with respect to outer space exploration and exploitation.

The professional work of the committee was acknowledged in the decisions of the International Telecommunication Union (ITU), particularly with respect to the implementation of a formula for calculating minimum disposal altitudes for space objects in GEO.[302] This international coordination improves the principles and regulations for transferring a non-functional object into a graveyard orbit without causing interference to functional space objects.

The decisions to adopt common guidelines or other norms in IADC are taken with consensus, which means that the work of

---

300 IADC Space Debris Mitigation Guidelines; p.5 point 3; Doc № IADC-02-01; http://www.iadc-online.org/Documents/Docu/IADC_Mitigation_Guidelines_Rev1_Sep07.pdf

301 Lotta Viikari, The Environmental Element in Space Law, 15, (2008).

302 ITU recommendation – ITU-R S.1003, point 3, (Dec. 2010).

the committee could be hindered by any of the participating space agencies.

The IADC Space Debris Mitigation Guidelines provide a brief systematization of the standard practices, and they are preceded by other lower-level detailed documents. An example of such a document is the Recommendation on Re-orbit Procedure for GEO Preservation.[303] Viikari and Perek are completely right about the assessment of the professionalism of IADC and that its Space Debris Mitigation Guidelines are the most comprehensive in the space sector.[304]

Another important document adopted by the Interagency Space Debris Coordination Committee is the "Protection Manual". It outlines recommendations for the design of space systems that will reduce the generation of space debris. The manual is regularly revised and improved in line with technological developments. These recommendations are necessary to reduce the formation of many small fragments, the tracking and removal of which is more difficult than the larger elements.

2.1.3. International cooperation in ITU

The International Telecommunication Union is the oldest specialized international organization at the UN, established in 1865, with 193 member states and more than 900 sectoral members by February 2023, most of which are representatives of the private sector. One of the main tasks of this international organization is to promote to coordinate efforts to eliminate harmful interference between radio stations of different countries.[305]

Viikari highlights the important role of ITU as an international organization in which are participating most of the existing states. She rightly concludes that certain regulations of the ITU, which aim

303 IADC Recommendation on Re-orbit Procedure for GEO Preservation, (1997).
https://www.iadc-home.org/documents_public/view/page/2/id/110#u

304 Lotta Viikari, The Environmental Element in Space Law, 95, (2008).

305 ITU Constitution, Art. 1.2. b)

to guarantee undisturbed telecommunication activities and effective use of GEO, result in environmental regulation of outer space activities.[306] She draws attention to the fact that space debris could cause harmful interference, and the ITU identifies the issue as a major challenge for preserving equitable access to GEO to be effective.[307]

The mission of this international organization is defined by two major legal instruments of ITU - the Constitution and the Convention. The highest governing organ is the Plenipotentiary Conference. Such a conference is convened every four years. In addition to the Plenipotentiary Conference, the International Telecommunication Union also convenes world radiocommunication conferences, telecommunication standardization assemblies, telecommunication development conferences, radiocommunication assemblies, and administrative radio conferences held at global, regional or particular levels. The organization has the authority to convene an extraordinary administrative radio conference.[308]

It is important to point out that the final agreements on the administrative radio conferences are legally binding for all member states.[309] Given that they are almost all UN member states, the legal significance of these universal treaties is enormous. The radio regulations are subject to frequent changes and updates with the technical advances in the use of telecommunications and the ability of more participants to access the geostationary orbit.

The ITU works in close cooperation with other relevant international organizations, such as UN COPUOS and IADC.

As a unique international organization ITU demonstrates that national and private stakeholders could work together for their mutual benefit and find working mechanisms to allocate frequency bands, allotment and assignment of radio frequencies for radiocommunication. The inclusiveness of the organizational structure and expertise in the decision-making process of ITU could serve

---

306 Lotta Viikari, The Environmental Element in Space Law, 85-93, (2008).

307 *Id.* at 88

308 ITU Constitution Art. 8, art. 13, art.22, art.32, art.43

309 ITU Constitution, Art. 4 par.3

as a positive example for the development of international legal cooperation to reduce the problem of space debris at least in the following ways:

Firstly, inclusiveness is crucial for achieving global influence and recognition of the international organization, because the adopted decisions are going to be applicable to all relevant states and their private organizations. The fact that most states are members of ITU and the radio regulations are legally binding illustrates the significant global governing capacity of the organization.

Secondly, in ITU are actively participating leading corporations, universities and other non-governmental entities, which gives them the opportunity to elevate the level of discussions and to present challenges and solutions for specific issues that they are facing. This, in turn, adds additional expertise and practicality to the texts of the adopted documents in order to achieve concrete results. The inclusion of the private sector in the decision-making process and the opportunity for non-governmental entities to participate in setting the agenda provide additional expertise and concreteness to the texts of the adopted documents. For ITU, the participation of the private sector is also beneficial with the membership fees that are an additional income for the organization and its mission.

An important legal obligation for member states is stipulated in article 44 par.1 of the ITU constitution and it is to limit the number of frequencies and minimum essentials of the frequency spectrum to provide the necessary service. The article also argues the states applying the latest technical advances as soon as possible.

The obligation to use frequencies and spectrum reasonably and sparingly has a direct bearing on the appropriate use of GEO and other orbits and the organization's ambition to ensure that satellites in orbit perform useful functions.

Space debris could not only jeopardize the safety of satellites but also the access to GEO and other orbits, which would hinder the use of the orbits by member states of ITU.

The efficient use of orbits with minimum space objects is another principle, which improves safety in outer space activities and ultimately statistically decreases the risk of a collision of space objects. The fewer the space objects, the lesser the risk of a collision. In the last decade, we are witnessing a huge increase in the launching of small satellites that is increasing the risk of a collision significantly.[310] This new reality requires additional space traffic management rules on a global level.

In 1982, at the UN-sponsored Second Conference on Exploration and Peaceful Use of Outer Space (UNISPACE II), a recommendation was made to the International Telecommunications Union to include in its regulations a rule requiring owners of satellites in GEO to remove those space objects that no longer function.

In 1993, the ITU adopted a recommendation for environmental protection in the GEO that stipulates that when satellites become dysfunctional, they must be relocated to a "super synchronous graveyard orbit". The same recommendation also stipulates that relocation should be done with particular care to prevent radio and telecommunication interference with active satellites. Despite its legally non-binding nature, the recommendation has a major effect and has been implemented by a large number of countries, which do have jurisdiction and control over satellites in the GEO.

Besides the function of an international regulator, ITU also plays an essential role as a coordinator between the Member States and private organizations. Part of the objectives of the international organization is "*to promote and enhance participation of entities and organizations in the activities of the Union and foster fruitful cooperation and partnership between them and Member States for the fulfilment of the overall objectives as embodied in the purposes of the Union..*"[311] Such coordination is carried out both at the expert technical level, as well as at the international political level.

The International Telecommunication Union facilitates the development of a regulatory regime that provides reasonable access to

---

310 Samantha Le May, S. Gehly, B. A. Carter & S. Flegel, *Space debris collision probability analysis for proposed global broadband constellations* 151 Acta Astronautica, 448-450, (2018).

311 ITU constitution, art. 1 par.3a)

orbital slots in Earth orbits for all countries and satellite operators under their jurisdiction and control. The desire to place satellites in orbit is steadily increasing, but the orbital slots are limited. These circumstances require the convening of conferences on the matter and the facilitation of an active dialogue with private organizations to seek new solutions that balance the interests of all participants in the debate on the use of the orbits of Earth.

The International Telecommunication Union responds promptly to attempts by separate countries to retain for themselves orbital slots, which they do not intend to use or which they will not use for the intended purpose but for leasing them. For example, the state of Tonga, with a population of 110,000, had applied to retain 20 satellite slots over its territory to meet its telecommunications needs in its 748 square km area. The US private corporation Unicorn, based in Colorado, was privileged to use the slots, which were rented from the company Tongasat. This problem with speculative requests to keep slots in orbit is known as the "paper satellite problem".[312] Subsequently, the ITU adopted stricter rules for the provision of slots, which stipulate that if a location is not used, the state shall lose the right to use it.[313]

At a plenipotentiary conference in Minneapolis, the USA, in 1998, the International Telecommunication Union discussed a gradual increase in fees to reduce speculative bids. As a result of these discussions, an *ad hoc* group for the reimbursement of satellite request costs is set up,[314] which adopts formulas for determining the fees to be paid when requesting the retention of slots in GEO. An important amendment of article 44 par.2 of the ITU constitution is made in 2001 that states that orbits and radiofrequency "*are limited natural resources and that they must be used rationally, efficiently and economically*".

312 Jannet C. Thompson, *Space for Rent: The International Telecommunications Union, Space Law and Orbit/Spectrum Leasing*, 62 J. Air L. & Commerce, 281, (1996).

313 Resolution 18 World Radiocommunication Conference, Res.18/WRC-95, (1995).

314 "Ad hoc group on Cost Recovery for Satellite Network Recovering"

This rule regulates that limited natural resources are all radio frequencies and associated orbits, not just GEO, as provided for in the International Telecommunications Union Conventions of 1973 and 1982. This amendment provides a legal basis for the more precise and complete legal regulation for the use of Low Earth and Medium Earth orbits.

2.1.4. International cooperation in UNISPACE conferences

Another significant international forum for discussing existing problems in space law, including the problem of space debris, is the UN conferences on space exploration and peaceful use. So far, three conferences have been convened, the last of which took place in Vienna in July 1999. The significance of these conferences is great, as they outline the principles of space law development.

The space debris issue was also discussed at the third conference, taking into account the achievements of other bodies addressing the issue, in particular the COPUOUS Scientific and Technical Subcommittee, the International Telecommunication Union and the Inter-Agency Space Debris Committee.[315]

During the Vienna Conference were analysed the work of the aforementioned areas and outlines were made for the next steps that the leading nations in space exploration should take. A recommendation for future action was made to improve the protection of Low-Earth space orbit and outer space environment by reducing space debris.[316] The UN General Assembly should consider and evaluate whether all the proposals made at the conference after five years have been implemented. Concerning the recommendation on space debris reduction, the UN General Assembly notes that no working group has been set up.[317]

315 Report on the third United Nations Conference on the exploration and peaceful use of outer space, Resolution 1 (v), A/CONF.184/6

316 Report on the third United Nations Conference on the exploration and peaceful use of outer space, Resolution 1 (v), A/CONF.184/, Recommendation 13

317 Review of the implementation of the recommendations of the Third United Nations Conference on the Exploration and Peaceful Uses of Outer Space;

The "Space Law Working Group of the 21st Century" was set up at the Vienna Conference. The conclusions and proposals of this working group emphasize the urgency of creating a guide to reducing space debris.[318] The Working Group recommends that the Legal Subcommittee and the Scientific and Technical Subcommittee of the COPUOS should discuss the matter. As stated in the previous subchapters, this recommendation has been respected by COPUOS, and the issue was discussed. The proposed guidelines for reducing space debris were not addressed in the Legal Subcommittee, and the guidelines themselves emphasize that they are not legally binding.

The third Space Conference concludes with a declaration known as the Vienna Declaration on Space and Human Development, which states that one of the problems to be addressed in the future is environmental damage as a result of space activities.[319]

The declaration stipulates that all space activities, in particular those that have a detrimental effect on the local and global environment, must be ensured, as far as possible, in such a way as to limit such effects and to take appropriate measures to avoid the detrimental effect.[320]

I believe that the objective that is set has unclear criteria as to whether it has been achieved, as the measures are carried out "to the extent possible". It also has an unclear designation, namely the division of the environment into "local" and "global". I consider this division of the environment methodologically incorrect for the following reasons:

Firstly, any object can be viewed through the prism of the local and global point of view, respectively, as part of a system that considers relationships with other elements in a larger system (local

---

A/59/174; Annex II recommendation 13.

318 Conclusions and proposals of the workshop on space law in the XXIst century, par. 5, (1999).

319 Report on the third United Nations Conference on the exploration and peaceful use of outer space, Resolution 1 (v), A/CONF.184/6

320 Vienna declaration on space and human development, Report on the third United Nations Conference on the exploration and peaceful use of outer space, Resolution 1 (v), A/CONF.184/6

view) and as a relatively closed system in which the details of the structure are the focus (global view). Therefore, I consider it inaccurate to divide one environment as global and another as local.

Secondly, the environment is an object of consideration in which interconnectedness and unity can be easily established since the pollution of part of it affects, to some extent, the entire environment. In this sense, outer space pollution with space debris, which can lead to the destruction of a satellite that performs soil monitoring functions, will affect the environment and the Earth's surface.[321]

From a legal point of view, I consider it is more appropriate to separate the environment according to the jurisdiction that is exercised in a given territory. Then we will look at the environment that is within the jurisdiction of a country, on the one hand, and on the other - the environment that cannot be nationally appropriated. This division is in line with Principle 2 of the Rio Declaration on Environment and Development from 1992,[322] which is of major political significance in international relations and environmental law. Under this principle, states have the sovereign right to exploit their resources in accordance with their national policies, but states have no right to damage the environment beyond their jurisdiction.

Outer space is precisely a territory beyond national jurisdiction. Since states do not have sovereign rights over outer space, the outer space environment should not be absorbed under national policies.[323] In practice, however, due to the lack of a legal entity to protect the interests of the outer space environment, states use outer space according to their national policies without protecting the interest of humankind.

We can summarize that the recommendations and proposals of the Third UNISPACE conference do not lead to a new international

321 Emil Konstantinov, *Outer Space Environment and Its Legal Protection*, Colloquium L Outer space, 100-102, (1989).

322 Rio Declaration on Environment and Development, UN Doc. A/CONF.151/26 (vol. I), 31 ILM 874 (1992)

323 Емил Константинов, Международноправни проблеми на практическото използуване на Космоса, 4 Бюл. СЮБ, 92-98, (1982).

legally binding regulation that addresses existing problems in space law, including space debris. The measures taken to implement these recommendations are not legally binding, which does not guarantee the resolution of the problem and the protection of the outer space environment.

Nevertheless, the importance of gathering all stakeholders in outer space activities to discuss major challenges and exchange views is a key step in reaching a breakthrough in international space policy and international space law development.

2.1.5. International cooperation in the Conference on Disarmament

The issue of the prevention of arms race in outer space (PAROS) was brought to the Conference of Disarmament's agenda in 1982, and since then, negotiations between states have been taking place on the topic without substantive results. The main reason is the severe opposition of the USA against a legally binding PAROS agreement.[324]

The issue of protecting the outer space environment from space debris is closely linked to the placement of weapons in Earth's orbit or on celestial bodies. The deployment of weapons of mass destruction in space is expressly forbidden in the norm of Article IV of the Outer Space Treaty. Nuclear, chemical, biological, and other types of weapons of mass destruction that may be created in the future fall within the scope of this prohibition.[325] Kolosov and Kusnetzov are correct that there is no international legal prohibition for the use of outer space for military, non-aggressive purposes, such as the maintenance of international peace and security, in accordance with Articles 42 and 51 of the UN Charter.[326]

---

324 Ranjana Kaul, *Relevance and Limitations of Outer Space Treaty in 21st Century, 50 years of the Outer Space Treaty*, IDSA, 53, (2017).

325 Генадий Жуков, 40 лет договору о принципах деятельности государств по исследованию и использованию космического пространства, включая Луну и другие небесные тела. Российский ежегодник международного права, 9, (2007).

326 Юрий Колосов, В. И. Кузнецов, Международное право, 327, (2004).

There is no explicit international legal prohibition on launching into outer space other types of weapons that are not considered for mass destruction.[327] In order to prevent an arms race in outer space, the UN General Assembly, in its Special Session on Disarmament, concluded that negotiations between states should take place in the international forum in Geneva, the Conference on Disarmament (CD).

On February 12, 2008, a formal proposal was made jointly by Russia and China that was a draft convention on "Prevention of the Placement of Weapons in Outer Space, the Threat or Use of Force against Outer Space Objects".[328] The main objective of the draft convention was "to prevent space from becoming an arena of military conflict and to ensure stability in space and the undisturbed functioning of space objects.[329] A revised draft treaty was presented in 2014. In 2017 a resolution was adopted by the General Assembly of the UN.[330] In this resolution was stipulated the establishment of a special forum named Group of Governmental Experts. In this forum, states are consulting and making recommendations on important aspects of an international legally binding treaty on the prevention of an arms race in outer space, including the prevention of the placement of weapons in outer space.

The prevention of the deployment of weapons in outer space has the primary purpose of guaranteeing the current principle in space law that space exploration and exploitation have to be carried out in the interest of maintaining international peace and security, and promoting international cooperation and mutual understanding.[331] Non-placement of weapons in outer space will also be beneficial to the outer space environment and the safety of space activities. If

327 Еимл Константинов, Международноправно ограничаване на милитаризирането на Космоса, 5 Междунар. отнош., 12-21, (1986). Malcolm Shaw, 5 ed. International Law, 482, (2003).

328 Report on the conference on disarmament to GAUN, CD/1853, point 40, (September 9, 2008).

329 Draft Convention, Introduction, CD/1839, (February 29, 2008).

330 A/RES/72/250

331 Outer Space Treaty, Article III, 1967

weapons are not placed in outer space, they will partially avoid the destruction that they could cause to other space objects, and also because these weapons could be potential targets for destruction from states in times of a military conflict.

The position of the US not to approve the proposal that was formulated and submitted jointly by Russia and China, argues that it does not include a ban on anti-satellite ground-based experiments. However, this criticism of the US is not supported with a counter-proposal or amendment. In this context, criticism of the proposal by the US representative which was declared unacceptable because it is unclear and does not include a ban on land-based anti-satellite and other weapons is untenable. It is important to emphasize that the United States does not propose the inclusion of ground-based anti-satellite weapons in the Prohibition Package, which would make the proposal exhaustive and guarantee the peaceful use of space. The lack of willingness on the part of the United States to participate in a constructive debate on the draft convention, which may propose and prohibit anti-satellite tests, points to the leading motive for its rejection. The American position has remained unchanged for decades, and it foresees that the US is not going to change "*its long-standing principle that arms control constraints or limitations on space-based systems or activities - beyond the existing in force regimes - are not in the national security interests on the United States.*"[332]

When any nation perceives its strength predominantly by the preservation of the unregulated international status quo, this could only lead to international insecurity, defence spending on behalf of its competitors, and technological innovation in the military sector. The reasons for the rejection of the proposal by the US are because of the fact that it explicitly prohibits the placement of weapons in outer space, regulates that space starts 100 km above sea level[333] and provides international legal guarantees that space will actually be explored and used for peaceful goals.

332 Point 22 from the official letter, expressing the US position on the proposal, CD/1847, (26 August 26, 2008).

333 Draft Convention, Art. 1, CD/1839, (February 29, 2008).

Mexico also supports the view that space should be explored and used for peaceful purposes only and is concerned that weapons may be placed in outer space.[334] Mexico's representative notes that the current legal system is inadequate and cannot guarantee the non-militarization of outer space.[335]

The first major problem is that the USA, as a leader in military spending[336] and weapons production and international trade, is not willing to achieve sustainable demilitarization, including in the space sector. According to the data collection of the Stockholm International Peace Research Institute (SIPRI) in the last two years global military spending is above 2.1 trillion dollars and USA continues to increase its military budget. The US military spending is driving other nations like Russia, China and India to increase their military budgets, conduct anti-satellite tests, and invest in space weapons in order to guarantee their national security.

The second major problem remains the absence of an independent international body to monitor the observance of international space law, and in particular, to oversee the objects, placed in outer space by states and private organizations. The lack of public information on space militarization raises the question whether weapons are already launched in outer space.[337]

Turkey also supported the proposal in principle. Its position is to guarantee the peaceful use of outer space and to strengthen international law to prevent a military race in outer space.[338]

---

334 CD, Final Record of the 1163 Plenary Meeting, Geneva, p.13 (January 19, 2010).

335 *Id.* at 14

336 SIRPI website, Improving transparency in military spending through disaggregated information, (August 30, 2022).

337 Владлен С. Верещетин, Несостоятельность американских правовых концепций применения силы в космическом про-странстве, Сб. Американский империализм-нарушитель международного права, 43-56, (1985).

338 CD, Final record of the 1131 pl. meeting, the Palais des Nations, 6, (March 12, 2009).

Canada and, in particular, Canada's Representative, Ambassador Marius Grinius, took the lead to change the status quo by conducting informal meetings with several state representatives in February 2009.[339] Canada's position urged states that have been blocking conference progress for more than a decade to rethink their position.[340] The USA remains the leading state that prevents the progress of the negotiations in the Conference of Disarmament.

German Representative Ambassador Hoffman noted that preventing military warfare in space is a matter of concern for all humanity.[341]

Brazil's position was also in favour of the proposal by Russia and China, with the Brazilian representative pointing out that this forum is of great importance in ensuring that outer space remains a peaceful space.[342]

The International Non-aligned Movement Organization, which has 118 member states also expressed its position in support of the Russian-Chinese proposal to guarantee peace in space and prevent a military race in outer space.[343]

It is visible that most countries, with the exception of the United States, had officially expressed their positions that an arms race in outer space should not be allowed and space should never become a battlefield.

It should be noted that the date of the Russian-Chinese proposal was months before the US presidential election. Possibly the contributing States to the draft convention hoped for a different US position on anti-satellite tests after this election.

The development after 2009 was also not encouraging for reaching a comprehensive, legally binding document on this issue. Although the European Union was ready to engage in a "meaningful discussion" on preventing the space arms race, in June

339 CD Report, CD/1879, point 43, (September 17, 2009).
340 CD Report, CD/1089. 11, (Feb, 2009).
341 CD Report, CD/PV.1148, 4, (August 6th 2009).
342 CD Report, CD/PV.1090, 4, (2009).
343 CD Report, CD/1875, 119-120, (2009).

2017, the EU Member States issued a statement to the Conference on Disarmament Working Group that they propose a multilateral **non-legally binding** instrument on Space Security.[344] Legally non-binding documents would be meaningless for guaranteeing long-term security in space, peace-building efforts and prevention of an arms race, particularly after the Russian invasion of Ukraine in February 2022.

With respect to cooperation between states on limiting the global threat from weapons of mass destruction, the extending of the bilateral international treaty on strategic arms reduction between the US and Russia (New START treaty) was a positive signal from the USA and Russia to limit their nuclear stockpile of weapons. The agreement does not cover new types of weapons. Analysing the motivation of states to continue this ban should not be seen as a sign of disarmament. This is because maintaining such a large number of nuclear weapons in both countries is politically unjustified, as these weapons cannot fully respond to contemporary threats and, on the other hand, are economically irrational. Despite the fact that on January 22nd 2021, the Treaty on the Prohibition of Nuclear Weapons entered into force, the nine states known to have nuclear programs have not signed the treaty.[345] However, outer space has not lost its strategic role for military use, most notably by the US and the preservation of the right to deploy weapons in it. With respect to the placement of weapons that are not for mass destruction in outer space, the US position remains unchanged and such weapons are technically allowed today.

The most positive and comprehensive result for the protection of the outer space environment, and in particular the prevention of space debris, resulting from the use of space weapons, would be a total ban on the placement of weapons in outer space, as well as a

344 Conference on Disarmament, WG, "Way Ahead" EU Statement on the Prevention of an Arms Race in Outer Space, (June 14-16, 2017).

345 Treaty on the Prohibition of Nuclear Weapons, UN Doc. A/CONF.229/2017/8, UN Doc. CN.476.2017.TREATIES-XXVI-9 [hereinafter Nuclear Ban Treaty]

ban on anti-satellite Earth-based experiments, surface, airspace and outer space. The adoption of a complete legally binding ban on the placement of weapons in outer space should be ensured by rigorous international monitoring from an independent expert international organization with its own technical equipment.

Maleev proposes the creation of a new special international organization within the UN structure to monitor and control the militarization of outer space.[346] I believe that the implementation of such a proposal will greatly contribute to the transparency of space activities and give further assurances that space is actually used for peaceful purposes. Presently, the predominant understanding among states is that there is not legally binding international norm that stipulates that outer space should be used exclusively for peaceful purposes.[347]

In my opinion, one of the most appropriate organizations whose experience can be used to carry out such monitoring is the CTBTO, which presently has an international system of 337 high-tech monitoring facilities.[348] The long-delayed entry into force of the treaty establishing the organization is a bad signal for the creation of an organization to monitor weapons in outer space.

Mowthorpe analysed the historical context of the competition in space between the USA and the USSR.[349] During the Cold War, the race between the US and the USSR was used for increasingly sophisticated weapons for the destruction of satellites, leading to an appreciation of the number of antisatellite tests conducted by the two superpowers, resulting in the creation of a lot of space de-

346 Юрий Н. Малеев, Военное использование космоса в интересах международной безопасности, Актуальные проблемы современного международного права, Российского университета дружбы народов, 56-58, (2005).

347 Bruce A. Hurwitz, *Israel and the Law of Outer Space*, 22.4 Israel Law Review, 457, 459, (1988).

348 Comprehensive Test Ban Treaty Organization, www.ctbto.org

349 Mathew Mowthorpe,The Militarization and Weaponization of Space, 13-78, (2004)

bris.[350] President Carter's administration had been active in seeking a ban on anti-satellite attempts in 1978-1979, but during this period, the USSR did not want to be banned from testing them, and three rounds of negotiations on the issue were held. The first round is in June 1978 in Helsinki, the second in January and February 1979 in Bern, and the third in April, May and June 1979 in Vienna. Following the invasion of the USSR in Afghanistan and the coming into power of President Reagan, whose administration is not so inclined to ban anti-satellite tests, the positions of the two countries changed diametrically.

After the collapse of the USSR, a tacit moratorium on testing anti-satellite weapons comes, and this is not stipulated in an international treaty. Not resorting to these attempts is not regarded as a legal obligation for states, which is why there is no *opinio juris* for this practice, and accordingly, there is no international custom that prohibits anti-satellite attempts, rightly concludes Hays.[351]

The absence of such an international legal ban leads to the political situation in which the newly emerging space powers, such as China and India, should consolidate their positions in international relations with a demonstration of their military-space potential. This poses an even greater threat to the outer space environment. Countries considering their national interests through the lens of consolidating their military power in space, including through actual testing of their anti-satellite weapons, have become a major threat to the protection of the space environment, and a legal ban on anti-satellite testing is much needed for the protection of outer space environment. This is the conclusion of many international legal experts, especially after the successful test of the first Indian anti-satellite test on March 27th 2019.[352] Bhat and Mohan are correct in their conclusion that an exclusive treaty to prohibit ASAT weapons and

---

350 *Id.* at 113-117

351 Peter Hays, United States military space: Into the twenty first century, USAF institute for national security studies, USAF Academy, 87-88, (2002).

352 Alexey Arbatov, *Arms control in outer space: The Russian angle, and a possible way forward*, 75:4 Bulletin of the Atomic Scientists, 151-161, (2019).

ASAT tests continues to be a "far fetched dream", considering the lack of political will among the concerned states.[353]

2.1.6. International cooperation in the Artemis Program

The Artemis Program and the Artemis Accords are at the same time a significant step in the utilization of outer space resources and also a controversial example of international cooperation that is centered around one nation, namely the USA. The accords are significant because concrete goals and plans have been set and funding for their achievement allocated.[354] The goal is to land the first woman and first person of colour on the Moon by 2024 and establish a lunar orbital station[355] and a lunar base,[356] which are later going to be used for the exploration of Mars and other celestial bodies in the solar system.

This form of international cooperation is relevant to the issue of space debris mitigation and the protection of the outer space environment because it sets new legally non-binding rules and standards, which are going to shape outer space activities on celestial bodies, starting with the Moon.

The fact that the Artemis Accords are designed as a US-centric form of exploitation of outer space resources is evident from NASA's official statement about the Artemis program: "*While NASA is leading the Artemis program, international partnerships will play a key role in achieving a sustainable and robust presence on the Moon.*"[357] The representative of the Russian Space Agency states

---

353 Sandeepa Bhat & V. Mohan, *Anti Satellite Missile Testing: A Challenge to Article IV of the Outer Space Treaty,* 2NUJS L. Rev., 205, 212, (2009).

354 NASA website, The US funding of the Artemis Program alone is 6.88 billion dollars for 2022, https://www.nasa.gov/sites/default/files/atoms/files/fy2022_budget_summary.pdf

355 NASA website, Gateway, https://www.nasa.gov/gateway

356 NASA website, Moon Base Camp, https://www.nasa.gov/feature/goddard/2021/nasa-s-artemis-base-camp-on-the-moon-will-need-light-water-elevation

357 NASA website, https://www.nasa.gov/specials/artemis-accords/index.html Last access 10.02.2023

this reason to dismiss the program.[358] The format of the accords is not multilateral but instead a collection of several bilateral agreements between NASA and the partnering country.

As of December 2022, twenty countries have signed the Artemis Accords. This represents a shift in the development of a global space economy.[359]

NASA confirmed not so much the US compliance with the international space law principles, but the consideration of the Outer Space Treaty, emphasizing that space resource extraction and utilization "*can and will be under the auspices of the Outer Space Treaty, with specific emphasis on Articles II, VI, and XI.*"[360] The usage of the verb "can" and the phrase "under the auspices" do not show confidence in the intention of NASA to comply with binding international space lawfully. The concretization of only three articles from the treaty is also problematic to the interpretation of the intention of the program. Other leading space-faring states that are not part of the Artemis Accords, like China, Russia and India, have no legal guarantees that the program is not going to be used in violation of Article IV of the Outer Space Treaty and specifically not placing weapons of mass destruction in outer space. The position of the President of the USA, expressed in the Executive order from April 2020,[361] attests the understanding of the US government that Article II of the Outer Space Treaty permits appropriation of space resources, complete rejection of the Moon Agreement, and objection to its capacity to reflect international legal custom.[362] Mosteshar rightly concludes that this is a unilateral attempt to circumvent the Outer

---

358 NASA website, https://www.space.com/russia-space-agency-chief-criticizes-nasa-moon-plans Last access 10.02.2023

359 Memme Onwudiwe & Kwame Newton. *Africa and the Artemis Accords: A Review of Space Regulations and Strategy for African Capacity Building in the New Space Economy*, 9.1. New Space, 42, (2021).

360 NASA website https://www.nasa.gov/specials/artemis-accords/index.html Last access 10.02.2023

361 Exec. Order No. 13,914, 85 Fed. Reg. 20,381 (Apr. 6, 2020)

362 Sa'id I. Mosteshar, *Artemis: The Discordant Accords,* 44 *J. Space L.*, 591, 596-597, (2020).

Space Treaty and general international law.[363] Even if we accept the argument that the initial bases on the Moon might be in compliance with art. II of the Outer Space Treaty, in time, that national settlement would lead to a violation of this norm that prohibits national appropriation and occupation of celestial bodies.[364] The norms of Article II of the Outer Space Treaty have been accepted as international legal custom, and they carry the obligations for non-appropriation and non-occupation of outer space to all states, private organizations and people.[365]

The establishment of a facility, which is also named Moon Base Camp, is also a clear violation of Article II of the Outer Space Treaty, as this is a form of occupation and appropriation of parts of the Moon. The purpose of the rejected Moon Agreement was to avoid such initiatives, which are led by a group of countries in competition with other groups of countries. The Russian and Chinese responses to the accords culminated in deeper cooperation between the two states and the formation of a strong Sino-Russian alliance. Both countries initiated the International Lunar Research Station, consisting of a space station in the Moon's orbit, a moon base, and mobile rovers and robots on the surface. Other countries are invited to join this initiative as well. It is of critical importance for the global influence of the accords to see the attitudes and political positions of India, Germany, and other European states. The Artemis accords received significant recognition after France signed the accords in 2022.

The Artemis program envisions a fundamentally different approach to the utilization of the Moon's resources than the one provided in the Moon Agreement. One of the major differences is that

---

363 *Id.* at 597

364 Antonio Salmeri, *Developing and Managing Moon and Mars Settlements in Accordance with International Space Law*, In Proceedings of the 71st International Astronautical Congress, IAF, 4, (2020).

365 А. Н. Вылегжанин, М. Р. Юзбашян & М. А. Алексеев, Международно-правовые перспективы использования природных ресурсов Луны и других небесных тел, 3.1. Горный информационно-аналитический бюллетень, 155, 156, (2021).

the Artemis accords are a non-binding policy document that is going to be implemented by several bilateral agreements[366] between the USA and its partners, whereas the Moon Agreement foresees a unique multi-lateral mechanism and the establishment of an international regime with appropriate procedures.[367] The aim of the last is to achieve equitable sharing by all state parties in the benefits from these resources.[368] Another important difference in the principles of usage of the resources of the Moon in both documents is that the Moon Agreement takes into consideration the interest of the present and future generations,[369] whereas the Artemis Accords do not have such an obligation. The common heritage of mankind principle, which is stipulated in the art. 11 of the Moon Agreement, usually foresees the establishment of an international legal regime that takes into consideration the interest of humankind and considers the interests of all nations.[370] The participation of Australia in both the Artemis Accords and the Moon Agreement brings a lot of controversial issues[371] and ambivalence that ultimately probably will result in Australia withdrawing from the Moon Agreement.[372] Such an act would signify the further deterioration of international space law because of the preferences of states to participate in alliances that compete with others instead of participation in mechanisms that legitimize equitable ways of distribution of resources.

The Artemis accords validate the transfer of competition and rivalry of mundane national relations in outer space instead of set-

366 Fabio Tronchetti & Hao Liu, *Australia's signing of the Artemis Accords: a positive development or a controversial choice?*, 75.3 Australian Journal of International Affairs, 243, 244, (2021).

367 Moon Agreement, Art.11 par.5, 1979

368 *Id.* at Art 11 par.7 d)

369 *Id.* at Art.7

370 Stephan Hobe, *Common Heritage of Mankind – An Outdated Concept in International Space Law?* 41 Colloquium on the Law of Outer Space of the International Institute of Space Law, 271-277, (1998).

371 Fabio Tronchetti & Hao Liu, *Australia's signing of the Artemis Accords: a positive development or a controversial choice?*, 75.3 Australian Journal of International Affairs, 243, 246-249, (2021).

372 *Id.* at 246-249

ting a new global venture, which is formed based on the common heritage of mankind principle.

The existence of at least two parallel programs with different participating organizations will result in dispersing the financial, technological, scientific, and human resources of all nations into similar activities. This means the creation of at least two times more space debris in the Moon's orbit and on the Moon's surface. The risk of accidental collision of assets of either program or even military conflict on the Moon would result to even more space debris, and this status quo would lower the safety of both space programs.

2.1.7. International cooperation on a regional European level

Presently, European Space Agency space debris requirements are defined in the standard ECSS-U-AS-10C/ISO 24113. The standard is applicable to all ESA projects by Space Debris Mitigation Policy.[373]

Historically, space debris has been identified as a serious issue by the European space sector and policy makers in the mid-1980s. It is being considered by both the European Space Agency (ESA) and the European Union, as well as at the level of national space agencies and national policymaking. Following the explosion of the third stage of the Ariana-1 H-10 V16 missile, a large amount of space debris[374] was generated, further emphasizing the need for international, and regional cooperation in Europe to reduce this problem.

In 1986, the ESA Director established a Space Debris Task Force to assess the various aspects associated with them. In 1988, the Working Party provided a report prepared by it. This report serves as the basis for the adoption of a resolution of the ESA Council that defines the Agency's space waste policy.[375]

This resolution sets out the main tasks for solving the problem. These tasks include: reducing the generation of space debris

373 ESA/ADMIN/IPOL(2014)2

374 Heiner Klinkrad, et al., *Space debris activities in Europe*, 587, 4th European Conference on Space Debris, 1, (2005).

375 Resolution of the European Space Agency, ESA/C(89)24, (1989).

to ensure safe access to space and reducing the risk of human and non-human flight; reducing the risk of the ground from entering objects; reducing the risk to GEO satellites; the acquisition of space waste information that is necessary to evaluate the spread of the problem and its consequences through the use of its own resources or as a result of cooperation with other space agencies; studying the legal aspects of space debris.

It is important to emphasize that all the agreements reached as a result of the European cooperation are in accordance with the applicable international space law. This is explicitly stated in the relevant final acts.[376] The principle that regional cooperation should comply with the guidelines of universal cooperation is of crucial importance to achieving higher safety standards and consistency in space policymaking.

Solving any environmental problem, including the problem of space debris, requires universal cooperation. The adoption of regional pollution control measures alone will not produce the desired environmental outcomes because they will reduce the competitive potential of the industry, which operates in the specific region. Higher safety standards are related to more investments, which will increase the price of the provided services.

If there are only regional restrictive environmental measures in place, this will encourage industry and customers in the area to reorient themselves to regions where such restrictions do not exist. Therefore, Europe's efforts are directed toward universal cooperation in the main UN space forum - the Committee on Peaceful Uses of Outer Space and in the main forum for the space agencies on this issue - the Inter-Agency Space Debris Committee.

There are areas of regional cooperation on space waste that can be undertaken at a regional level. Such areas of cooperation in Europe are the creation of a European space situational awareness system that resembles the US system. The planned system capacity

376 ESA Space Debris Mitigation for Agency Projects; 3 reference documents [RD-4] United Nations Treaties and Principles on Outer Space, ESA/ADMN/IPOL(2014)2, (2014).

includes 98% cataloguing of objects in near-Earth orbit, mid-earth orbit, and geostationary orbit already in US catalogues.[377] ESA also directs efforts to develop collision computing systems[378] as well as systems to provide in-orbit particle protection about 1 cm in size. These efforts culminate in the creation of a comprehensive preliminary program called the "Space Situational Awareness preparatory programme".

This provisional program was adopted in November 2008 by the ESA Council of Ministers and began working on January 1st, 2009.

The main aim of the programme is that Europe could acquire the independent capability to watch for objects and natural phenomena that could harm satellites in orbit or infrastructure such as power grids on the ground. By providing timely and accurate information and services on the outer space environment, the risk of collisions with space objects and the loss of life of astronauts could be reduced.

The information that the systems provide includes space debris, asteroid particles, and the adverse effects of space weather. This program ensures that information on the location and characteristics of space debris is not shared and made available by non-EU countries, which provides a level of security independence for the EU and ESA member states.

Close international cooperation within Europe is a key element in the successful implementation of the program and the achievement of its objectives. This cooperation includes national agencies of European countries, ministries of defence, the European Commission, the European Defence Agency, the European Maritime Safety Agency, research units and others.

In addition to working closely at the regional European level, the program also collaborates with NASA, as well as UN bodies and other international agencies.

---

377 Heiner Klinkrad, et al., *Space debris activities in Europe*, 587, 4th European Conference on Space Debris, 26, (2005).

378 ESA website, The system DEBIE-1, installed on the satellite PROBA and system DEBIE-2 installed on the satellite EuTEF, https://space-env.esa.int/r-and-d/instrumentation/standard-in-situ-impact-detector-debie/ last access 10.02.2023

All these high-tech systems, developed on the basis of European cooperation, do not impede efforts to reduce the problem of space debris at the level of universal cooperation but guarantee the technological independence of Europe and are a strategically important step in European foreign and defence policy.

The legally non-binding nature of the European Code of Conduct creates uncertainty that it would be applied to legally binding contracts between ESA and private corporations. Therefore, it is logical that the European Space Agency's Director-General prepared ESA regulations for the reduction of space debris that apply to all space projects under the authority of the Agency. These acts are legally binding and enter into force immediately upon their issue.[379]

An important part of the European Code of Conduct with respect to the design requirements, is the prohibition of the deliberate destruction in orbit of a space system or part of it.[380] Since anti-satellite tests are a type of intentional destruction in orbit, it may be logical to raise the question of whether they are also included in the scope of this prohibition rule. ESA is a regional international organization for space research cooperation exclusively for peaceful purposes, and the organization has no authority to conduct anti-satellite tests or to regulate this matter legally. Such powers are vested in States, and this internal ESA ban does not prevent nation-states from continuing to make such tests.

The problem of space debris has been raised by ESA and has been extensively discussed at five European conferences on space depletion. The fifth conference was held in Darmstadt, Germany, from March 30th to April 2nd 2009. The conference was widely represented, with 330 participants from 21 countries, making the conference the largest forum in the world to discuss the problem of space debris. The agenda of the conference included both technical issues - space environment modelling, collision prediction, orbit

---

379 ESA Space Debris Mitigation for Agency projects, ESA/ADMIN/IPOL(2014)2, (2014).

380 European Code of Conduct, measure 4.1.2, SD-DE-04 (2004).

and entry risk analysis, protection and protection, and legal issues related to space debris policy analysis, existing legal documents and guidelines.

Particular attention is paid to the European Space Situational Awareness Program and the role of the program to guarantee Europe's autonomy and independence in access to information on space objects. An important result of the conference is the unification around the thesis that the current international and national guidelines for reducing space debris are only a first step towards ensuring a safe space environment. The next necessary step outlined at the conference is the active removal of orbital debris.

Cooperation between national space agencies in Europe, ESA, the private sector and representatives of European international legal doctrine would not be enough if there were no EU political positions on space development and, in particular, the protection of the outer space environment from space debris.

In 2003, as a result of close cooperation between the EU and ESA, a Green Paper on a European space policy was prepared. This document sets out the EU's top priorities for space. At the forefront of these priorities is securing and maintaining European access to space, backed by long-term funding.[381] The Green Paper is a policy framework document, but not a legal one. It gives impetus to the debate on a formal European Space Policy. The Green Paper does not explicitly mention space debris, but it is a major barrier to access to space, and it can therefore be concluded that this problem has been indirectly addressed. Building on the Green Paper on a European Space Policy, in 2003, the European Commission published a White Paper on Space: A New European Frontier for an expanding Union.[382]

In its essence, the White Paper is a concrete action plan for drawing up a formal European Space Policy. Space debris is mentioned in the document, noting that Europe must have the capacity

381 Green Paper European Space Policy, **COM/2003/0017**, 9 and 18, (2003).
382 White paper - Space: a new European frontier for an expanding Union - An action plan for implementing the European Space policy, SEC, 1249 (2003).

to provide critical users with critical information about solar eruptions, Low-Earth objects and space debris.[383]

The emphasis put on space debris in the White Paper is to provide information about them, but not to mitigate them, safety standards and a long-term policy for protecting the outer space environment. It states that Europe must have a capacity. That does not mean the European Union or any of the Union's agencies, nor does it a priori suggest that this capacity must be achieved in ESA. This formulation leaves the door open for the development of this capacity by various European institutions and European international organizations each to achieve technological development in its field.

The next step in EU and ESA cooperation happened in 2004 with the signing of a framework agreement between the European Community and ESA. The main objective of the Framework Agreement is to promote the creation of a coherent European Space Policy and to build a common basis for EU-ESA cooperation.[384] The Framework Agreement does not explicitly mention the problem of space debris, and this is fully justified since the purpose of the document is to set common goals and priorities, not to fix specific issues of concern.

Article 8 of the agreement provides for the coordination of joint activities between the two organizations to be carried out at regular joint meetings between the EU Council and the ESA Council at the ministerial level. This general council is called the Space Council.[385]

The creation of the European Space Council was an important step in European cooperation for space exploration and exploitation. The Space Council was not a formally constituted body but a forum for coordinating meetings between the EU Council and the ESA Council. This special status of the Space Council is required

383 *Id.* at 18

384 Framework agreement between European Comunity and European Space Agency, Art. 1.1 and Art. 1.2, Official Journal of the European Union, L 261/64, (Aug. 6th 2004).

385 *Id.*

because of the need for coordination between the bodies of two separate and very different legal entities - the EU and ESA.[386] This special status of the Space Council was required because of the need for coordination between the bodies of two separate and very different legal entities - the EU and ESA.

A Secretariat was set up at the European Space Council to monitor the implementation of the Cooperation Agreement and to facilitate the implementation of acts adopted by the Space Council. These acts are resolutions that are subsequently introduced by the adoption of the relevant legal instruments in the European Union and in the European Space Agency. Article 11 of the Cooperation Agreement provides for a dispute settlement procedure, which guarantees the correct implementation of EU and ESA Space Council resolutions, as well as the settlement of disputes between representatives of the two organizations.

In this way, through the Framework Cooperation Agreement, a *de facto* new European body was created to shape European Space Policy.

On May 22nd 2007, at the fourth meeting of the Space Council, a resolution was adopted approving the European Space Policy. The act mentions space debris, stating that Europe supports the continued efforts of the Committee on the Peaceful Uses of Outer Space at the United Nations to mitigate and prevent space debris.[387]

This wording formulation means that for Europe, the problem of space debris is serious, but it must be fully regulated at a universal level, not regionally. The most likely reason for this position is the desire not to restrict the European Space Industry alone and not to create additional economic burdens for it alone. Another reason for Europe's demand for universal cooperation is its continued dependence on the United States and, to a certain extent, on Russia for information on the situation in space. As mentioned above, the importance of this information is crucial because, without it, the

386 *Id.*

387 European Space Policy article I, Space Council resolution, ESA BR 269, (May 22th 2007).

security of access and the presence of space systems and humans in outer space cannot be guaranteed.

Thirdly, protecting and securing the outer space environment from only one regional space force will not significantly contribute to the trends of space debris pollution, nor will it protect Europe's space systems from collisions with other space objects.

For the European Union, outer space is of great importance. Accordingly, European Space Policy is one of the Union's priorities. This is evidenced by the norm in Article 189 (1) of the Treaty on the Functioning of the European Union.[388]

It states that to support scientific and technical progress, industrial competitiveness and the implementation of its policies, the European Union shall develop a European Space Policy. To that end, it may promote joint initiatives, support research and technological development and coordinate efforts needed for space exploration and use.

The logical conclusion of this statement is to ensure the safety of humans and space systems in space; the risk of one of the most serious outer space problems — the space debris pollution should be reduced.

Until 2020, the program was managed by ESA, and its funding was provided by the ESA Member States and EU. Since April 2021, the EU has confirmed the transformation of the European Space Program and adopted more coherent and comprehensive functions. The Space Programme aims to ensure the continuity and evolution of the three existing flagship programmes, Galileo, Copernicus and EGNOS. It will also support new initiatives on space surveillance (SSA), including Space Surveillance and Tracking (SST), Space Weather and Near-Earth Object (NEO), and satellite communications (GOVSATCOM).[389]

In 2021 the European Commission presented its priority to improve space traffic management which, inturn, is directly related to the issue of mitigation of space debris and a safe outer space envi-

---

388 The Treaty on the Functioning of the European Union, 2008/C 115/01

389 EU Commission official website https://ec.europa.eu/defence-industry-space/eu-space-regulation-ready-take-2021-04-28_en last access on 10.02.2023

ronment.[390] The reason is that investments to improve space traffic management systems lead to the avoidance of collision events that may result from the proliferation of satellites and space debris.

When we envision clearing waste, the most obvious solution would be to capture it and remove it for processing. This view could also be applied in outer space as the European Space Agency (ESA) is planning to collaborate with the company ClearSpace for similar activities. The signed contract envisions that ClearSpace, at the beginning of 2025, will use a giant mechanical claw to grab a large piece of debris and propel it towards the lower levels of the atmosphere, thus burning and melting the space object.[391] This mission is a service contract and not a direct procuring, as ESA applied in the past. This is a sign that ESA is attempting to resolve problems in outer space by creating a fundamentally new sector of commercial activities and that the cleaning of space debris could also become a business initiative for companies in the space sector.

The regional cooperation on a European level, which included the relationships between member states of ESA and EU and its members predominantly, illustrates clearly that common efforts could lead to better projects. Concrete steps to improve space traffic management, space situational awareness systems and investments in debris removal projects cannot be achieved by any of the EU or ESA member states alone. The experience and good practices of European regional cooperation in outer space could be used to establish global cooperation between more states in the world, which could lead to better international institutional mechanisms.

2.2. International cooperation at a non-governmental level

International cooperation at a non-governmental level is important to be researched as it provides perspectives, analyses and

390 EU Commission official website https://ec.europa.eu/commission/presscorner/detail/en/IP_21_651 last access on 10.02.2023

391 ESA website, http://www.esa.int/Safety_Security/ESA_purchases_worldfirst_debris_removal_mission_from_start-up Last access on 10.02.2023

proposals that are not necessarily bound by political positions and national interests. The scientific approach is inherent to both COSPAR and the International Law Association, two key organizations, that produced indispensable proposals for the mitigation of the problem of space debris.

2.2.1. International cooperation in COSPAR

The Committee on Space Research was established in 1958 by a resolution of the International Council for Science. This Committee is an international non-governmental organization whose main purpose is to ensure international cooperation in outer space research. Although not an intergovernmental organization, the Committee plays a significant role in the relationship between states with respect to space exploration and exploitation, which is why it is important to explore its activities and input in cooperation. The Committee's task is also to ensure the exchange of research results, and information on space and to be a forum that is open to all scientists who research on space exploration issues.

The Committee pays close attention to the problem of space debris and environmental pollution resulting from space activities. These can be actions that damage the outer space environment, but they can also be activities in outer space that damage the environment on the Earth's surface. The organization has created a panel for potentially environmentally damaging activities in space. This panel deals with the problems that accompany the formation of space debris in Earth's orbits. The panel operates on an *ad hoc* basis, and its reports serve as additional expertise and analysis to support policy-making within the relevant authorities. The main body that is consulted on these reports is the UN Committee on the Peaceful Use of Outer Space.

The Committee on Space Research pays particular attention to the danger of space debris or operating space systems bringing potentially infectious space organisms to Earth. Biological contagion to Earth from space debris are not sufficiently addressed in the policies of space-faring nations and relevant international organizations. The norm of article IX of the Outer Space Treaty stipulates that states should avoid harmful contamination and adverse changes in the environment of the Earth resulting from the introduction of extraterrestrial matter and shall adopt appropriate measures for this purpose. No comprehensive international measures have yet been taken to ensure that such an infection can be prevented.

In October 2002, the Space Research Committee adopted a policy to protect the planet, which was later updated.[392] It is not legally binding, but it is an important scientific analysis and a set of measures that can be accepted by States as legally binding. The main purpose of the document is to prevent biological contamination resulting from space exploration and to provide recommendations and standards in this field that are consistent with the terms of the Outer Space Treaties and other applicable international agreements.[393]

The Planetary Protection Policy adopted by the Committee states that, for certain missions, pollution control must be undertaken in accordance with a number of measures. The document classifies five mission categories, each of which provides a package of measures.[394] These categories, in practice, represent degrees of risk that the respective mission and the object of that pollution mission carry, which may adversely affect living organisms. From Category I - for missions with no risk of contamination to Category IV, which has a very high risk of contamination and Category V, which is designated for missions that return to Earth.

The document recommends that committee members provide information on the procedures and calculations used to protect the planet in each flight. The period within which the information is to

---

392 COSPAR Planetary Protection Policy, 2002, amended 2005: http://cosparhq.cnes.
fr/Scistr/Pppolicy.htm. Cf. J.D. Rummel et al., 'COSPAR's Planetary Protection Policy: A
Consolidated Draft' (2002).

393 COSPAR website, http://cosparhq.cnes.fr. Planetary Protection Policy, Preamble, (2002).

394 *Id.* at 2-5

be provided is six months from the launch. The role of the Committee is to keep these reports, make them public, and submit to the UN an annual report of the processed reports received for the relevant period. The planet's defence policy also envisages seven requisites that each report should have. There is no barrier to including additional information.

The activities of the Committee on Space Research are often based on anticipating situations that have not yet arisen and recommendations for taking measures to prevent theoretically possible risks. In my opinion, this approach is needed in future regulation. It would be positive to apply preventive management strategies to the discussions in the relevant international governmental organizations dealing with pollution issues resulting from space exploration.

Since the organization is a non-governmental scientific organization, its decisions are not legally binding, and the expert recommendations and conclusions are only advisory. The members of the organization are scientific experts in their field, which is why the activity of the organization is important for the provision of expert standards and environmental protection measures to support international governmental organizations or countries.

One of the weaknesses of current international space law is the lack of adequate international rules to regulate the contamination of terrestrial biological organisms resulting from space activities.

2.2.2. International cooperation in International Law Association

The problem of the international law regime of space debris was raised by the International Law Association (ILA) in 1986 at the conference in Seoul. From this point on, the issue is inevitably on the agenda of the Space Law Committee of the Association and is considered a priority even before the topic of placing weapons in space. The analysis of the legal regime and proposals from ILA is a significant contribution to possible future regulation.[395]

395 Maureen Williams, *Safeguarding Outer Space: on the Road to Debris Mitigation*, 31 Security in Space: the Next Generation Conf. Report, 84, (2008).

In 1990, at the sixty-fourth conference in Queensland, a legal instrument was discussed to regulate the issue. This conference outlines the main legal points that should be included in the future legal instrument. The basic principles include a general obligation to cooperate; negotiating in good faith; an obligation to ensure that activities in outer space do not cause harm to humans, space objects or the environment of other countries or in areas outside national jurisdiction; an obligation to exchange information and to consult, an obligation to prevent, control, and reduce space debris. To achieve effective legal regulation of space debris, the need to clarify and define the concepts of pollution, contamination, and space debris is emphasized.

In 1994, at its meeting in Buenos Aires, the Space Law Committee of the Association adopted a preliminary draft of the "Legal Instrument for the Protection of the Environment from Damage from Space Waste", also known as the Draft Space Debris Convention.[396]

The document contains 16 articles and has been prepared in accordance with the principles outlined above. Article 1 of the legal instrument sets out the definitions of the concepts of space debris, pollution, and contamination. An important clarification is made in paragraph (b), which provides that the concepts of pollution and contamination will be regarded as synonymous.

The definition of space debris serves as the foundation of future definitions, which will emerge in COPUOS, IADC and other international forums. It states that space debris means man-made objects in outer space other than active or otherwise useful satellites when no change in these conditions can reasonably be expected in the foreseeable future.[397] The legal instrument is applicable to space debris that is likely to cause harm and those that have already caused

396 Karl-Heinz Bockstiegel, *ILA Draft Convention on Space Debris/ILA Konventions-Entwurf zu Weltraumtrummern/Un Projet de Convention de l'ILA sur les Debris Spatiaux*, 43 ZLW, 395, (1994).

397 International Instrument on the Protection of the Environment from Damage Caused by Space Debris, Article 1c)*, 66th Conference (1994). [hereinafter ILA instrument]*

harm.[398] This damage can be to the environment, persons or to objects. Viikari points out that the scope of the rules in the document also covers indirect damages, which is a broader application than envisaged in the Liability Convention.[399]

Article 3 of the draft convention sets out the general obligation to cooperate. This cooperation is regulated at a horizontal level - cooperation with countries and international governmental organizations and at a vertical level - cooperation for the prevention, reduction, and control of damage or material risks that could cause space debris to activities under the jurisdiction and control of the respective state or international organization.[400] Vertical cooperation allows the exercise of governmental control over the private organizations associated with it because most of these space activities are carried out by private corporations, but the responsibility lies with the respective countries to which the organizations are affiliated.

Article 5 of the draft convention stipulates that the rules in the legal instrument will be compatible with other international treaties. The draft convention is thus a further step in interpreting the principles already established in international space law and refining the rules relating to the pollution of space and space debris.

The legal instrument explicitly states that states will bear international responsibility in accordance with the rules provided in the legal instrument, Outer Space Treaty and Liability Convention.[401] A significant innovation in the proposed draft convention is that international fault liability for States will arise in any harmful environmental change in areas within and outside national jurisdiction or control.[402]

Article 9 pays special attention to the dispute settlement rules that require the parties to consult on issues related to the interpretation and application of the rules in the legal instrument. If the parties

398 *Id.* at Art. 2

399 Lotta Viikari, The Environmental Element in Space Law, 103, (2008).

400 ILA instrument, Article 3b) *(1994).*

401 ILA instrument, Article 6, article 7, article 8, (1994).

402 *Id.* „any adverse modification of the environment of areas within or beyond national jurisdiction or control", (1994).

fail to reach an agreement within twelve months of the invitation to consult, they may seek arbitration or a court of justice to settle their dispute, in accordance with the rules of the draft space convention for the settlement of space law disputes.

Probably due to the stricter rules of international responsibility that would force States and the space industry to invest in the safety of the space environment, the legal instrument fails to become a legally binding international treaty. The document has political weight and contains various recommendations for drawing up an international treaty that guarantees the protection of outer space from pollution by space debris.

The question remains whether certain rules of the document are legally binding norms, the source of which is customary international law.[403] As stated, the conduct of anti-satellite attempts is not prohibited by customary international law. These attempts are a harmful change to the environment, according to the definition of harm in the legal instrument, which means that the rules for harm in Article 1f) are not considered a valid law.

Malanczuk raises an important question that remains unanswered today. If there is damage to the outer space environment, which state or group of states are entitled to claim international liability from the damaging state?[404]

Another important contribution of ILA to improve the legal norms that preserve outer space environment is visible in the Sofia Guidelines for a Model Law on National Space Legislation.[405] Article 7 of ILA Model law deals with the protection of the environment. The norm of Art.7. Paragraph 1 foresees that space activities should not directly or indirectly cause environmental damage on Earth or in outer space. This comprehensive approach is beneficial as it points out that outer space environment should also be included in the scope of protection. However, Bhat is correct

403 Lotta Viikari, The Environmental Element in Space Law, 102, (2008).

404 Peter Malanczuk, *Review of the regulatory regime governing the space environment*, 45 ZLW, 37, 56, (1996).

405 Res. №6/2012, 75th Conference of International Law Association

that the lack of precise threshold of environmental damage creates uncertainty whether the states will protect the environment at all and if such obligations are more stringent than those stipulated in art. IX of ther Outer Space Treaty.[406] The requirement of environmental impact assessment is also a positive step that was made in the ILA Model Law.[407] At the same time, if the parameters of the assessment has to be decided by the states, without any common standards, uniformity and international legal obligations, this could incentivize some states to have less rigorous requirements and minimalistic approach in order to attract private space actors.[408] Article 8 of the ILA Model Law stipulates that "*space activities should be carried out in such a manner as to mitigate to the greatest possible extent any potential space debris*". The lack of precise technical standards leads to ambiguity and vague obligations of states, which will not result in adequate protection of outer space environment. The ILA Model Law contributed in developing national legislation, projects, procedures and good practices to mitigate space debris. The national practices for reducing space debris, reviewed in subchapter 1.5. also take into considerations of the ILA Model Law. Developing states with newly established space policies and space programs could use the ILA Model Law as a basis to achieve adequate space project management and safety of their space missions.

The ILA has adopted a liberal approach in its Draft Convention on the Settlement of Disputes related to Space Activities. It includes the right of private organizations not to request the state that has jurisdiction over the space object to be a party to the dispute on their behalf in an international tribunal.[409] If such a proposal is accepted by states, this would mean that states agree to introduce a new inter-

406 Sandeepa Bhat. "*A Discourse on the Remodeling of Ila Model Law on Nation Space Legislation.*" 41 *J. Space L.*, 1, 12, (2017).

407 Art. 7 par.2 ILA Model Law, 2012

408 Sandeepa Bhat. "*A Discourse on the Remodeling of Ila Model Law on Nation Space Legislation.*" 41 *J. Space L.*, 1, 13, (2017).

409 Lotta Viikari, *International Law Association´ s Draft Convention on the Settlement of Disputes related to Space Activities*, 14-17, (2021).

pretation of Article VI from the Outer Space Treaty and the norms of the Liability Convention.

2.3. Main challenges in international cooperation to resolve the issue of space debris

With the development of the space sector, all space-faring nations and humankind became much more dependent on outer space. At the same time, there is an increase in vulnerability because military and economic dependence on outer space has not translated into a centralized strategic vision for space to guide international policy-making.[410]

We are witnessing separate approaches by groups of states to initiate lunar scientific stations and other smaller lunar projects. China and Russia have published their roadmap for the future International Lunar Research Station.[411] The USA also plans to explore and even exploit the Moon with allied states that will comply with the Artemis accords. The lunar orbit "Lunar Gateway" is planned to become a global international lunar space station, but not all countries agree with the rules and vision, which is proposed by the USA. Roscosmos and NASA announced joint cooperation in 2017 only to end in January 2021 because Roscosmos viewed the program as too "US-centric".[412] Japan, India, Turkey and EU countries are also investing in small-scale Moon projects. These activities of states clearly show that the level of international cooperation is low, and

---

410 Patricia K. McCormick, *Space debris: Conjunction opportunities and opportunities for international cooperation,* 40.6 Science and Public Policy, 810, (2013).

411 Roscosmos website http://en.roscosmos.ru/22170/ (June 16th 2021). in St. Petersburg, The Roscosmos State Space Corporation and China National Space Administration (CNSA) held a joint session on the auspices of the Global Space Exploration Conference (GLEX 2021), dedicated to the presentation of the Roadmap for the creation of the International Lunar Research Station (ILRS).

412 SPACENEWS website, Russia skeptical about participating in lunar Gateway., (October 12th 2020). https://spacenews.com/russia-skeptical-about-participating-in-lunar-gateway/ Last Access 10.02.2023

that the institutional formula has not been found so far. The future of outer space activities will require long-term projects, which means significant investments and high risk. The combination of the two could serve as an incentive for states to improve their present relations and resolve the main political issues in front of them. This general improvement of relations of the space-faring nations is the basis of resolving all pending issues of addressing space debris.

It is evident that the world has become multipolar, and consequently, the competition between space-faring nations has become more diverse.[413] In order to address the coordination problem due to an absence of communication, it is ideal for creating focal points of diplomatic communication.[414] The focal points system of organized communication would serve states better, because they would know what is expected from them and what to expect from each other.[415]

Space debris management is an issue of primal importance that states could work to resolve even if they have a low level of bilateral relationship. As analysed in chapters I and II, the indiscriminate generation of space debris is an imminent threat to all space activities, and it could jeopardize military operations and activities for civil purposes. If the threat is of such a large scale and the experts and political leaders are understanding it well, what might be the reason for inactivity and irresponsible actions, such as leaving non-functional satellites in outer space for so long?

First, active debris removal projects are expensive initiatives, and they cost millions of US dollars.[416] At the same time, the effect is very often beneficial for the whole outer space environment, and

413 Ram S. Jakhu & Joseph N. Pelton, eds. Global Space Governance: an international study, 20, (2017).

414 S. G. Sreejith & Yugank Goyal, *Institutional cost of international space law*, 41 J. Space L., 70, (2017).

415 *Id.* at 70-72

416 Space.com website, ESA signed a $104 million (€86 million) contract with ClearSpace to accomplish this feat. The team will use the ClearSpace-1 robot to capture Vespa from Low Earth orbit and drag it down into Earth's atmosphere, where both spacecraft will burn up. https://www.space.com/esa-startup-clearspace-debris-removal-2025 Last access 10.02.2023

it is not fair for the burden of the costs (which are coming from the public budget) to be for one or even a few space agencies. The most comprehensive solution for this challenge is a global international organization or a fund, which budget is made by equitable instalments by member states and by private actors. The political will for such an initiative is still not present.

There are several main factors that are leading to the absence of comprehensive regulation on protection of the outer space environment and mitigation of the risks from space debris. Firstly, in order to be comprehensive, such legal framework has to include the majority, if not all, space-faring nations. The competition among the leading space-faring nations is leading to efforts to invest in space capabilities, and not in the long-term protection of the outer space environment, which will be beneficial to all states. States and their private corporations prefer to utilize their space assets in orbit as much as possible and not to deorbit their space objects when they become non-functional, because the space assets will provide more services and therefore more economic and strategic gain in short-term.

Focusing on the competition for the resources of outer space could provide a short-term strategic advantage for the "winner". However, in the long term, it would jeopardize its relationships with other groups of states. The leaders in space exploitation should be able to find wisdom in cooperation based on mutual respect. Through the already established diplomatic and military channels, the political leaders of all space-faring nations should find a working formula for equitable distribution of outer space resources, acceptable by all states. If this is not done, the risk of escalation between states in outer space is going to be high.

Secondly, we are not witnessing comprehensive regulation of the outer space environment for the same reason we are not seeing such thorough regulation for the Earth environment, even when the political and economic leaders are aware of the detrimental effects of climate change. The attitude of states and companies to exploit their environment for economic resources and with negligence to the environmental degradation from their activities.

Chapter 3

Doctrinal proposals to mitigate and resolve the challenges from space debris

The difficulties of international cooperation to resolve or mitigate the challenges from space debris are explored in the previous chapter. The absence of a coherent and comprehensive approach to resolve and adequately manage the issue of space debris has led to the emergence of doctrinal proposals to resolve the issue.

The important contribution of legal scholars to create meaningful theoretical solutions to the existing problems in international space law and make proposals for the new legal regime and international institutions is key to overcoming the deterioration of international space law in the last four decades. These theoretical solutions are valuable for space law development as they could inspire future political leaders to conduct necessary changes, instead to adopt convenient and less significant proposals. The small changes of international regulation would not shift the present paradigm and they would preserve the *status quo*. The result would be more crashes of space objects in outer space.

Considering the challenges on an international level, many representatives of the international legal doctrine have contributed their proposals to fill the gaps in international space law. This chapter analyses these proposals by distinguished representatives of international space law doctrine.

These proposals include 1) legal analysis and optional protocols to interpret the existing legal treaties and other instruments; 2) proposals for the adoption of new legal treaties to resolve or mitigate the space debris problem.

The amendments of the outer space treaties are extremely difficult procedural processes, as they require consensus in the UNCOPUOS and such approval of a resolution would be very challenging.[417]

A possible solution is not to amend the treaty itself but to adopt specialized protocols to the treaties which interpret the norms and the obligations of the states.[418] Such protocols would be optional, and their ratification could be done by individual states when they have the political will to do so.

One possible solution for interpreting articles of the Outer Space Treaty is elaborated by Sachdeva, and it is the draft of a limited-purpose resolution of UNCOPUOS, which is later presented as a resolution in the General Assembly of the UN.[419] This procedure for clarification of the Outer Space Treaty was used previously in regard to the application of the concept of a launching state[420] and on the issue of registration of space objects.[421]

With respect to existing international legal practice on space debris, the focus is on the applicability of Article IX of the Outer Space Treaty. Among the legal proposals the establishment of new international institutions – international organizations, a specialized court of justice, specialized funds and others are analysed.

---

417 Ram S. Jakhu, *The Future of the Outer Space Treaty.* Fifty Years of the Outer Space Treaty, 185, 186, (2017).

418 Gurbachan S. Sachdeva, *Outer Space Treaty: An Appraisal*, Fifty Years of the Outer Space Treaty, 24, 42-43, (2017).

419 Gurbachan S. Sachdeva, *Space Mines: Dialectics of Legality*, 7.2 Astropolitics, 135, 146, (2009).

420 Resolution 59/115 (December 10th 2004). Application of the concept of the "launching State"

421 UN GA resolution, A/RES/62/101 Recommendations on enhancing the practice of States and international intergovernmental organizations in registering space objects, (Dec. 17th, 2007).

3.1. Proposals for amendments of article IX of the Outer Space Treaty

Chapter I explores the history of the negotiations for the adoption of Article IX of the Outer Space Treaty. When it comes to protecting the outer space environment, the rules in Article IX are unsatisfactory as they do not create clear legal obligations for the state parties. The lack of a clear deadline or time frame for the stipulated "consultations" means that discussion could continue indefinitely, and during that time, serious damage could take place.[422]

What is "harmful contamination"?; What is included in the wording "due regard to the corresponding interests of all other States Parties to the Treaty"?; What changes in the Earth's environment are considered "adverse" as a result of the "introduction of extraterrestrial matter"?; What a hypothetical or real extra-terrestrial biological entity is referred in the treaty?; What should be the appropriate measures?

All of these questions have been raised in international space law forums[423] because the exact obligations of many states and international organizations remain unclear. For this reason, several representatives of the international legal doctrine have made proposals for amendments to Article IX or further clarifying and interpreting the scope of its norms.

Robinson is concerned about the contamination of the outer space environment with microorganisms from Earth and makes recommendations to ensure the physical and biological integrity of celestial bodies.[424] He defends his position of empowering a public organization, supported by all space-faring states.[425] The obligations

---

422 Maureen Williams, *Safeguarding Outer Space: on the Road to Debris Mitigation*, 31 Security in Space: the Next Generation Conf. Report, 86, (2008).
423 Nandasiri Jasentuliyana, *Space debris and international law* 26 J. Space L., 139, 140-142 (1998).
424 George Robinson, *Forward contamination of international space and celestial bodies: risk reduction, cultural objectives and the law*, 3 ZLW, 388-397, (2006).
425 *Id.* at 397-399

of this new international public body should include the adoption of a research protocol, that sets the limits of minimal risk in the study of extraterrestrial life.

The existence of such an international organization is becoming urgent to resolve major present and future problems of international space law, including the problem of space debris.

Robinson also points out that these studies should be conducted following the international regulation of research experiments, standards of usage of equipment, and obligations to follow procedures.[426] In its proposal to amend Article IX, he provides that the Member States of the Treaty should be represented by COSPAR (or another body) on all matters of contamination from Earth to other celestial bodies. In his view, COSPAR should determine the levels of risk that are acceptable to ensure the controlled intervention or interaction of humanity with an open extraterrestrial life form and that all Member States of the Treaty should respect these minimum standards.

In my assessment, Robinson's proposal is valuable as it finds a way to create such an authority. It emphasizes the need for highly professional expertise that protects transnational interests, including the protection of the outer space environment, health and life of human beings in outer space and on Earth.

Robinson's proposal focuses on outer space contamination, which is biological of nature and its source is from Earth. Adopting transparent public international rules and procedures to prevent biological contamination from Earth is not a premature action, as the existence of methane-based extraterrestrial life forms has already been recognized by some NASA scientists and by astrobiologists.[427]

Fernandez argues that the abandonment of objects can be interpreted as harmful contamination of outer space and a violation of Article IX of the Outer Space Treaty.[428] He points out that space

---

426 *Id.* at 397-399

427 NASA website, www.nasa.gov/topics/solarsystem/features/titan20100603.html last access on 10.02.2023

428 Sanz Fernandez, *Space station and space debris*, The 42rd Colloquium on

debris is not "for the benefit of mankind", is not "in the interest of all countries" and impedes free access to space. Therefore, countries that abandon any type of waste violate the treaty.

I consider this interpretation of Art. IX to be too broad and not sufficiently precise since outer space activities have always been linked to the separation of space debris. Moreover, in the sixty-year practice of states performing space activities, no country has classified abandonment of objects in outer space as a violation of the norm of Article IX. This calls for the creation of a new norm in international space law that explicitly prohibits the abandonment of non-functional objects in outer space.

3.2. Proposals for the establishment of a Space Debris Convention

The logical course of continuing to codify international space law and resolve existing problems should be through international treaties that are congruent with the existing and operational space treaties. As early as the early 1990s, proposals were made for an international space debris convention. In 1991, Hobe stated that it was best to address the inadequate regulation of the current legal regime for space debris with a separate international convention, aiming to regulate the protection of the outer space environment.[429] He proposed that this convention should be drafted in the same way as other space treaties - agreed by the COPUOUS, first examining the technical parameters of the Scientific and Technical Subcommittee, and then moving to the adoption of legal norms in the Legal Subcommittee.

Hobe analyses the national space policies and the dynamic of the international space cooperation three decades ago and at that time he did not believe that it was realistic to accept such a convention, and it would be more probable for states to agree on le-

the Law of Outer Space, 73-74, (1999).

429 Stephan Hobe, *Space debris: A proposal for its international legal regulation*, 34 Colloquium on the Law of Outer Space, 194, 198-200, (1992).

gally non-binding principles. Three decades later, this prediction is fully justified, demonstrating the lack of political will on the part of several states to resolve problems in outer space regulation by adopting a modern (if necessary radically new) international legal framework. In developing the general principles of his proposal for a convention, Hobe states that emphasis should be placed on rules that prevent the generation of space debris. Compensation rules should exist, but they should be considered of a secondary nature.

Preventive rules should be given priority in international space law, as they will advocate for higher standards of treatment of the outer space environment. Even considering the space debris problem solely from an economic point of view, waste prevention in space, where possible, is much cheaper than its subsequent removal. It should be noted here that the absence of an independent international space tracking system creates the prerequisites for unequal and biased application of the accepted compensation mechanisms, depending on which state is the pollutant and which state is damaged. Considering the competitive and often adversarial nature of international relations, such scenarios should never be excluded. Next, Hobe proposes that the new convention should be fully in compliance with the existing space law. The proposal draws attention to collecting and sharing of information on space objects, including space debris. Hobe stresses the need to expand the scope of the mandatory information, which must be provided by the launching states to the UN Secretary-General. The proposal states that this information include the type of materials that the space object is made of, the design parameters, and the pre-calculated end of the mission. Hobe goes on to mention that the next step could be to create traffic rules and suggests that satellites have to be removed from orbit at the end of their mission. He reaffirms that states, which have jurisdiction and control over space objects, should be obliged to inform the Secretary-General of the United Nations, and potentially the states concerned. If they fail to fulfil this obligation, they will be presumed guilty of the damage unless they prove that the damage would have occurred even if they had notified the concerned states and the Secretary-General of the United Nations. Hobe also proposed that the existing regime of international liability should be adapted to space debris by explicitly stating that they are space objects. The scope of the term "damage", according to him, should be extended to include properly justified costs for space exploration, and search and rescue operations to the Earth's surface.[430]

Considering the difficulties of accurately identifying the space debris that caused destruction in outer space, in the airspace or on the Earth, Hobe also justifies the proposal to establish an international compensation fund. This fund should aim to compensate the injured parties when it is impossible to determine which country is responsible for the damage. The proposal stated that the fund should be a legal entity and have at least two bodies - a general assembly in which the member states of the fund participate, and the second body is the manager of the fund. Each country launching a space object should contribute an amount to the fund. He pointed out that the amount should be proportional to the risk from launching this space object (the greater the risk of a space object, the greater the amount the state had to pay in the fund). This requirement further stimulates states to reduce the risk of a space launch, both during and after the mission. The creation of a specialized compensation fund would resolve the challenge for a damaged country to identify the ownership of the space junk that caused the damage.

The proposal for a Space Debris Convention, which was published by Imburgia, includes the establishment of a Space Sustainability Authority with the purpose to aid space debris mitigation and removal activities.[431] The proposal envisions that the organization to have its own financial resources, which are not made exclusively by payments of member states. It is extremely needed to have an international organization that is capable to react immediately to mitigate the results of a space debris collision.

---

430 *Id.* at 199

431 Joseph S. Imburgia, *Space debris and its threat to national security: a proposal for a binding international agreement to clean up the junk*, 44 Vand. J. Transnat'l L., 640, (2011).

In 2007 Senechal proposed a draft convention on space debris, which consisted of twelve articles. He substantiates the need for his initiative with the global scale of the problem and the drastic increase in countries launching space objects. Senechal advocates the Space Debris Convention to be a necessary legal instrument, not voluntary mitigation recommendations that do not have a legally binding effect on the states. He also logically points out that such a convention must be ratified by all "space nations".[432]

The main objectives of the draft convention are four. First, the author proposes to regulate the independent tracking and cataloguing of space debris. He points out that it is risky for countries to rely on other countries for the provision of information since the information may be delayed, and manipulated, especially in the event of a major incident. Because of these risks, Senachal proposed to set up an independent intergovernmental tracking system at the UN or another independent organization.

In my opinion, Senechal's proposal focuses on one of the most important problems in international space law that is directly related to space debris, namely: the absence of an independent body to ensure the sharing of reliable information on what is happening in space. As mentioned in the previous chapter, only a few of the countries that are leading space exploration have their own space monitoring system. The risk that information will be withheld is too great, and the guarantees that this is not the case today are too small.

The second major objective cited by the French author is the adoption of legally binding standards for space debris mitigation. The arguments put forward are that competition, and the imminent emergence of new actors into outer space activities will endanger the safety in outer space.

The third objective was to introduce a "space preservation" clause. This means that certain areas of space, such as Geostation-

432 Thierry Senechal, *Orbital debris: drafting, negotiating, implementing a convention*, Diss. MIT, 13, (2007).http://www.pon.org/downloads/ien16.2.Senechal.pdf

ary and Low-Earth orbits, will be protected from major pollution in those areas, and countries that deviate from this obligation will be subject to penalty payments.

In my opinion, this proposal has significant merit because it envisions the protection of the outer space environment to become a principle whose breach entails international sanctions.

Senechal also offered a mechanism for the conditional granting of a license to launch space objects by space operators. The condition that must be fulfilled in order to be licensed is that the space operator accepts mandatory space debris mitigation procedures. The same measures he proposes to apply to military activities in outer space. To achieve the goal of space preservation, a proposal for a convention includes a quota mechanism for space-debris pollution that is similar to that of the 1995 emission of the United Nations Acid Rain Program.[433] The fourth aim of the proposal for a draft convention included an international liability regime, compensation, and a dispute settlement system. Establishing a working and acceptable dispute settlement mechanism is of key importance to resolving issues between states in outer space[434] in the event of a collision with space debris or destruction of space debris on Earth. Senechal mentioned that it is necessary to regulate the issue of international liability and compensation for damage, both in space and in space-related damage to the Earth's surface. The proposal acknowledged the international liability regime provided in the Liability Convention, and he concluded that it has to be extended to include damages from space debris.

In my opinion, such an extension of international liability would cause confusion since the current Liability Convention provides international liability for damage from space debris, but the challenge is that some of the non-functional objects cannot be

433 Thierry Senechal, *Orbital debris: drafting, negotiating, implementing a convention*, Diss. Massachusetts Institute of Technology, 23, (2007). http://www.pon.org/downloads/ien16.2.Senechal.pdf

434 Yijun Zhang, *An Analysis of the Regulations on Environmental Damage to Outer Space Caused by Space Debris*, 1.1. Journal of Frontiers of Society, Science and Technology, 139, (2021).

identified. Even if absolute international liability for damage from space debris in outer space is introduced, which means a change in the existing international space legal regime, it will not be practical because it will still not be possible to identify space debris fragments unambiguously.

In addition to the absolute liability for damage to the Earth's surface and to the airspace provided in the Liability Convention, Senechal also proposes the introduction of a compulsory insurance system.[435]

With regard to disputes that may arise, he proposes the introduction of a new dispute settlement mechanism - the Dispute Settlement Board. Unlike other dispute settlement mechanisms (such as mediation), which require fair cooperation between participants, the board would act as an international court of justice, whose decision is "final and not subject to review by the policy-making authority". Such a measure would indeed discipline the countries and establish guarantees for compliance with the negotiated international norm. Unfortunately, at this stage of international relations, it is difficult to imagine that states will voluntarily restrict themselves and will subordinate their space activities and research policies to an independent international body. I share the conclusions of this proposal that states need independent international control of their activities, as guarantees are needed to ensure that space law is respected. At present, there is no political will on the part of the leading nations to coordinate their national space policies and much less desire to submit themselves to independent monitoring. Senechal's proposal also includes an optimistic timetable for the adoption of the convention, which stipulates that by 2012 the UN General Assembly may adopt it. The UN did not acknowledge the proposal.

The Stimson Centre for Space Security, along with non-governmental organizations from Canada, the US, Russia, France and Japan, proposed to agree on a common manual between countries

---

435 Thierry Senechal, *Orbital debris: drafting, negotiating, implementing a convention*, Diss. Massachusetts Institute of Technology, 24, (2007). http://www.pon.org/downloads/ien16.2.Senechal.pdf

engaged in space activities and space research. The objective of the document was to prevent incidents and dangerous military activities in outer space.[436] The proposal for this manual reaffirmed the current principles of space law and the existing international space treaties. They are accompanied by an obligation to develop space-based traffic rules, which needs to be followed by all countries; to deepen cooperation on space situational awareness; an obligation to reduce the generation of space debris, in accordance with the guidelines of IADC and COPUOS.

In my view, the merits of this proposal are that it addresses the problem of pollution of space and the formation of space debris in close connection with other outstanding issues in space law.

To overcome the problem of space debris, it is not enough to reduce their formation in space when performing space activities. It is also necessary to introduce traffic rules for the movement of space objects in outer space to ensure better safety in space activities and avoidance of collisions. There are representatives of space law doctrine, such as Lafferranderie, who are arguing that it is urgent to adopt simple and concrete provisions that can be further developed later and for the time being, give them international recognition instead of proposing a whole new Space Debris Convention.[437]

3.3. Proposal for establishing an international organization for the usage of Earth's orbits

Safety in outer space includes adequate traffic management and the creation of common rules for the movement of all space objects. A comprehensive national definition of space traffic management, we can find in section 2b) in the USA Space Policy Directive-3, National Space Traffic Management Policy. The definition of space traffic management is "planning, coordination, and on-orbit syn-

---

436 Michael Krepon, *A code of conduct for responsible space-faring nations*. 55 Space Security and Global Cooperation, 165-173, (2007).

437 Gabriel Lafferranderie, *Space debris and related legal issues*, 473 European Space Agency Publications-ESA SP, 856, (2001).

chronization of activities to enhance the safety, stability, and sustainability of operations in the space environment".[438] This definition is comprehensive, and it could be used on a global level to describe the term.

In 1998, Supankana made two alternative proposals for international institutional regulation of the issue. The first was to create a new international organization to handle all aspects related to the use of Earth's orbits.[439] To this hypothesis, he suggests that it was possible to extend the powers of an already existing international organization to include these functions. In my opinion, the most suitable organization would be ITU since it is responsible for the allocation of frequency bands, allotment, and assignment of radio frequencies for terrestrial and space radiocommunication.

Supankana's second alternative proposal is to create a coordination mechanism between already existing organizations.[440] This proposal envisions a deeper form of cooperation between countries to protect the outer space environment.

Supankana's proposals re-emphasizes the need to regulate and control the placement of space objects in outer space and to regulate their movement. These are important aspects in the prevention of collisions and the protection of the outer space environment. In my view, it is imperative that an international organization carries out these activities in Earth's orbits. An expert group that presented in COPUOS in its 49th session a comprehensive report on active debris removal envisions a similar proposal.[441] The report identified three main elements of an operational and regulatory framework for

---

438 USA Space Policy Directive-3, National Space Traffic Management Policy, Section 2 b, (June 18th, 2018).

439 Supancana, I.B.R. The international Regulatory Regime Governing the Utilization of Earth Orbits, Rijk universiteit te Leyden, 1998, p.286

440 I.B.R. Supancana, *The international Regulatory Regime Governing the Utilization of Earth Orbits*, Rijk Universiteit te Leyden, 287, (1998).

441 Report Active Debris Removal - An Essential Mechanism for Ensuring the Safety and Sustainability of Outer Space, International Interdisciplinary Congress on Space Debris Remediation and On-Orbit Satellite Servicing, A/AC.105/C.1/2012/CRP.16, (2012).

space debris remediation. The first one was establishing an intergovernmental organization based on the early Intelsat model[442] to perform removal and servicing operations on a commercial basis and to support the development of technological innovations for active debris removal. The need for such an organization is essential to include the same standards and practices for all states, coordinate the efforts and resources in the development of ADR systems and achieve an institutionalized cooperation mechanism that has to guarantee that states shall regard the interest of other states and private actors in outer space activities.

The second element of the proposal consists of signing an agreement of states to procure on a commercial basis the removal of space debris created by their own national space activities.[443] After that, the subscribed states are allowed to impose a national space "garbage" collection tax on final users of space-based commercial services available in the country. This proposal is an example of a good application of taxation policy as a tool for incentivizing the removal of space debris from Earth's orbits.

The third element is related to improving national licensing rules so that they include an assured removal clause that should apply to space systems and relevant launcher upper stages. The private company should be required to demonstrate that the system is capable of performing a safe, controlled re-entry (or placement in graveyard orbit) at the end of its mission or that the operator has contracted a commercial removal service to carry out removal operations at the end of the mission.[444] Such requirements would be extremely useful for changing the culture of the utilization of outer space that has been developed by private space actors.

---

442 The period when Intelsat was an intergovernmental organization and before it was privatized.

443 Report Active Debris Removal - An Essential Mechanism for Ensuring the Safety and Sustainability of Outer Space, International Interdisciplinary Congress on Space Debris Remediation and On-Orbit Satellite Servicing, A/AC.105/C.1/2012/CRP.16, 40, (2012).

444 *Id.* at 40-41

3.4. Proposals for the establishment of an international fund for the damages caused by space debris

In addition to Hobe's proposal outlined above, several other proposals for the establishment of an international compensation fund for damages from space objects, including space debris. The proposed regime is not included in the international space legal liability regulation. Proposals have been made for the creation of funds, both for compensation for damages from space debris and for funds aimed at protecting the outer space environment.

According to Viikari, the compensation fund should include the "space nations", and their commitments should be proportionate to their involvement in outer space activities.[445] In practice, this means developed countries should establish an international mechanism to ensure that all damages caused by space objects are compensated. The creation of such a fund, similar to the International Fund for Compensation for Oil and Pollution Damage,[446] has its positives, but it also has its weaknesses. I consider it a positive step to have a compensation mechanism in place to ensure that the concerned countries are compensated. This will save the difficulty of identifying the fragments that caused the destruction of the space system. The issues that such a fund could not address are related to environmental protection and preventive actions. If such a fund exists, it will encourage countries that have little or no involvement in the fund not to take rigorous space conservation measures and they will not insure their space endeavours. The disadvantage of such a fund is that it will create inequalities in international relations since the damage will be borne by a small number of developed countries, even though they may not be liable for the damage.

Next, the direct effect of the creation of such a fund will be the emergence of new economic safeguards and subsequent com-

---

445 Lotta Viikari, The Environmental Element in Space Law, 195-202, (2008).

446 Convention on the Establishment of an International Fund for Compensation of Oil Pollution Damage, 1953 UNTS 330, (November 27th 1992).

pensation, rather than preventative measures to avoid crashes and protect the outer space environment. If prevention is a priority, then a larger percentage of the funding should be allocated to projects for prevention. Guided by this principle, Viikari proposes the creation of an international fund as a preventative mechanism to support the introduction of measures to reduce space debris before its formation. Her proposal states that it is unrealistic to expect the space sector to adopt such a proposal in the near future since the principles of such a preventative fund will not always be in line with current economic feasibility.[447] Considering the way outer space is exploited so far, I also agree that such a fund is unlikely to be introduced. There is currently an international trust fund for the UN Programme on Space Applications, which Viikari concludes is not effective enough.[448] One of the tasks of this fund at the UN is to ensure the safety of the outer space closest to Earth's surface. It is protected through further research and implementation of space debris mitigation measures. Viikari's conclusion is that the capacity of this trust fund does not allow a wide range of activities, which is why she proposed the creation of a trust fund, together with other mechanisms, to protect the outer space environment.[449] Viikari argues that raising money for the fund should be done by introducing a tax called an "environmental space tax".[450] The purpose of this tax is to prevent the reluctance of states to donate money to an outer space environmental fund. Viikari also drew attention to the management of such a fund by pointing out good and bad practices in the management of environmental trust funds. This proposal emphasized the need for a financial commitment from countries to protect the environment, and the introduction of an environmental space tax would be a real step in international cooperation for the protection of their space systems.

Another significant proposal was made to find a means of protecting the outer space environment by the authors Lial and Larsen,

---

447 Lotta Viikari, The Environmental Element in Space Law, 202, (2008).

448 *Id.* at 226

449 *Id.* at 227

450 *Id.* at 228

who also justified the imposition of a tax for the use of the geostationary orbit.[451] This tax is stipulated by both authors to be annual or one-off. Such a fee would not violate the principle of free access to outer space, which is enshrined in Article I, paragraph 3 of the Outer Space Treaty, which stipulates that outer space is free for exploration.

3.5. Proposal for the establishment of an International Space Authority

Yun Zhao proposed to set up an International Space Authority that functions similarly to the International Seabed Authority, established under the United Nations Convention on the Law of the Sea.[452] According to Zhao, the principles that the International Space Authority should step on are the economic profits of organizations exploiting outer space and the service of humanity. The author stipulated that these two principles should be in balance. The comparison between the seabed and outer space reveals several common characteristics. They both are areas beyond national jurisdiction, both are not subject to national appropriation and declaration of sovereignty; both have enormous economic potential. Koch argues that the International Seabed Authority provides a precedent for the sustainable and equitable commercial development of global commons (the deep seabed).[453] The risks of conducting mining activities on the Moon, Mars, and other celestial bodies are related to the fact that these are relatively new territories for exploitation. Mining and other commercial activities could contaminate and destroy their essential scientific value.[454]

451 Lyall & Larsen, Space law: a treatise, 241, (2009).

452 Yun Zhao, *An International Space Authority: A Governance Model for a Space Commercialization Regime*; 30.2 Journal of Space Law issue, 287-296, (2004).

453 Jonathan Sydney Koch, *Institutional Framework for the Province of all Mankind: Lessons from the International Seabed Authority for the Governance of Commercial Space Mining*, 16.1. *Astropolitics*, 7, (2018).

454 *Id.* at 16

Mining mineral resources from celestial bodies is an invasive act, which leads to pollution and possible depletion of non-renewable resources.[455] In the case of the International Seabed Authority, the Central Data Repository manages the designation of areas of environmental interest, which are reserved for marine scientific research. Companies that are interested in commercial activities in those areas are required to receive an extraction license. Koch concludes that a similar embargo on specific sites in outer space could be feasibly considered.[456]

Zhao proposes the establishing of an International Space Authority. This body should have a Council that includes a broad and balanced representation.[457]

The author further elaborates his proposal by describing a formula of thirty-six members: four representatives of the largest importers of products, four of the largest exporters, four representatives of the states that have made the largest investments in the preparation of commercial activities in the area, six representatives of developing countries, and the rest to be distributed on a fair geographical basis. The proposal also states that decisions should be taken unanimously and, where this is not possible, by a qualified two-thirds majority. The transfer of technology to developing countries should not be compulsory, and the argument for this proposal was that these technologies must be able to continue to generate profits for their owners. Zhao also suggests that developing countries can receive these technologies at market prices.[458] The inclu-

455 Gurbachan S. Sachdeva, *Space Mines: Dialectics of Legality*, 7.2 Astropolitics, 135, 146, (2009).

456 Jonathan Sydney Koch, *Institutional Framework for the Province of all Mankind: Lessons from the International Seabed Authority for the Governance of Commercial Space Mining*, 16.1. *Astropolitics*, 16, (2018).

457 Yun Zhao, *An International Space Authority: A Governance Model for a Space Commercialization Regime*; 30.2 Journal of Space Law issue, 289, (2004).

458 Yun Zhao, *An International Space Authority: A Governance Model for a Space Commercialization Regime*; 30.2 Journal of Space Law issue, 289, (2004).

sion of developing countries is important not only from an altruistic perspective. An excluded nation can make unilateral claims to space resources and create a property dispute that could impede the development of future treaties.[459]

Another feature of the organization is to preserve the use of space for commercial purposes. The author also pointed out that transparency of access to outer space and its resources as well as easy access to information must be guaranteed. The proposal stipulated that the International Space Authority should try to balance the interests of resource-using countries with those of developing countries.[460]

Additional organs to the Council of the International Space Authority are proposed to be the Finance Committee and the Technical and Legal Committees. The sum of interests of various states and private organizations described by Zhao has not helped to preserve the outer space environment. The allocation of resources between states and private organizations with the proposed formula does not guarantee that these resources will be used for the interests of developing countries or the interests of all humanity. Zhao's proposal focuses on the use of space resources by certain countries and private organizations compared to protecting the outer space environment, which seems of secondary importance.

The academia of international space law clearly addressed the ethics of space use. The need for open and close cooperation between countries in the pursuit of space activities, including the full exchange of information, is a vital element for the peaceful use of space and the protection of the outer space environment.[461]

Maria de Cocca made a significant proposal to create an "organization for administration and justice" that represents humanity

---

459 Robert C. Bird, *Procedural Challenges to Environmental Regulation of Space Debris*, 40.3 American Business Law Journal, 651, (2003).

460 *Id.* at 291

461 Maria de las Mercedes de Cocca; Liability and responsibility for space debris, abandoned and unregistered space objects, and for damages caused during rescue operations, Proceedings of the 43 Colloquium on the Law of Outer Space, 359-362, (2000).

and has jurisdiction in outer space, including the geostationary orbit, the Moon, and other celestial bodies.[462] To achieve this, Cocca continues that it is necessary to set up a commission to study the creation of an international space body. In addition to setting up an institution, she also proposes to consider the abandonment of a space object as a violation of outer space.

With the development of space technology, it becomes possible the production of space debris to be minimized.[463] It is strongly desirable that states take the utmost care not to release space debris into space and to bring back non-functioning space systems. Unfortunately, as already mentioned, there are currently no such international legal obligations.

3.6. Proposal for the Establishment of an International Air and Space Law Court of Justice

In addition to the creation of international organizations for the protection of the outer space environment, the allocation of space resources and the regulation of traffic in space, representatives of the international legal doctrine proposed the creation of a specialized international court of justice on air and space law.[464]

In his proposal, Kim points out that such an international court of justice is necessary in order to guarantee the speed of work and the fairness of the process in air and space law cases.[465] In his reasoning for the creation of a specialized court, the author included the enormous amount of losses incurred by operators and the fact that incidents often turn into catastrophes, which always have an international character.[466] Kim also mentioned the incidents caused

---

462 *Id.* at 367

463 Э. Василевская, Правовые аспекты обеспечения безопасности полетов в космос, Международное научное сотрудничество и правовые вопросы освоения космоса; Академии наук СССР, 89, (1984).

464 Doo Hwan Kim, Proposal for establishing an international court of air and space law, 3 ZLW, 362-370, (2010).

465 *Id.* at 362

466 *Id.* at 363

by space debris, focusing on disputes and uncertainties that arise after such collisions. The international court of justice that the author proposed would have a global jurisdiction and would act as a "world court".

The jurisdiction of the court is to concurrently resolve disputes and provide advisory opinions. Kim also proposes a court structure that includes fourteen judges, elected jointly by the bodies of the International Civil Aviation Organization and the UN Committee on the Peaceful Uses of Outer Space. Seven of the judges are legal experts in aviation law, and the other seven are legal experts in space law.

Court decisions should be in accordance with international law. The decisions are final and binding only between the parties to the dispute.[467] Only states may be parties to the dispute. The proposal explicitly states that the international court should settle disputes arising out of damage caused by space debris. The establishment of the court, Kim proposes to happen through an international convention, and the first step should be the creation of a draft convention.[468]

3.7. Significance of the doctrinal proposals

The proposals for amendment of article IX and other provisions of the existing treaties were a smart approach to avoid the complex procedure of adopting a new treaty. However, this approach is not going to be successful, until the leading space-faring states do not have the political will and economic interest to agree on new interpretations of the same norms. Amendments to the present outer space treaties could bring unpredictable developments in the future implementation of the norms, and for this reason, many states are not willing to initiate such changes.[469]

---

467 Kim, Doo Hwan. *Proposal for establishing an international court of air and space law*, ZLW, issue 3, 371, (2010).

468 *Id.* at 365

469 Ram S. Jakhu, *The Future of the Outer Space Treaty.* Fifty Years of the Outer Space Treaty, 185, 186, (2017).

Despite justified proposals for the adoption of a convention on several representatives of international legal doctrine, there is no prospect of this happening until there is a dramatic change in the vision of the leading states regarding the outer space environment and their responsibility for protecting it. Nevertheless, one of the most important tasks of legal academia is to formulate legal and political proposals that are comprehensively resolving major issues, such as space debris mitigation and the protection of the outer space environment. The formulation of the solution and its promotion is an important step toward raising awareness of the issue among the public, which could lead to a shift in the priorities of the decision-makers.

Levying taxes for the protection of the outer space environment is an important aspect of the academic proposals, as it provides funding for needed activities, and serves as an incentive to states and private companies to protect the environment. The inclusion of the issue in the financial budgets of states could reinforce economic cooperation to invest in preventive international space activities.

In addition to levying taxes to protect the outer space environment, legally binding international standards and rules for a higher ecological culture should also be established for all outer space activities. If the breach of these rules also entails significant financial penalties, the preventive effect of space pollution would be vastly improved.

In view of all the specificities of outer space, I fully share the need to create an international space authority, but to be effective, the national interests of states need to be deeply interconnected and complementary, not in a state of competition or conflict in relation to outer space exploitation. Even before Zhao's proposal, other representatives of the international legal doctrine illustrate the need to create a special international body empowered to address a wide range of existing problems in space law.[470]

In my opinion, the creation of an international court of justice would be positive from the point of view of achieving impartiality

470 Э. Василевская, Правовой статус природных ресурсов луны и планет, 47-50, (1978).

in the resolution of disputes arising from collisions of space objects in space, airspace or on Earth. There is currently no legal obstacle to resolving these international disputes in the UN International Court of Justice or through the procedure in the Liability Convention of establishing a Claims Commission.[471] The practice has so far shown that states do not wish to resort to international litigation to resolve a collision of space objects or damage from space debris.

471 Liability Convention, Art. XIV-XX

Chapter 4

Author's proposals to resolve the problem of space debris

"We cannot solve our problems with the same thinking we used when creating them."

Albert Einstein

Based on the analysis and conclusions from the previous chapters, the answer to the first part of the research question (that is if there is a comprehensive international legal regulation of the space debris issue) is that there is no such international legal regulation. The second part of the research question that talks about the reasons for the absence of comprehensive international legal regulation of the issue of space debris was analysed in detail in the previous chapters. The most significant reason is shortsightedness in national and international space policy development from the early stages of developing space activities. Examples of this shortsightedness are the lack of economic incentives for the private space sector to invest in preventive technologies; legally allowing anti-satellite testing; low level of coordination and cooperation to develop space traffic management rules and the absence of common standards for reducing space debris among space-faring nations. The absence of a common vision to explore and use outer space in the interest of humankind, all states, and private space industry is another significant reason for states not to adopt comprehensive international legal regulation.

In my opinion, the proposals for a new international legal regulation should first address the question: Does the proposal solve major problems in outer space through implementation of an adequate legal mechanism? All political considerations and subjective opinions about how realistic it is the proposals to be implemented should not be an argument for not creating the proposals. The pessimistic view about innovative proposals is most often based on the status quo of the present understanding of the national interests of space-faring nations and the expectation that a new type of political leadership and policy-making is not going to emerge.

Secondly, if we want to find solutions to the problem of space debris, the proposals and recommendations should be formulated from a different mindset and not from the same mindset that is creating the issue in the first place.

Thirdly, if the issue of space debris is perceived together with other major unresolved issues of international space law, then comprehensive, holistic solutions could be envisioned and adopted if there is the political will among space-faring nations to protect the outer space environment and secure safe space activities.

4.1. The interdependence of the issue of space debris with other issues in space law

The problem of the increasing risk of space debris creation is not isolated and should be addressed together with several other existing problems in international space law. Some of these issues have been addressed in previous chapters. For example, the absence of a clear legal mechanism or international body to protect the outer space environment and the Earth from various dangerous activities or extraterrestrial biological threats from outer space created the preconditions for significant environmental pollution in Earth's orbits and risks of back contamination on Earth. While there are technological options for the safe return of non-functional space objects, states and private organizations continue to abandon them in outer space for most of their missions. Although this inaction is a major source of pollution, it does not lead to international sanctions. The absence of an international legal ban on anti-satellite weapons testing also creates legal uncertainty in space and is directly related to the increase in space debris.

Another pending problem in space law, which is directly related to space debris, is the regulation of outer space traffic. Presently, there are many participants in space activities, not just a few countries, as it was in the first two decades of outer space exploration and exploitation. The capacity of many more states and private organizations, which are willing to use the benefits of outer space, has already increased significantly. Organizations, such as the International Telecommunication Union, are responsible for the regulation of activities related to sending satellites into outer space. At the same time this international organization does not control outer space traffic and is not responsible for providing information about the situation in outer space. There is a strong need to introduce comprehensive, legally binding rules for the movement and deorbiting of space objects.

Due to the physical characteristics of outer space, objects move at a velocity of several kilometers per second (different speeds in different orbits), and virtually any collision with a solid space object larger than 1 centimeter leads to the destruction and hence formation of space debris. The above-mentioned circumstances further necessitate the creation of an international body to regulate outer space traffic.

Directly related to the movement of space objects and the formation of space debris are also the principles of distribution of slots in outer space. As stated, geostationary and other orbits are limited resources that must be used rationally and fairly. These requirements do not necessarily mean that market principles should dominate together with the rule of "first come, first served". The freedom to explore and exploit outer space, as set out in Article I of the Outer Space Treaty, is a principle that should be interpreted as freedom within certain clearly regulated legal boundaries that are exercised to protect outer space environment and to ensure that access to space is not impeded by all states or private organizations. An example of such responsible behaviour is the recommendation of the International Telecommunication Union to member states to move their non-functional satellites from the geostationary orbit to a "graveyard orbit".[472]

The safety of all space flights should also be ensured by the introduction of mandatory standards for the construction, armour and other components of space objects for all states and private organizations.

Another problem directly related to the threat of space debris is the lack of an international body to disseminate information on activities happening in outer space. An international body responsible for the timely and accurate dissemination of the relevant information ensures that collisions (such as that between the Iridium 33 and Cosmos 2251 satellites in 2009) could never happen again because of negligence.

Furthermore, the absence of a legal mechanism to guarantee the Earth's protection against outer space contamination with biological organisms, which may occur through the return of space debris, preserves the risk of this threat against humanity.

Another important reason for the growing problem of space debris and other problems in space law is the inconsistency of the general prescriptions in outer space treaties with their specific implementation in space exploration and exploitation. All states and private organizations that are conducting outer space activities should carry them out in a simultaneous implementation of several international legal principles established in public international law, including international space law.

---

472 ITU Recommendation, ITU-R S.1003 point 3, (1993).

For the legal exploration and exploitation of outer space, it is imperative for states to observe several principles stipulated in the Outer Space Treaty.

In my view, to safeguard the outer space environment and to ensure the safe and equitable development of space exploration, it is necessary to establish a new international organization that is authorized to synchronize national interests between states and those of private organizations in such a way that they do not violate the interests of humankind. I believe that such an international organization is the key to resolving the problem of space debris, as well as addressing other important issues in space law for the future.

4.2. The need for International Space Agency

Space exploration and other activities in the future will continue to evolve towards the colonization of celestial bodies. The symbolic ramming of national flags on the Moon, planets or asteroids should remain in the past.

If we do not have an organization to improve the relationships between states regarding outer space activities, the current separatist and limited approach will likely be preserved for the future. If International Space Agency (ISA) is not created, the issues that are not directly related to the national interests of states will not be resolved in the future. Such issues are: 1) pollution of the high seas with space debris; 2) preservation of dangerous space debris in Earth's orbit, which is expensive to be removed; 3) environmental degradation of celestial bodies; 4) bioethical risks with experiments with extraterrestrial biological entities; 5) non-informing a rival state about an imminent threat from outer space; 6) lack of significant support for the developing countries to improve their space capacity; 7) initiating projects that are solely for the benefit of a few nations and are not in the interest of humankind as a whole.

The creation of an International Space Agency, which includes most of the nations on the globe and is dedicated to protecting the interest of humankind as well as those of states and private actors, would provide an opportunity to resolve many of the current problems in outer space policies, including the issues of space debris and the protection of the outer space environment.

For the present research, the proposals and analysis are limited to the topics of space debris and the protection of the outer space environment.

Such an international organization should avoid becoming another forum for discussions of states but should have a supranational character and should be governed by people who are independent of national and corporate interests. This organization should not repeat the work of ITU and COPUOS. It should be established in such a way that it can be protected from the domination and influence of any particular country, group of countries or private organizations.

Presently, the public and academia rely on a few space-faring nations to share their discoveries in outer space, based on governmental compliance with Art. XI of the Outer Space Treaty. There are no monitoring mechanisms and space assets owned by an international organization that serves the interest of humankind and not a specific state or group of states. If an extraterrestrial biological matter is found, there are no guarantees that this discovery would be publicly shared with everyone, and that the research would be performed in the best interest of humankind. If such extraterrestrial life forms exist, there remains the risk of non-publicly disclosed research and engagement by states with the aim of pursuing national interests that seek to prevail over other countries. Such a scenario could be extremely dangerous for the interests of humankind and could lead to the exposure of dangerous biological organisms to Earth through the return of space objects or reentering of space debris.

Unless the interest of humankind is not incorporated and defended by a specific organization, outer space activities will continue to be pursued, taking into account only the national and corporate interests. This means a continuation of policies that aim for supremacy and domination in international space policy. Sharing of information will be conducted based on achieving strategic advantage over adversaries. Outer space resources will be unevenly shared on "first come, first served" rule.

The purpose of the International Space Agency is to prevent these negative effects that result from national confrontation and adversarial mentality. Instead, the future of outer space exploration and exploitation should be for the benefit of all human beings, all states, and with due regard to the environment of Earth and outer space, including celestial bodies. An important task for ISA should be to ensure that all results of space exploration are made public and that space activities are carried out in full transparency. Global transparency is required as each person needs to know what activities and discoveries are taking place in outer space. Transparency of information and independent monitoring of space objects are key aspects to avoid collisions of space objects in outer space and to minimize the creation of space debris.

The need for the International Space Agency to resolve the issue of space debris is strong because over the last five decades states have demonstrated that they are not willing to achieve deeper level of cooperation. In the last forty-five years states have shown that they are unwilling to clearly regulate all matters of international space law, including the issue of space debris. At present, there is no independent global monitoring mechanism that observes whether the countries fulfil the requirements of the "due regard" principle of other states, as set out in Article IX of the Outer Space Treaty. This is because states may not realize that their national interests are being negatively affected because there is no legal certainty about them being informed about all activities of other states and private organizations. Even if states were timely informed about these activities, there is no effective legal mechanism to ensure that another state will cease its national space activities that threaten foreign national interests. As analysed in Chapter II, the international consultation procedure provided in the same Article IX of the Outer Space Treaty has no obligation to achieve a specific result. This is the reason why countries do not resort to this procedure. The possibility to establish a Claims

Commission stipulated in the Liability Convention has also never been used.

The International Space Agency could also resolve the issue of space debris by introducing high safety standards and the legal obligation of states and private actors to use technologies that are friendly to the outer space environment. The new organization, which is not constrained by national policies and short-term interests, could set such rules that aim to protect the outer space environment and improve the safety of space activities in the long term.

4.3. Purpose and goals of the International Space Agency

The logical approach of establishing a global space agency is the next step to international cooperation in outer space. It would provide immense opportunities for resolving the present and future challenges in space exploration and exploitation, including minimising the risk of collisions between space objects and the production of dangerous space debris.

This new organization should clearly formulate its mission, long-term goals and objectives.

The mission of the International Space Agency should be to develop a global space program, which serves the interest of humankind, integrates the interests of all participating states and the scientific community and be the leader in outer space exploration and exploitation.

The first long-term goal is to adopt a common view of outer space, standards, and practices of outer space activities among nations and private organizations, including minimizing the threat from space debris.

The organization should accept states as its members only upon adopting a common view of outer space and accepting the standards and best practices for space activities as legally binding for the state and its corporations. The organization should achieve legally binding delimitation of airspace and outer space and common legally binding definitions of all relevant terms, including "space object" and "space debris" in outer space for its member states. These issues remain unresolved, and common international legally binding definitions exist only on a regional European level. A similar organizational approach is used in the enlargement of the European Union. The applicant states are attracted by the economic, financial and political benefits that the EU is providing for them, and they need to change their national legislation to be compliant with EU law and EU principles. This approach guarantees that states are voluntarily changing their legislation, and that new rules are not imposed upon them, and sovereignty is respected.

Through this new global space agency, many developing countries would be able to participate much more in the utilization of services from outer space and benefit from space research and investments in space projects. If the International Space Agency attracts developing states to become its members, this would become a guarantee that the development of their national space sector and space policies would be done with the care of the outer space environment and with minimal space debris production. There is no legal constraint on ISA and developed states to support financially and with technological transfer the developing states, so that they could adopt higher environmental standards.

The use of shared resources and infrastructure would lower the costs significantly for developing countries to participate in space activities.[473] The lack of coordinated efforts among less developed states results in not using the benefits from outer space services and becoming dependent on space-faring nations to have access to those services. The establishment of ISA would provide an opportunity for every nation to invest a relatively small amount of financial resources in the form of a fee, which is a certain percentage of their annual GDP or similar fair formula. With this funding and other source of income, the International Space Agency would be able to

473 Memme Onwudiwe & Kwame Newton. *Africa and the Artemis Accords: A Review of Space Regulations and Strategy for African Capacity Building in the New Space Economy*, 9.1. New Space, 43, (2021).

develop its own strategic space projects to function independently. Such projects should be a global navigational satellite system, space situational awareness system, remote sensing satellites, telecommunication satellites, space stations, systems for deorbiting space debris, and a lunar base.

The second long-term goal of the organization should be to include all nations in outer space research. ISA should aim to facilitate good relationships among states and common view on space activities, which are performed in the interest of humankind. This goal will be beneficial for the outer space environment and for the safety of space activities.

The concept of considering humanity as a separate legal subject is not new. Nenovski proposes the vision for humanity as a separate legal entity, justifying it with the need to protect human rights.[474] Trindade argues even that humankind has already emerged as a separate legal subject, coexisting with states.[475] I do not agree with this statement, as humankind does not have an organization that formulates and protects its interest. Such organization will be capable to formulate and manifest the will of humanity as a separate group.

Presently, there is no international or supranational organization that truly represents humanity and has the authority to act on its behalf. The UN Convention on the Law of the Sea stipulates that "*the area of the seabed and ocean floor and the subsoil thereof, beyond the limits of national jurisdiction, as well as its resources, are the common heritage of mankind, the exploration and exploitation of which shall be carried out for the benefit of mankind as a whole, irrespective of the geographical location of States*".[476] The International Seabed Authority is the organization through which state parties to the convention govern the area that is a common heritage of

---

474 Нено Неновски, Права на човека и права на гражданина. Към въпроса за съдържанието на понятията, 3 Правна мисъл, 28, (1993).
475 Antonio Trindade, International law for humankind: towards a new jus gentium, 275-276 (2010).
476 Preamble of the UN Convention on the Law of the Sea, Dec. 10, 1982, 1833 U.N.T.S. 397.

mankind.[477] The organization itself does not represent humankind, understood as an independent group, consisting of all human beings from past, present and future generations. It serves as a forum for the nations to manage those resources according to national interests not according to the interests of humankind.

The International Space Agency should take into consideration what should be included in the scope of the legal interest of humankind to distinguish it from national interests. Then outer space resources could be managed in the interest of humankind. One guiding principle with respect to outer space can be indicated here and it is consistent with the applicable international space law. It foresees that: "*Outer space is an area of all humankind, which is explored and used to advance the interests of humankind*".

Many positive outcomes could happen by the establishment of an organization that is governed in the interest of humankind and for the benefit of all nations. For the present research, its scope will be limited to outer space activities and the protection of outer space environment, including minimization of the dangerous effect of space debris.

Since the beginning of the space age, the outer space environment has been unnecessarily polluted by countries because non-functional satellites were left in orbit. If, in the early years of space exploration, this behaviour would be justified, then from the beginning of the 21st century, space activities threatened the safe use of outer space, the integrity of space objects, and the safety of human beings on Earth and in outer space. The legal obligation to return all non-functional space objects is a logical and necessary step that would allow ISA to protect the outer space environment. The current practice of all space-faring nations and corporations to abandon non-functional satellites in space is a cost-effective measure that is in line with their respectively short-term national and corporate interests. This behaviour is violating the interest of humankind, as it will make outer space hardly accessible and dangerous for future generations.

477 *Id.* Art.157 par.1.

Another goal of the International Space Agency should be the adoption of good practices and high safety standards for launching, and operating space objects.

In contemporary international relations, national conflicts or competition between states are also carried in outer space. The stronger the economic and energy competition is among states on Earth, the harsher it is in outer space.[478] Space exploration continues to evolve in first place because it provides a military advantage of one state over another. All space-faring states develop their national space policies and place objects in outer space according to their national interests, including national security. This has led to the situation in which many states and private organizations deploy their own space systems, which duplicate the performance of functions of other space systems. The desire for autonomy, self-sufficiency, and the preservation of technological advantage, which guarantees military dominance or independence, is the reason for the development of several projects for a global navigation satellite system. Today there are four global GPS systems operating in outer space instead of one with independent operational control. Because of this understanding of national interests, we see more than a hundred satellites in the Middle Earth Orbit instead of fewer than forty.

The creation of an International Space Agency would provide a much better example of compliance with the obligation of states to conduct outer space activities "for the benefit and in the interests of all countries", stipulated in Article I of the Outer Space Treaty. At the same time, the decisions of the organization and its plans for space activities would guarantee that the national activities of one state are not violating the sovereignty of another.

The third long-term goal of ISA should be to train its own team of experts, who can act adequately in a possible collision of space objects, including space debris on Earth. This would be the first team of specialists, who would have the duty to clean the high seas

---

478 В. В Буряк, Освоение космоса и международная безопасность. 24.1. Ученые записки Крымского федерального университета имени ВИ Вернадского. Социология. Педагогика. Психология, 172, (2011).

from returning space objects. Presently, space-faring nations are not allocating significant resources for such global environmental policies, because their focus is to govern their national territory.

The fourth long-term goal is to establish a decision-making process and governing body, which takes into consideration recommendations from the most advanced scientific organizations. Examples of such organizations are COSPAR and International Law Association. Such synergy between expert non-governmental perspectives and national and international political perspectives is needed to use available resources to develop international space policy management. Presently, plans for mining activities and projects of space tourism do not take into consideration all relevant scientific areas that those activities could hinder or permanently destroy. All relevant scientific areas of peaceful space research have to be considered. The optimal way of achieving such a comprehensive decision-making process is to apply holistic governance and include all relevant stakeholders in the discussion and decision-making process.[479]

In order to achieve the above-mentioned goals, the organization has to define its functions and establish an appropriate structure.

4.4. Functions of the International Space Agency

The functions of the International Space Agency should be established to adequately authorize the organization to achieve its ambitious goals and not overlap with the functions of other international organizations, such as the COPUOS and ITU. The functions of the organization have to correspond to its goals.

4.4.1. Adopting legally binding definitions

With the creation of the organization, it would emerge an opportunity for the legal regulation of all terms, including "space ob-

479 Aleksandar Milanov, *Holistic globalization—alternative socioeconomic model*, The Globalization Conundrum—Dark Clouds behind the Silver Lining, 310-321, (2019).

ject", "space debris", "lawful and unlawful contamination", "harmful interference", "peaceful use of outer space", and "militarization of outer space". The fact that these terms are not legally regulated shows the inability of states to complete this important task. The process of formulating the definitions should consider the proposals of different states, representatives of international legal doctrine, and experts in space sciences. The definitions should be a continuation of the development of current space law. Since many of the member states of the UN COPUOS were unwilling to provide information and participate in similar initiatives for clarification of legal definitions,[480] it is evident that a new approach is required, and different organization has to complete this task. Presently, the European Space Agency has adopted many definitions of the terms, which are binding for the member states in Europe. The International Space Agency could use this good example on a global level and adopt the terms for all its members.

4.4.2. Delimitation of the boundary between airspace and outer space

More than sixty years since the start of outer space activities, the boundary between airspace and outer space has not yet been legally determined. Different countries have different national interests and visions of the boundary between airspace and outer space.

A typical example of such differences was the provocative position of the equatorial states, as expressed in the Bogota Declaration of 1976 that states that "*they regard the geostationary orbit as an integral part of their sovereign territory*".[481]

Despite the withdrawal of the countries from this position, the declaration clearly demonstrates the differences in attitudes toward the extension of national sovereignty in desired orbits and the prin-

480 For example in relation to adopting legal definitions to aerospace objects - UN COPUOS, „Questionnaire on Possible Legal Issues with Regard to Aerospace Objects"; A/AC.105/787

481 The Declaration of the First Meeting of Equatorial Countries, Art.5 par.2, (December 3th 1976). [hereinafter Bogota Declaration]

ciples of delimitation of outer space and airspace. If the International Space Agency is established, the organization could lead the process of official legal delimitation of both areas. This would be beneficial for space debris management in LEO because there will not be conflicting views among the member states of the space debris being in airspace or in outer space.

The demarcation of this boundary would be carried out for all member states of the organization, and later ISA could negotiate with other states to adopt the same demarcation to achieve a unified global view of the legal boundaries of airspace and outer space.

4.4.3. Providing slots for space objects on principle "The most suitable orbit."

Determining the optimal way of distribution of slots in outer space so that the risk of collisions is minimized is key to improving space traffic management and decreasing the risk of collisions of space objects.

At present, states and private organizations select the slot in which they desire to place a satellite on a first-come, first-served basis.[482] This principle enables technologically and economically more advanced countries and private organizations to fill slots in outer space that are in correspondence with their interest without considering that these spaces can be used more rationally for the needs of other entities. The saturation of Low Earth Orbit with thousands of more satellites in the last few years exacerbates the problem further requiring an immediate change in the principle of slot distribution. Different slots in space are of different importance, and a higher perspective than the national one is needed to assess the most suitable location to place a space object to optimize the use of Earth orbits. Countries that launch objects into space are largely guided by the principles of national security, combined with the financial economy. Sometimes the launch is intended to be an international demonstration that the state possesses a certain technology.

482 Nandasiri Jasentuliyana, International space law and the United Nations, 267-277, (1999).

As noted in previous chapters, the current legal regime and practices have made it possible to abandon satellites in outer space once they are no longer functional. The absence of comprehensive regulation is leading to the accumulation of space debris for which no country or international organization is internationally liable before a collision happens.

The International Space Agency should take into consideration these issues among its members and should plan the launchings of space objects to be compliant with the principle of "the most suitable orbit". This principle includes calculations and analysis to find the optimal orbit for a space object without interfering with other space missions and even complimenting them whenever it is possible. If certain slots are more important for other purposes and for future projects, they should be preserved for them. ISA can advocate the implementation of the principle among all states but can make it legally binding only for its members. Duplication of programs should be avoided to decrease the number of objects in outer space, which would lower the risk of space debris creation. An important function of ISA should be to provide slots for satellites or other space objects, guided by the principle that the placement of the space object should not violate the interest of humankind but to further develop it. This means that the safest technology should be used.

The member states of ISA or their private organization, which are registered in the member states, should make an application stating the purpose of its mission and the tasks of the space object. The state could propose a certain orbit and present the justifications for its choice, but the final word should be of ISA to distribute the orbit, achieving the optimal fulfilment of the criteria, so that the services are provided as desired by the applicant. Such limitation is absolutely required to achieve successful long-term management of space traffic and provide optimal services for all member states. The criteria for choosing the most suitable orbit should be provided and explained in advance by ISA. Principles like "functionality", "safety", "economic efficiency", and "due regard to the interests of other member states" are extremely important, and they must be defined in detail for the member states and their private organizations. The implementation of this new principle of slot distribution would provide much more advanced planning of utilization of outer space and much better coordination of space activities in the long term. The avoidance of interference between the systems and the regard of other space projects would make outer space exploitation and exploration much safer from collisions and would minimize the creation of space debris.

Besides slot distribution, the International Space Agency must choose the optimal way for launching space objects to a specific location. This choice should also take into consideration the least polluting technology and method of sending the space object to the desired orbit or a celestial body. In addition, ISA would also monitor the operation of the object and, if needed, deorbit the space object to avoid polluting outer space, avoiding collisions, providing a slot for a different space object, or for another reason. Investments in space assets for deorbiting space systems are key to achieving this goal of the self-sufficiency of the organization to perform all required tasks.

4.4.4. Legal regulation for intentional destruction of space objects

The lack of a precise international legal mechanism to govern the question of whether a state is allowed to destroy space debris in space or a functioning space system of a foreign country under certain conditions creates potential tensions in international relations. The progress of the work of the Conference of Disarmament analysed in Chapter II clearly illustrates that an anti-satellite ban could not be achieved through conventional forms of international cooperation. The absence of a legally binding agreement for banning anti-satellite tests and other forms of planned destruction illustrates that the present international mechanisms and organizations are not sufficient for the resolution of this source of space debris creation. For this reason, the International Space Agency should implement internal rules regulating the intentional destruction of space objects. The general rule should be the one that is prescribed by most of the representative of the academia, researching outer space safety and anti-satellite weapons usage: The intentional destruction of space objects should be legally banned.

There are scenarios in which intentional destruction could be useful and needed to avoid a disaster, for example, if there is a chance for larger space debris to survive the lower levels of the atmosphere during return to Earth. In this case, intentional destruction would be positive for the safety of people on Earth. The International Space Agency should be the final authority to decide in which cases to perform such preventive measures. They should be implemented taking into consideration all safety requirements and the interests of all parties. This internal regulation of ISA is complementary to the present international space law. It is achieving the goal of predictability of space activities and non-usage of space technology for the destruction of space objects. The violation of the internal legal rule of the deliberate destruction of space objects without the permission of the International Space Agency would lead to internal sanctions for the member state. The most severe among those sanctions should be the freezing of the membership of the state.

The advantage of implementing internal regulation in an international organization over classical international legal liability is that the consequences for the state would apply much faster and in such a way that the state would experience the negative effect of its space industry and lack of utilization of outer space through ISA. Membership in ISA should be beneficial for a state, which is going to be a strong incentive for compliance with the internal rules of the organization.

4.4.5. Management of outer space traffic

To reduce the risk of space debris and to increase the safety of space exploration and exploitation, the International Space Agency should be authorized to regulate both access to outer space and traffic management. Evidence of this need is the current absence of rules on space traffic, the absence of an international organization that has an obligation to inform all actors, which could be affected by a movement of a space object, possible interference, and other relevant information to preserve the safety of space missions. The creation of a classical intergovernmental international organization would not protect the interests of humankind, the interests of the outer space environment and ultimately the long-term interests of states and private organizations. The integration of those interests can be achieved by establishing a sui generis International Space Agency.

The present monitoring of space traffic led to the incident between the satellites Iridium 33 and Cosmos 2251 in February 2009. This collision demonstrated that the lack of adequate legal regulation of space traffic is extremely dangerous for the space sector. It illustrated that states could not perform all necessary activities to protect the outer space environment and space systems. The space debris generated had significantly polluted outer space, but no state or international organization has an international responsibility for the destruction of the satellites, for polluting the outer space environment and for increasing the risk for space missions.

The International Space Agency should be tasked to monitor space traffic and inform the potentially affected parties in a timely manner. ISA should also inform third parties about possible collisions and support them to avoid accidents. This would increase the credibility of the organization to protect the interests of humankind and with the help of experts and technology to perform all necessary tasks diligently.

The International Space Agency should invest in its own technological equipment to locate, monitor, and remove space objects.

Outer space is now available to more and more private actors for space tourism. The safe conduct of this activity requires an international body to provide all the necessary information on the activities in outer space to ensure that safety measures are properly adopted and that the outer space environment is protected. The provision of non-pertinent information and other services for third parties, which are not members of the International Space Agency, could be professional and bound by a specific fee. The organs of the ISA should decide the appropriate policy of cooperation with third parties.

If a space object launched by ISA landed on any territory on Earth, including the high seas, a specially trained team of experts will be entitled to collect it and negotiate with the respective state on which territory the object is. This is very beneficial for developing nations and least developed countries, which are members of ISA, as they are not going to spend additional resources than their membership fee. For space-faring nations, which are not members of ISA, this could be expensive and time-consuming. It could lead to international liability and severe financial compensation.

Adequate space traffic management requires constant investments in better technology, maintenance of the existing systems, and training of personnel to recover space objects. This requires significant financial resources, and it could be achieved better by an organization that combines the resources of many states and private actors.

4.4.6. Adoption of mandatory safety standards for space objects

Governments' intentions to explore and exploit outer space could sometimes not be in correspondence with their technological capabilities. This is leading to an increase in risk of unfortunate incidents occurring during the launch of space objects. Secondly, if the space objects are not with optimal design, chemical structure and shielding, it would lead to easier destruction in outer space and the production of more space debris compared to technological innovations if used in these scientific areas.

There are not any international legal obligations of sovereign states to apply any safety standards and usage of specific technology for their space missions.

The International Space Agency should adopt safety standards that are legally binding on all states and private organizations, which would like to have access to outer space. Presently, as analysed in chapter II, the common practice is that states and private organizations comply with standards and guidelines, which are voluntary. An example of such legally non-binding measures is the COPUOS space debris mitigation guidelines and IADC guidelines.

Without legally binding obligations and without an existing working mechanism to impose sanctions, when necessary, the behaviour of states and private actors could not be coordinated properly, and unsafe exploitation and exploration of outer space will continue.

The requirement of the International Space Agency to improve and innovate safety standards and to support the creation of better technology for utilization of outer space would provide support for the scientific community to focus on those positive aspects of technological development instead of the advancement of weapons and defence systems. Under the present legal regime and international relations, technological developments in the space domain are often initiated and framed by military interests.[483]

The creation of a global space agency, which could function self-sufficiently with its own technological systems and which protects the interest of humankind, would lead to the allocation of more resources to scientific projects for peaceful use than states are willing to provide today.

An example of a scientific goal that should be stated by ISA is to develop technology that is capable of tracing small space debris that is presently undetectable. As was analysed in chapter I, particles under 4 cm cannot be detected presently in Low-Earth orbit, and particles bigger than 1 cm could destroy a space object.

Improving shield protection and detection of small space objects should be a priority task for ISA to improve the safety of outer space activities and minimize the risk of space debris.

If ISA achieves this goal and the technology for shielding is improved, then it should adopt a legally binding standard for its use among its member states to guarantee better protection of the space systems.

483 Christian Brünner & Alexander Soucek, eds. *Outer Space in Society*, 8 Politics and Law, 180, (2012).

4.4.7. Reaction at risk of back contamination

In the late 1950s, NASA established a planetary quarantine program and a special planetary quarantine office.[484] This program aims to prevent or minimize the spread of infection to extraterrestrial worlds where life may exist.[485] The main focus of the program is to prevent forward contamination[486] from Earth of extraterrestrial life forms in outer space. In July 1969, NASA also published national measures to protect the Earth from extraterrestrial contamination, which established the policy of the US space agency to protect the Earth's environment from adverse changes and contamination resulting from the return of personnel or space objects.[487] Robinson rightly pointed out that the publication of these national quarantine regulations should have been done much earlier, and there was a delay of more than ten years.[488]

It is important to emphasize that in implementing these measures, NASA "complies with security obligations, restrictions and safeguards that are in the interest of national security."

I believe that the protection of the environment and the life of all human beings on Earth should not come second to the national interests of any country, which is why it is imperative to create a global organization that intergrates the interests of all member states with the interest of all humankind.

Such an organization should adopt a set of global measures, including global quarantine protocols to protect Earth and life on it from back contamination.

---

484 Charles R. Phillips, *The planetary quarantine program: Origins and achievements, 1956-1973.* Vol. 4902, 21-33, Scientific and Technical Information Office, National Aeronautics and Space Administration, (1974).

485 Id.

486 Stephen Gorove, *Pollution and Outer Space: A Legal Analysis and Appraisal*, 5 NYUJ Int'l L. & Pol., 55, (1972).

487 George Robinson, *Article IX of the Outer Space Treaty:Extraterrestrial Back Contamination, the U.S. Constitution, and the "Politics" of U.S. Regulatory Authority*, EILENE Galloway Symposium, Cosmos Club, Washington, 6, (2010).

488 *Id.* at 6-7

National measures are taken in correspondence with the national interests of a country, which, as analysed above, are not always in line with the interests of humankind. Other examples of such discrepancies are budgetary savings in creating better procedures for protection, lack of significant investments in research, and classifying information about space objects and about specific activities in outer space. In the national interests of some countries, the spread of the infection among the population of citizens of other countries can even be considered acceptable.

Each quarantine protocol includes the detention, examination, and decontamination for an indefinite period of time of people and property, based on the likelihood that an infection that is suspected to be dangerous may spread. These restrictions predispose national quarantine protocols to become legal instruments through which human rights could be violated. A global quarantine protocol and other measures should be planned by ISA to protect the interest of humankind, which means not violating the set of human rights of all human beings.[489]

The adoption of all measures that are limiting the freedom of movement of people and are limiting other human rights is very important to comply with the principles of derogation of rights: a temporary exception, which measures are prescribed by law and information about the planned measures is sent in advance to the relevant body of monitoring human rights.

At present, there is no adequate international legal framework to protect against the contamination of the Earth and its entire biological species from dangerous outer space organisms. One possible way for such organisms to get to Earth is through space debris that survived entering the atmosphere. In Chapter I was illustrated that that the contamination of Earth with such organisms is a real threat, which makes it necessary for ISA to create a global planetary quarantine protocol for the Earth, which

---

489 Aleksandar Milanov & George Penchev, *The Need for Establishing a New United Nations Body to Protect Earth from Back Contamination and Outer Space from Forward Contamination*, 9 IJCS, 925, 929, (2020).

would be binding on its members and open for accession by third parties.

Purposefully, the proposal does not contain a recommendation for the adoption of an international agreement, respectively the preparation of an international quarantine protocol, for the following reasons:

In the first place, countries have different visions in terms of environmental protection and treatment of people. The national interests of the leading states are based on the desire for supremacy over other states, and there is a danger that the adversarial states will not cooperate adequately to quickly control a possible infection from space.

Second, the countries that have the potential to respond adequately to such danger are less than other countries. An adequate response to a crisis of this magnitude implies well-trained professionals working in a team, who possess scientific knowledge in various fields and who have modern technology to prevent the spread of the infection. Most developing countries do not have a national policy to respond to such a problem. The untimely and erroneous response of states to space contamination can endanger the lives of many people, including those outside that country.

Thirdly, if an infected extraterrestrial organism lands on the high seas, where no country has exclusive jurisdiction to act, it is not certain that countries will commit to preventing possible contamination, as sending teams and equipment will be costly. The International Space Agency should be responsible for the training of a recovery team, which must also act in the high seas. The existence of such a team of experts, capable of acting on a global level should not be limited to the member states of ISA. If states, which are not members of ISA, are willing to recover space debris and implement quarantine procedures for the space object and affected area, ISA should be able to provide assistance and guidance when asked.

The introduction of national quarantine protocol procedures by the United States and other economically developed countries, and the achievements of organizations such as the International Council of Scientific Unions, COSPAR, and the World Health Organization are positive steps that create good and bad practices. However, these national steps are insufficient to ensure the safety of the whole Earth. Robinson also stressed that it is imperative that national measures for adequate protection and threat mitigation procedures should be adopted worldwide.[490] I agree with this conclusion, believing that the most appropriate legal mechanism for realizing this goal and resolving the problem of this potential threat is the creation of a sui generis organization that acts on a global level and is capable of adopting global quarantine protocol procedures.

In order to carry out its function of protecting the Earth from space contamination, teams of scientists from all over the world (astrobiologists, chemists, ecologists, lawyers, human rights specialists, and others) should be brought together at the International Space Agency to act accordingly and serve the interest of humankind. Those teams should have a shared jurisdiction to act on the territory of a member state and its respective governmental structures. These teams should also act on the high seas if in these territories there is a suspicion of contamination from outer space. The selection of these scientists working for ISA should be made based on clear non-discriminatory criteria, and it should provide professionalism in the respective field and readiness to work in the interest of all humankind and of the member states of ISA.

The global quarantine protocol should contain a system of rules that ensure, that the infection is not spread and regulate the relations between ISA and its member states and ISA and non-member states.

Firstly, among these rules should be included an obligation of ISA to inform its member states about new discoveries in outer space, the status of activities and information about the orbit of all monitored space objects, including space debris. Such information should be provided to third parties, including states, academia and the general public, as stipulated in art. XI of Outer Space Treaty.

490 George Robinson, *Interplanetary contamination: the ultimate challenge for environmental and constitutional lawyers?*, 31.1. J.S.L. Issue, 119, (2005).

The difference is that article XI provides that the information should be provided "*to the greatest extent feasible and practicable, of the nature, conduct, locations and results of such activities.*"[491] The information to the member states should be provided immediately, and in full capacity.

Secondly, ISA and the member states must define the nature of their shared jurisdiction when ISA experts are working in the territory of a member state. In my opinion, the ISA team should be led by a representative of the government for the recovery or decontamination of a space object. In this way, expert knowledge, technology, and appropriate procedures would be available for the member state to use in order to act accordingly to the threat.

Thirdly, the ISA team would be able to conduct a threat assessment together with the experts from the member state and adopt the most appropriate containment measures to avoid the distribution of the threat to other countries.

4.4.8. Adoption of rules of safe exploration and exploitation of outer space and celestial bodies

In addition to the danger of infecting the Earth with extraterrestrial organisms, there is a danger of contamination and pollution of the celestial bodies, which can be detrimental to the outer space environment.

The "polluter pay principle", stipulated in principle 16 of the Rio Declaration, should be further developed by ISA in its internal rules. Specifically, clarifications should be made on what type of pollution is legally allowed because of the current development of technologies and what type of pollution should not be legally allowed. Although it is allowed under international space law rules, the creation of unnecessary space debris in outer space, including on celestial bodies should be qualified as prohibited pollution in the internal rules of the organization. ISA would have to take action to remove the space debris and clean the respective area of outer space.

---

491 Outer Space Treaty, Art. XI, 1967

If member states and their private organizations are polluting the outer space environment that stands in violation of the internal rules and standards of ISA, they should remove the produced debris. If they do not possess the technology to do that, they could use the resources of ISA, according to the conditions of the organization.

The International Space Agency should establish and monitor compliance among the member states with the internal rules of space exploration to minimize pollution of outer space. The experiments that countries do in outer space are very often inconsistent with the interests of humankind and the protection of the outer space environment. An example is the competition for testing nuclear weapons in space between the USSR and the USA.

Some of these nuclear tests in space were performed by the United States and the Soviet Union between 1958 and 1962, in particular the "Argus" series of tests by the United States.[492] And the series of tests "K Proekt" of USSR.[493]

In 1963, with the entry into force of the Treaty Banning Nuclear Weapons Tests in the Atmosphere, Outer Space and Under Water, these tests were banned only for the USA and USSR, which are States Parties to the Treaty, but not for those states that are not members of it.

The norm of Article IV of the Outer Space Treaty prohibits the launch of all types of weapons of mass destruction into orbit around the Earth and on celestial bodies but applies only to states that have ratified the treaty. Even if we assume that all states are bound by an international legal ban on nuclear weapons testing from this treaty or from the existing norm of international legal custom, a violation of this international legal prohibition will entail sanctions that the

---

492 Argus I – 27.08.1958, height 200km; Argus II – 30.08.1958 height 240km; Argus III 06.09. 1958 height 540 km, SMDC Monitoring Research [http://www.rdss.info/database/nucex/report/explosion.pdf]

493 Projects K-1 and K-2 – 27.10.1961, height respectively 300 km and 150 km; K-3 – 22.10.1962,height 290 km; K-4 – 26.10.1962, height 150 km; K-5 – 01.11.1962, height 59 km, which is lower than the commonly accepted boundary between airspace and outer space of 100 km, SMDC Monitoring Research [http://www.rdss.info/database/nucex/report/explosion.pdf].

state may be willing to bear. The reason is that the government can determine how many and which of its citizens will distribute the burdens of these sanctions. Denouncing international treaties that are part of the global architecture of security has already been done. An example is the US withdrawal from the Intermediate-Range Nuclear Forces Treaty, announce on August 2nd, 2019.

For example, a country like North Korea may decide to test its nuclear weapons not only on its territory but also in outer space. This legal situation creates potential risks for other nuclear tests to be performed in outer space and this is not in the interest of humankind. We are witnessing how international liability and sanctions are not capable of guiding the government of North Korea into complying with the basic principles of the UN Charter and other international legal norms.

ISA should have the authority to determine which studies and experiments are permitted and do not harm the outer space environment. Respectively, ISA should be able to ban experiments that could cause serious damage.

4.5. Structure of the International Space Agency

The creation of an adequate structure for the International Space Agency is crucial for properly achieving the ambitious goals and execution of all tasks. In my proposal, ISA should integrate the interests of member states and humankind. The representatives of the organization and the expert teams should be independent of any national and corporate interests that might convolute their actions. For this reason, my proposal of the structure of the organization is developed in three separate bodies. These are 1) General Assembly; 2) the Executive Board; 3) Supervisory Authority.

Member states logically should form the General Assembly, and its purpose should be to determine the goals of ISA, overall budget, and membership fees, and to select the member of the Executive Board, according to predetermined criteria, which should make sure that the most qualified candidates are filling the positions.

The Executive Board should be able to function independently from the General Assembly, and its director should not become a "Servant of the Member States", as is the UN Secretary-General.[494] The Executive Board should be free to choose the projects and missions with which to achieve the declared goals of the GA. The Executive Board should take into consideration the national policies of the states and their national interests, but its actions should serve with priority the interests of humankind. The Executive Board should be able to adopt the internally binding rules and standards that must be confirmed by the General Assembly with a qualified majority, for example, 2/3 of the member states. The Executive Board should be capable of finding other sources of funding besides the fees from the members of ISA. It should also be able to establish supplementary organs and institutes to fulfil its tasks.

The Supervisory Authority should include a representative of the most qualified international scientific organizations and be approved by the General Assembly. Such organizations are the Committee on Space Research, the International Council for Science, the Space Law Committee of the International Law Association, the International Standardization Organization, the International Science and Technology Center, the International Astronomical Union, and others. The function of the members of the Supervisory Authority should be to monitor whether the activities of the Executive Board are in correspondence with the best scientific practices. The decision-making process of ISA should provide the opportunity for the Supervisory Authority to veto the most important decisions of the Executive Board and to propose better options for the Board. After that, the Executive Board should adopt a new decision, which takes into consideration the recommendations of the Supervisory Authority. The second decision could be in force if it is not vetoed by 2/3 of the members of the Supervisory Authority. If a second veto is made to the decision, an internal dispute settlement mechanism should be applied to find the most com-

494 Vesselin Popovski, Reforming and innovating the United Nations Security Council. Hague Institute for Global Justice, 9, (2015).

prehensive solution, which should be implemented later by the Executive Board.

The role of the private actors should be only as contractors of the Executive Board, when necessary.

In my opinion, such a *sui generis* structure is needed to include all relevant interests and integrate them accordingly.

It should be noted that an organization that protects the interests of humankind and aims to operate with its own space assets, budget, and internal rules, should not be established within the UN system of bodies. This is because the UN is an international organization in which national interests are reconciled and cohered. The arithmetic sum of all national interests is by no means identical to that of all humankind,[495] and an independent decision-making process is key for the proper functioning of the International Space Agency.

A typical example of the discrepancy between the two types of interests (the sum of national and that of humankind) is the exploitation of the environment and the attitude to natural resources. All countries exploit the resources on their territory, as well as the resources that are the common heritage of all mankind, depending on their own national environmental and development policies, and the economic benefits of these resources are distributed on a commercial basis, which does not mean that every human being can benefit from them. The resources of Earth and outer space are not used and properly managed with respect to the interests of future generations of human beings. Visible proof of this statement is the increased risk from space debris for all space activities.

Another example of a major contradiction between national interests and the interest of humankind is the recourse to military action to resolve disputes. From the point of view of humankind, any war is unacceptable because humans are suffering and dying, regardless of their citizenship, ethnicity, or political views. The International Space Agency should have the goal to promote peace among nations and peaceful utilization of outer space.

495 Aleksandar Milanov, *International legal status of humankind*, 2 Bulgarian Journal of International Law, 94, 2009

The structure of ISA and the decision-making process should not be a result of a compromise between space-faring nations and should not become a "hostage" of national interests. The structural challenges that COPUOS is experiencing have shown that the organization could never produce legally binding acts as long as the USA and other countries are not willing to comply with such a legal framework.

4.6. Relationship between International Space Agency, national space agencies and private organizations

International Space Agency should establish different types of relationships with nations that are member states and with third countries. The International Space Agency should have jurisdiction and control of the space systems that it launches. The participation of the European states in the European Space Agency does not result in the dismantling of their national space programs and agencies. Similarly, the International Space Agency would not preclude the opportunity for nations to develop their own space programs and national space projects. The relationship between ISA and the national space programs and national space laws of the member states should include at least the following principles:

1) The member states should apply for their national space program the same standards and practices as the International Space Agency. Every member state of ISA must apply the same interpretation of the international legal framework and the definitions and interpretations that are adopted by ISA.

2) The membership of a state in the International Space Agency should provide much more benefits for it than individual space projects. This membership should require its member states to reform their space legislation and space programs accordingly. The continual refusal of a state to adopt those legal requirements should result in a measure of freezing its membership and access to the benefits of the ISA space program. This would serve as a guarantee that all states would fulfil their commitment to inter-

national legal treaties, updates of standards, implementation of good practices, and other obligations that the states had previously declared.

3) The private actors registered in the member states of ISA should be closely monitored by the national states and by a specialized monitoring body of ISA. Since the standards and other obligations are mandated by ISA, the organization should be allowed to monitor whether they are properly implemented by private organizations.

4) The ISA representatives should work in the spirit of cooperation and initiate dialogue and projects with many states. At the same time, ISA leadership should be acknowledging the possibility of all states that are not members of ISA to join the organization in the future, if they are willing to accept the principles and internal rules of the organization.

The policy of open gates toward all states is logical, considering the aim of ISA to protect the interest of humankind. ISA should aim to become the leading space agency in the world and should invest in those critical systems that would make the organization self-sufficient. This means that in conducting projects with third countries and their private organizations, ISA should not rely on foreign technology for a long period of time. ISA could provide paid services for third parties, if their space mission is not violating international space law and ISA regulations. With respect to developing countries, which are not members of the organization, ISA should establish different forms of cooperation and capacity-building mechanisms, such as associate agreements, which could "pave the road" for future membership of the country.

The role of private organizations should be limited to subcontractors and businesses in the field of the space sector, which are regulated by states. Their activities should be closely monitored by national space agencies, as mentioned in art. VI of the Outer Space Treaty. The private organizations with headquarters in member states of ISA should also be monitored by ISA.

4.7. Political Factors for the Institutionalization of the International Space Agency

National policies and international relations are mutable and dynamic. The present political factors for the emergence of ISA indicate that the leading space-faring nation – the USA-- would not be willing to support such an initiative. If the USA is not leading the organization or if it is not capable of significantly affect its institutional mechanisms, it is expected that the USA is not going to support the establishment of ISA. The reason is that ISA would compete with Artemis Program and other US space projects.

The failed proposals of Chinese, Russian and some European delegations to adopt global legal ban on antisatellite testing in outer space is due to the vision of the USA that such complete legal ban would jeopardize their national security and would eliminate a strategic military advantage that USA has over other states. The result is higher risk for destruction of space assets and more dangerous space debris for all states. This example illustrates that new international space treaties and new international organizations in space are possible after major shift in the understanding of national interests in the USA or with the exclusion of the USA as a founding member state of a future treaty or international organization.

The deterioration of the work of the COPUOS, the lack of progress in the Conference on Disarmament, the absence of attempts to set an agenda for the next UNISPACE conference signifies that there is lack of political will in the USA to resolve the international legal problems in space law, including the major topic of space debris regulation.

The attempts of the USA to dominate in international relations and to set plans for colonization and mining of celestial bodies are in contradiction to Art. II of the Outer Space Treaty. This provides an opportunity for other space-faring nations like Russia, China, possibly India, African countries, South American countries and even European countries to look for an alternative form of leadership that is based on equality and service of interests of all member states and the interest of humankind. This alternative could be the International Space Agency.

The European example of establishing a regional space agency could be very useful in analysing the good and bad practices since the ESA's emergence in 1975. The key principle for establishing ISA should be the independent members of the Executive Board not to be influenced by conflicting international relations of states. The organization should aim to adopt comprehensive policies to protect the outer space environment from dangerous space debris.

Conclusion

The goal of achieving a safe outer space environment and mitigating the risks from space debris is impossible without achieving the improvement of international cooperation between competing space-faring nations. The present research establishes the legal gaps in international regulation, including the absence of legal definitions, and blocked international processes to adopting needed international legal norms. There is no comprehensive international legal regulation of the space debris issue. The reasons for its absence are many, but the most important one is the competition between states, which degrades the level of international cooperation. The need for states to synergize their interests with those of humankind would not be achieved as long as the mentality to compete prevails over the attitude to work together.

The identification of the different types of space debris and the need for a separate approach to their legal regulation is a key finding of the research. An analysis is made of the weakness of international cooperation, and comprehensive proposals are provided to address and overcome them. Conclusions are made on the effectiveness and the direction of work of the leading international organizations on the topic. Proposals to improve the regulation of space traffic are analysed together with the need to adopt mandatory standards for launching space objects and ensuring the protection of the outer space environment and the safety of people on Earth. In the research is proposed the adoption of new international rules and principles to serve as a minimum standard, is mandatory for all space actors–

states and private corporations. The implementation of the principle "The most suitable orbit" instead of the present rule "First come, first served" with respect to the distribution of orbital slots could pave the way for holistic space traffic management and better use of Earth's orbit. The author concludes that to achieve a safe outer space environment, all identified legal gaps have to be addressed at the same time with the adoption of a new sui generis global organization, namely the International Space Agency. This approach will lead not only to the legal regulation of space debris issues but could provide an answer for the principles of future exploitation of celestial bodies and their resources.

Bibliography

Publications in Cyrillic (Bulgarian and Russian)

1. Анастасов, Ангел. "Договорът за всеобхватна забрана на ядрените опити- въпроси на влизането в сила и временното изпълнение." Изд. Научни трудове на Института за Правни Науки, том V (2008):5-27.

2. Буряк, В. В. "Освоение космоса и международная безопасность." Ученые записки Крымского федерального университета имени ВИ Вернадского. Социология. Педагогика. Психология 24, no. 1 (2011).

3. Василевская, Э. "Правовой статус природных ресурсов луны и планет." Наука, (1978).

4. Василевская, Э. "Правовые аспекты обеспечения безопасности полетов в космос; Международное научное сотрудничество и правовые вопросы освоения космоса". Академии наук СССР, (1984).

5. Васьков, С.А. , Малков, С.П. "Нормативно-правовое обеспечение космической деятельности". СПбГУАБ, (2003).

6. Верещетин В.С. "Несостоятельность американских правовых концепций применения силы в космическом пространстве. Американский империализм-нарушитель международного права." Москва, Издательство ВНИИТЭМР, (1985).

7. Вылегжанин, А. Н., Юзбашян, М. Р., & Алексеев, М. А."Международно-правовые перспективы использования

природных ресурсов Луны и других небесных тел.” *Горный информационно-аналитический бюллетень,* (2021): 155-172.

8. Ганев, Маргарит. Специализираните организации от системата на Организацията на обединените нации, Институт по международно право, София, (2005).

9. Жуков, Генадий. “40 лет договору о принципах деятельности государств по исследованию и использованию космического пространства, включая Луну и другие небесные тела.” Российский ежегодник международного права, Москва, (2007).

10. Колосов, Юрий; Кузнецов, В.И. “Международное право” Изд. НОРМА, Москва, (2004).

11. Колосов, Юрий Михайлович, and Сергей Геннадьевич Сташевский. *Борьба за мирный космос: правовые вопросы*. “ Международные отношения, 2014.

12. Константинов, Емил. “Международноправни проблеми на практическото използуване на Космоса”. Бюл. СЮБ № 4 (1982): 92-98

13. Константинов, Емил. “Международноправно ограничаване на милитаризирането на Космоса.” Междунар. отнош. 5, (1986): 12-21.

14. Малеев, Юрий Николаевич. “Военное использование космоса в интересах международной безопасности.” *Актуальные проблемы современного международного права. Материалы межвузовской научно-практической конференции/ отв. ред. АЯ Капустин, АХ Абашидзе*. (2005).

15. Малков, С. П. “Международное космическое право: учеб. пособие. СПб.” (2002).

16. Неновски, Нено. “Права на човека и права на гражданина (Към въпроса за съдържанието на понятията).” Правна мисъл 3, (1993).

17. Рубанов, Август. Взаимосвязь гражданского права России и международного космического права: вопросы теории, Государство и право №4, Москва, (2006).

Publications in English

18. Akers, Agatha. "To infinity and beyond: Orbital space debris and how to clean it up." *U. La Verne L. Rev*. 33 (2011): 285.

19. Akhmetov, Vladimir, Vadym Savanevych, and Evgen Dikov. "Analysis of the Indian ASAT test on 27 March 2019." arXiv preprint arXiv:1905.09659 (2019).

20. Ansdell, Megan. "Active Space Debris Removal: Needs, Implications and Recommendations for today's geopolitical environment." *Journal of Public & International Affairs* 21 (2010).

21. Atney-Yurdin, Irene. Space debris legal research guide. *Pace yearbook of international law*. Vol. 3 (1991): 167-198.

22. Arbatov, Alexey. "Arms control in outer space: The Russian angle, and a possible way forward." Bulletin of the Atomic Scientists 75, no. 4 (2019): 151-161.

23. Baker, Howard. *Space debris: legal and policy implications*. Springer, 1989.

24. Baslar, Kemal. *The concept of the common heritage of mankind in international law*. Vol. 30. Martinus Nijhoff Publishers, 1998.

25. Beard, Jack M. "Soft Law's Failure on the Horizon: The International Code of Conduct for Outer Space Activities." U. Pa. J. Int'l L. 38 (2016): 335.

26. Benkö, Marietta, and Kai-Uwe Schrogl. "Space Debris in the United Nations: Aspects of Law and Policy." In Second European Conference on Space Debris, vol. 393. 1997.

27. Benko, Marietta, Gerhard Gruber, and Kai Uwe Schrogl. "UN Committee on the Peaceful Uses of Outer Space: Adoption of Principles Relevant to the Use of Nuclear Power Sources in Outer Space and Other Recent Developments," ZLW 42. (1993): 35.

28. Benkö, Marietta, Kai-Uwe Schrogl, Denise Digrell, and Esther Jolley, eds. *Space law: current problems and perspectives for future regulation*. Vol. 2. Eleven International Publ., 2005.

29. Bhat, Sandeepa, and V. Mohan. "Anti Satellite Missile Testing: A Challenge to Article IV of the Outer Space Treaty." *NUJS L.*

Rev. 2 (2009): 205-212.

30. Bhat, Sandeepa. "A Discourse on the Remodeling of Ila Model Law on Nation Space Legislation." *J. Space L.* 41 (2017): 1-28.

31. Bird, Robert C - Procedural challenges to environmental regulation of space debris. / In: *American business law journal*; vol. 40. 3 (2003): 635-685.

32. Bordunov, Vitaliy. "Rights of States as Regards Outer Space Objects." *Proceedings of the 24th Colloquium on the Law of Outer Space*. 1981

33. Böckstiegel, Karl-Heinz / ILA Draft Convention on Space Debris In: Zeitschrift für Luft- und Weltraumrecht; vol. 43.4 (1994): 395-400.

34. Brearley, A. Reflections upon the notion of liability: the instances of Kosmos 954 and space debris, Journal of space law, Volume 34 issue 2 (2008): 291-319.

35. Brünner, Christian, and Alexander Soucek, eds. Outer space in society, politics and law. Vol. 8. Springer Science & Business Media, 2012.

36. Carns, Marc G. "Consent Not Required: Making the Case that Consent is Not Required under Customary International Law for Removal of Outer Space Debris Smaller than 10CM." AFL Rev. 77(2017): 173.

37. Castronuovo, M. Marco, Active space debris removal—A preliminary mission analysis and design. Acta Astronautica, 69(9-10) (2011): 848-859.

38. Cheng, Bin. "The commercial development of space: the need for new treaties." J. Space L. 19 (1991): 17.

39. Cheng, Bin. Studies in international space law. Clarendon Press, 1997.

40. Cheng, Bin. "Article VI of 1967 revisited: 'International Responsibility', 'National activities', and 'The appropriate state'.", Journal of Space Law, issue 26/1, (1998): 7-32.

41. Cheng, Bin. "The legal status of outer space and relevant issues: Delimitation of outer space and definition of peaceful use."

J. Space L. 11 (1983): 89.

42. Chimni, Bhupinder S. "International institutions today: an imperial global state in the making." European Journal of International Law 15.1 (2004): 1-37.

43. Christol, Carl Q. "International liability for damage caused by space objects." American Journal of International law 74.2 (1980): 346-371.

44. Cocca, María de las Mercedes Esquivel. Liability and responsibility for space debris, abandoned and unregistered space objects, and for damages caused during rescue operations. *Proceedings of the 43rd Colloquium on the Law of Outer Space* 43 (2001): 359-368.

45. DeLuca, L. T., Bernelli, F., Maggi, F., Tadini, P., Pardini, C., Anselmo, L., ... & Chiesa, S. "Active space debris removal by a hybrid propulsion module." Acta Astronautica 91 (2013): 20-33.

46. Dembling, Paul G., and Swadesh S. Kalsi. "Pollution of Man's Last Frontier: Adequacy of Present Space Environmental Law in Preserving the Resource of Outer Space." Netherlands International Law Review 20.2 (1973): 125-146.

47. Diederiks-Verschoor, L.H. Legal aspects of environmental protection in outer space regarding debris, *Proceedings of the 30th Colloquium of Law of Outer space*. 1987.

48. Diederiks-Verschoor, Isabella HP. "The Legal Aspects of Space Activities with Potentially Harmful Effects on the Earth and Space Environments." *Proceedings of the 15th Colloquium of Law of Outer Space*. 1972.

49. Diederiks-Verschoor, Isabella Henrietta Philepina, and Vladimir Kopal. *An introduction to space law*. Kluwer Law International BV, 2008.

50. Fernandez, Sanz. "Space station and space debris." *Proceedings of the 42nd Colloquium on the Law of Outer Space*. 1999.

51. Forshaw, Jason L., et al. "The active space debris removal mission RemoveDebris. Part 1: From concept to launch." *Acta Astronautica* 168 (2020): 293-309.

52. Goehring, John S. "Can We Address Orbital Debris with

the International Law We Already Have? An Examination of Treaty Interpretation and the Due Regard Principle." *J. Air L. & Com.* 85 (2020): 309.

53. Golrounia, Ali Akbar; Bahrami, Mohsen - The draft of the International Law Association for a Convention on Space Debris (Buenos Aires): can it meet the needs of the 21st century/ In: *Proceedings of the 42rd Colloquium on the Law of Outer Space* 39 (1996): 223-228.

54. Gorove, Stephen. "Interpreting article II of the outer space treaty." *Fordham L. Rev.* 37 (1968): 349.

55. Gorove, Stephen. "Pollution and Outer Space: A Legal Analysis and Appraisal." *NYUJ Int'l L. & Pol.* 5 (1972): 53

56. Gorove, Stephen. Toward a Clarification of the Term Space Object-An International Legal and Policy Imperative. *J. Space L. 21* (1993): 11.

57. Hacket, George T. "*Space debris and the corpus iuris spatialis*." Vol.2. Atlantica Séguier Frontières, 1994.

58. Hall, Loretta. "The history of space debris." (2014).

59. Hall, R. Cargill. "Comments on salvage and removal of man-made objects from outer space." *Journal of Air Law and Commerce* 33.2 (1967): 288.

60. Hays, Peter. *United States military space: Into the twenty first century*, USAF institute for national security studies, USAF Academy. Air university press, 2002.

61. Hermida, Julian. *Legal basis for a national space legislation*. Vol. 3. Springer Science & Business Media, 2004.

62. Hitchens Theresa, U.S.-Sino Relations in Space: From "War of Words" to Cold War in Space?" *China Security* 3.1 (2007): 12-30.

63. Hobe, Stephan, Geradine Meishan Goh, and Julia Neumann. "Space Tourism Activities-Emerging Challenges to Air and Space law. " Journal of Space Law 33 (2007): 359.

64. Hobe, Stephan. "Space Debris: A proposal for its international legal regulation." *Proc. 34th Colloquium L. Outer Space*, published by AIAA, 1992

65. Hobe, Stephan, and Jan Helge Mey. "UN Space Debris Mitigation Guidelines." *ZLW* 58 (2009): 388.

66. Hobe, Stephan."Common Heritage of Mankind – An Outdated Concept in International Space Law*?" Proceedings of the 42nd Colloquium on the Law of Outer Space*. (1998): 271–277.

67. Hurwitz, Bruce. The legality of space militarization. North Holland, 1986

68. Hurwitz, Bruce A. "Israel and the Law of Outer Space." Israel Law Review 22, no. 4 (1988): 457-466.

69. Imburgia, Joseph S. "Space debris and its threat to national security: a proposal for a binding international agreement to clean up the junk." Vand. J. Transnat'l L. 44 (2011): 589.

70. Jakhu, Ram S. "The legal status of the geostationary orbit." VII Annals Air & Space L. (1982): 333.

71. Jakhu, Ram S. and Singh, Karan, "Space Security and Competition for Radio Frequencies and Geostationary Slots" ZLW 58 (2009): 74

72. Jakhu, Ram S. and Paul Stephen Dempsey, eds. *Routledge Handbook of Space Law*. Taylor & Francis, 2016.

73. Jakhu, Ram S. "The Future of the Outer Space Treaty." Fifty Years of the Outer Space Treaty, IDSA, 2017

74. Jakhu, Ram S. and Joseph N. Pelton, eds. Global Space Governance: an international study. Springer International Publishing, 2017

75. Jakhu, Jasani and McDowell, Critical issues related to registration of space objects and transparency of space activities, Acta Astronautica. 143 (2018): 406-420

76. Jasentuliyana, Nandasiri. *International space law and the United Nations*, Kluwer Law International, 1999

77. Jasentuliyana, Nandasiri. "Space debris and international law." *J. Space L.* 26 (1998): 139.

78. Jasentuliyana, Nandasiri. "Environmental impact of space activities: an international law perspective." *Proceedings of the 26th Symposium on the Law of Space*. 1984.

79. Jiang, Yu. "Debris cloud of India anti-satellite test to Micro-

sat-R satellite." *Heliyon* 6.8 (2020): e04692.

80. Johnson, N. "A new look at nuclear power sources and space debris." *The Fourth European Conference on space debris.* 2005.

81. Johnson, Nicholas L., and Heiner Klinkrad. "Space debris environment remediation concepts." *5th European Conference on Space Debris*. No. JSC-17611. 2009.

82. Julienne, Marc. "China's Ambitions in Space: The Sky's the Limit." *Études de l'Ifri* (2021): 23-25.

83. Kaul, Ranjana. "Relevance and Limitations of Outer Space Treaty in 21st Century". *50 years of the Outer Space Treaty, IDSA.* 2017

84. Kellman, Barry. "Space: The Fouled Frontier: Adjudicating Space Debris as an International Environmental Nuisance." *J. Space L.* 39 (2013): 227.

85. Kim, Doo Hwan. "Proposal for Establishing an International Court of Air and Space Law" *ZLW* 59 (2010): 362.

86. Koch, Jonathan Sydney. "Institutional framework for the province of all mankind: Lessons from the international seabed authority for the governance of commercial space mining." *Astropolitics* 16.1 (2018): 1-27.

87. Konstantinov, Emil. Outer Space Environment and Its Legal Protection. *Proceedings of the 32nd Colloquium on the Law of Outer Space*. 1989

88. Koplow, David A. "ASAT-isfaction: Customary international law and the regulation of anti-satellite weapons." *Mich. J. Int'l L.* 30 (2008): 1187

89. Lachs, Manfred. *The Law of Outer Space: An Experience in Contemporary Law-Making by Manfred Lachs, Reissued on the Occasion of the 50th Anniversary of the International Institute of Space Law*. Martinus Nijhoff Publishers, 2010

90. Lafferranderie, G. Space debris. *Proceedings of the 45th Colloquium on the Law of Outer Space* 45 (2003): 44-50.

91. Lafferranderie, G. "Space debris and related legal issues." *Space Debris* 2 (2001): 853-856.

92. Lambeth, Benjamin S. *Mastering the ultimate high ground: next steps in the military uses of space*. Rand Corporation, 2003.

93. Lampertius, James P. "The Need for an Effective Liability Regime for Damage Caused by Debris in Outer Space." Mich. J. Int'l L. 13 (1991): 447.

94. Larsen, Paul B. "Solving the space debris crisis." *J. Air L. & Com*. 83 (2018): 475.

95. Larsen, Paul B. "Outer space arms control: can the USA, Russia and China make this happen." Journal of Conflict and Security Law 23, no. 1 (2018): 137-159.

96. Lee, Edward G., and D. W. Sproule. "Liability for Damage Caused by Space Debris: The Cosmos 954 Claim." Canadian Yearbook of international Law/Annuaire canadien de droit international 26 (1989): 273-279

97. Le May, Samantha, S. Gehly, B. A. Carter, and S. Flegel. "Space debris collision probability analysis for proposed global broadband constellations." Acta Astronautica 151 (2018): 445-455.

98. Lim, Jonathan. "The Future of the Outer Space Treaty–Peace and Security in the 21st Century." *Global Politics Review* 4.2 (2018): 72-112.

99. Lyall, Francys & Larsen Paul. *Space law: a treatise*. Ashgate publishing, 2009

100. Makarov, Yury, et al. "Major trends for space debris mitigation in near-Earth space in the Russian Federation." *Proceedings of the 68th International Astronautical Congress, IAC*. (2017): 3601-3612.

101. Malanczuk, Peter. "Review of the Regulatory Regime Governing the Space Environment-The Problem of Space Debris." *ZLW* 45 (1996): 37.

102. McCormick, Patricia K. "Space debris: Conjunction opportunities and opportunities for international cooperation." Science and Public Policy 40. 6 (2013): 801-813.

103. McDougal Myres S., Harold D. Lasswell, and Ivan A. Vlasic. Law and public order in outer space, Yale University Press, 1963

104. Mejía-Kaiser, Martha. Out into the Dark: Removing Space Debris from the Geostationary Orbit - Revised (October 25, 2019). Proceedings of the IISL Colloquium on the Law of Outer Space, Washington, D.C., USA, 2019

105. Milanov, Aleksandar. "Legal status of humankind in international law". Bulgarian journal of international law 3 (2009).

106. Milanov, Aleksandar. "Holistic globalization—alternative socioeconomic model." *The Globalization Conundrum—Dark Clouds behind the Silver Lining: Global Issues and Empirics* (2019): 295-321.

107. Milanov, Aleksandar, and George Penchev. "The Need for Establishing a New United Nations Body to Protect Earth from Back Contamination and Outer Space from Forward Contamination." IJCS (2020): 925-929

108. Mirmina, Steven A. "Regulation of Orbital Debris through National Measures, The." *Air & Space L.* 29 (2004): 137. Morgan, Richard A. "Military use of commercial communication satellites: a new look at the Outer Space Treaty and peaceful purposes." *J. air L. & com.* 60 (1994): 237.

109. Morin, Jean Frédéric, and Benjamin Richard. "Astro environmentalism: Towards a polycentric governance of space debris." *Global Policy* 12.4 (2021): 568-573.

110. Mosteshar, Sa'id. "Artemis: The Discordant Accords." J. Space L. 44 (2020): 591.

111. Mowthorpe, Mathew. *The militarization and weaponization of space*. Lexington Books, 2004.

112. Nagai, Yuichiro, Mukund Rao, Hideaki Shiroyama, K. R. Murthi, Motoko Uchitomi, and Baldev Raj. "Policy Analysis: Space Programmes of Japan And India." (2015): 1-14.

113. Onwudiwe, Memme, and Kwame Newton. "Africa and the Artemis Accords: A Review of Space Regulations and Strategy for African Capacity Building in the New Space Economy." New Space 9, no. 1 (2021): 38-48.

114. Perek, Lubos. "Space debris mitigation and prevention: how to build a stronger international regime." Astropolitics 2, no. 2

(2004): 215-226.

115. Phillips, Charles R. *The planetary quarantine program: Origins and achievements, 1956-1973.* Vol. 4902. Scientific and Technical Information Office, National Aeronautics and Space Administration, 1974.

116. Popova, Rada, and Volker Schaus. "The legal framework for space debris remediation as a tool for sustainability in outer space." Aerospace 5, no. 2 (2018): 55.

117. Popovski, Vesselin. *Reforming and innovating the United Nations Security Council.* Hague Institute for Global Justice, 2015.

118. Pusey, Natalie. "The case for preserving nothing: The need for a global response to the space debris problem." Colo. J. Int'l Envtl. L. & Pol'y 21 (2010): 425.

119. Roberts, Lawrence D. "Addressing the Problem of Orbital Space Debris: Combining International Regulatory and Liability Regimes." *BC Int'l & Comp. L. Rev.* 15 (1992): 51.

120. Robinson, George S. "Interplanetary Contamination: The Ultimate Challenge for Environmental and Constitutional Lawyers." *J. Space L.* 31 (2005): 117.

121. Robinson, George S. "Forward Contamination of Interstitial Space and Celestial Bodies: Risk Reduction, Cultural Objectives, and the Law." *ZLW* 55 (2006): 380.

122. Robinson, George. "Article IX of the Outer Space Treaty:Extraterrestrial Back Contamination, the U.S. Constitution, and the "Politics" of U.S. Regulatory Authority." EILENE Galloway Symposium, Cosmos Club, Washington. (2010)

123. Roeben, Volker. "Responsibility in international Law." Max Planck Yearbook of United Nations Law Online 16, no. 1 (2012): 99-158.

124. Rossi, Alessandro, et al. "ReDSHIFT: A global approach to space debris mitigation." *Aerospace* 5.2 (2018): 64.

125. Sachdeva, G. S. "Space Mines: Dialectics of Legality." *Astropolitics* 7.2 (2009): 135-149.

126. Sachdeva, G. S. "Outer Space Treaty: An Appraisal." Fifty years of the Outer Space Treaty (2017): 24

127. Salmeri, Antonino. "Developing and Managing Moon and Mars Settlements in Accordance with International Space Law." *Proceedings of the 71st International Astronautical Congress, 2020.*

128. Sattler, Rosanna. "Transporting a Legal System for Property Rights: From the Earth to the Stars." Chi. J. Int'l L. 6 (2005): 23.

129. Schrogl, Kai-Uwe, and Charles Davies. "New Look at the Concept of the Launching State-The Results of the UNCOPUOS Legal Subcommittee Working Group 2000-2002." ZLW 51 (2002): 359.

130. Schwetje, F. Kenneth - Liability and space debris/ In: International space law miscellanea : liber amicorum honouring Prof. dr. Andrzej Górbiel / ed. by Edward J. Palyga (1995).

131. Scott, William B. "Commission lays foundation for future military space corps." *Aviation Week & Space Technology* 154.3 (2001): 433-433.

132. Scott, William B. "Wargames underscore value of space assets for military ops." *Aviation Week & Space Technology* 146.18 (1997): 60-61.

133. Sénéchal, Thierry. "Space Debris Pollution–A Convention Proposal." *Protocol for a Space Debris Risk and Liability Convention.* 2008.

134. Seymour, Jennifer M. "Containing the Cosmic Crisis: A Proposal for Curbing the Perils of Space Debris." *Geo. Int'l Envtl. L. Rev.* 10 (1997): 891-914.

135. Shaw, Malcolm. International law. 5th edition. Cambridge, 2003

136. Smirnov, N. N., V. F. Nikitin, and A. B. Kiselev. "Peculiarities of space debris production in different types of orbital break-ups." *Second European Conference on Space Debris*. Vol. 393. 1997

137. Solomon, Lewis D. *The privatization of space exploration: Business, technology, law and policy*. Routledge, 2017.

138. Sreejith, S. G. "Unmaking a National Space Legislation for India: Indigenizing Space Law through the Organic Science of the Indian Space Program." *J. Air L. & Com.* 83 (2018): 109.

139. Sreejith, S. G., and Yugank Goyal. "Institutional cost of international space law." J. Space L. 41 (2017): 57.

140. Sreejith, S. G. "Whither International Law, Thither Space Law: A Discipline in Transition." Cal. W. Int'l LJ 38 (2007): 331.

141. Supancana, Ida Bagus Rahmadi. *The international regulatory regime governing the utilization of Earth-orbits*. Diss. Rijkuniversiteit te Leiden, 1998.

142. Thompson, Jannat C. "Space for rent: The international telecommunications Union, Space Law, and orbit/Spectrum leasing." *J. Air L. & Com.* 62 (1996): 279.

143. Trindade, Antônio Augusto Cançado. "International law for humankind: towards a new jus gentium." *International Law for Humankind*. Brill Nijhoff, 2010.

144. Tronchetti, Fabio. *The exploitation of natural resources of the Moon and other celestial bodies: a proposal for a legal regime*. Vol. 4. Martinus Nijhoff Publishers, 2009.

145. Tronchetti, Fabio, and Hao Liu. "Australia's signing of the Artemis Accords: a positive development or a controversial choice?." Australian Journal of International Affairs 75, no. 3 (2021): 243-251.

146. Vereshchetin, Vladlen S., and Gennady M. Danilenko. "Custom as a source of international law of outer space." *J. Space L.* 13 (1985): 22.

147. Vereshchetin, Vladlen. "International control and the concept of "open skies". From Coexistence to Cooperation: International Law and Organization in the Post-Cold War Era." Martinus Nijhoff Publishers, 1991

148. Vidal, Florian. *Russia's Space Policy: The Path of Decline?*, 2021.

149. Viikari, Lotta. *The environmental element in space law: assessing the present and charting the future*. BRILL, 2008.

150. Viikari, Lotta. "International Law Association′s Draft Convention on the Settlement of Disputes related to Space Activities." Arbitration. ru Magazine (2021): 14-17.

151. Wassenbergh, Henri A. *Principles of outer space law in*

hindsight. Martinus Nijhoff Publishers, 1991.

152. White, Wayne N. "Real property rights in outer space." *Proceedings, 40th Colloquium on the Law of Outer Space*. Vol. 370. 1998.

153. Williams, Maureen. "Perceptions on the definition of a "launching state" and space debris risks". Proceedings of the 45th colloquium on the law of outer space. Vol. 45 2003

154. Williams, Maureen. "Safeguarding Outer Space: on the road to debris mitigation." en United Nations Institute for Disarmament Research (ed.), Security in Space: the Next Generation, Geneva: United Nations (2008): 81-103.

155. Williams, Maureen. "2. Outer Space." *Yearbook of International Environmental Law* 26 (2015): 237-239.

156. Williams, Christopher D. "Space: The Cluttered Frontier." *J. Air L. & Com.* 60 (1994): 1139.

157. Williamson, Mark - Planetary spacecraft debris : the case for protecting the space environment. *Proceedings of the 42nd Colloquium on the Law of Outer Space*. Vol. 42, 2000.

158. Wright, Wright, David. "Orbital Debris Produced by Kinetic-Energy Anti-Satellite Weapons." *en United Nations Institute for Disarmament Research (ed.), Celebrating the Space Age* 50 (2007): 155-164.

159. Young, Andrew John. "Space transportation systems." (1984).

160. Zhang, Yijun. "An Analysis of the Regulations on Environmental Damage to Outer Space Caused by Space Debris." Journal of Frontiers of Society, Science and Technology 1, no. 1 (2021): 134-141.

161. Zhao, Yun. "An international space authority: A governance model for a space commercialization regime." *J. Space L.* 30 (2004): 277

Printed in the USA
CPSIA information can be obtained
at www.ICGtesting.com
LVHW060744100124
768537LV00002BA/10

9 786199 083499